as I saw it

a reporter's intrepid journey

MARVIN SCOTT

BEAUFORT BOOKS

as i saw it

FIRST EDITION

Library of Congress Cataloging-in-Publication Data On File
Hardcover: 9780825308420

For inquiries about volume orders, please contact:
Beaufort Books
27 West 20th Street, Suite 1102
New York, NY 10011
sales@beaufortbooks.com

Published in the United States by Beaufort Books
www.beaufortbooks.com

Distributed by Midpoint Trade Books
www.midpointtrade.com

Printed in Canada

Book designed by Mark Karis

To Lorri

The woman beside me, who inspires me every day

To my grandchildren Jake, Alexandra, Nathan

They are our future, for whom this book is written so they have some vision of the past

Marvin and Lorri Scott

TABLE OF CONTENTS

acknowledgements

*i*t takes a lot of effort to recount events that took place over the course of 50 years. The notes and recordings I saved from major events proved a tremendous asset to me in preparing this book, jogging my memory bank to bring the past into clearer focus. However, an undertaking like this book would not be possible without the encouragement, support and assistance of others as well.

James Carpenter is an editor extraordinaire, a true grammarian who accepted my colloquial style and made sure I didn't have any dangling participles. His work ethic, patience and late-night telephone editing sessions have helped to make this what I hope you will find an enjoyable read.

My wife Lorri is my first line of defense. If my writing passes muster with her, then I'm ready to send it on to my editor. She is a true blessing—my inspiration, my mentor, my friend. This book would not have been possible without her beside me.

I also want to acknowledge my agent of nearly 40 years, Richard Leibner, for his loyal support. More than an agent, he's been a friend and mentor to me—as well as my shrink at times.

It is such an honor to have had Dan Rather write the Foreword to this book. Dan has been an inspiration to me, and to so many other broadcast journalists. He certainly sets the gold standard for excellence in reporting.

I would like to thank my dear friend Rita Cosby for encouraging—or more accurately, pushing—me to write this book, and for her introduction to my publisher at Beaufort Books.

I must also recognize Ted Kavanau for giving me my first real break in television news in New York. I told him not to believe a word I had written in my résumé, and to give me the true test: a couple of news assignments. He did, beginning a 10-year run at WNEW-TV, Channel 5—and the rest is history.

Similarly, I say thanks to John Corporan for his belief in me, which began a relationship at WPIX-TV, Channel 11 that has now spanned 37 years of my professional life.

Thanks also to Karen Scott, the army-brat news director who said yes to my idea to spend five Christmas holidays with our soldiers in Iraq and Afghanistan. My appreciation to Tribune Broadcasting VP Communications Jessica Bellucci and WPIX News Director Amy Waldman for permitting the use of the television screen images highlighted on the following pages.

No television reporter or anchor can succeed without the backup of a multitude of talented camera people, producers and editors, without whom we could never bring these stories to air. My gratitude to all of those I've worked with, with particular thanks to cameraman David Kimmel for giving up five Christmas holidays to venture off to war zones with me, and to producer Ellyn Marks, who always worked tirelessly to secure the best guests for my weekly public-affairs program.

My indebtedness also to the tens of thousands of people I have interviewed, for trusting me to tell their stories.

And finally, to my children Steven and Jill, my love to you—and thanks for your understanding for all those dinners I missed while out chasing the news.

preface

BY DAN RATHER

Dan Rather and me, circa 1980.

*m*ark Twain once remarked that the difference between the right word and the almost-right word is the difference between the words *lightning* and *lightning bug*. The dictionary defines *intrepid* as "being of resolute fearlessness, fortitude and endurance." That is exactly the right word to describe Marvin Scott's journey as a lifelong reporter—and to describe the man himself. It fits Marvin like a bespoke suit.

He has traveled his intrepid journey almost entirely in local television news, which is a jungle of fierce competition, especially in the ultimate media market that is New York. He has survived and thrived for a long time, through talent and sheer force of will.

While doing so, he never backed up, never backed down, never turned around—and, remarkably, never lost his civility or his sense of humor. He sought to be, then became and now remains, dedicated to quality journalism of integrity, always trying to be accurate and fair while at the same time pulling no punches and playing no favorites.

As a reporter, he's hard-nosed but softhearted, skeptical—especially of power and powerful people, as a good reporter should be—but never cynical. He's always seen himself as a kind of "honest broker of information" for viewers and listeners. To continue to be that, he uses what some now would call old-fashioned methods (he sees them as *traditional*—never out of style): working the phones, wearing out shoe-leather, developing sources. He knows what goes on in police precinct houses after midnight and hospital emergency rooms on weekends, as well as inside Trump Tower and City Hall. Marvin knows because he's been there, many times, for many years. Because of that, he's hard to herd, and impossible to stampede.

In other words, and for short, Marvin's a pro. This collection of some of the more unique and memorable stories he's covered, and interviews he's done, is a primer for aspiring young television journalists and anyone who wants to know what goes on—what *really* goes on—in local television news, and how a pro works at his craft.

introduction

*e*xcept for the sound of birds dancing between the trees, it was quiet as I stood beneath the Victory Arch in Baghdad's Memorial Park, a symbol of Saddam Hussein's long, oppressive rule. A loud, rumbling sound broke the tranquility of the moment. It was an Iraqi tank crunching and clanking over the cobblestone roadway as it edged ever so slowly over the bomb-wracked street. The sound reminded me of the loud clackety-clack of the little red wagon I once toted along the cobblestones of the Grand Concourse in the Bronx, waking people along the way as I delivered morning newspapers back in the days when my life as a reporter was a distant dream. I was only 13.

Back then I was an inquisitive kid with a passion for photography, and it was a raging fire that sparked my interest in what would become a lifelong career. I was allowed beyond the fire lines to get a dramatic picture of the inferno, and afterward got details of the fire from a battalion chief. Suddenly I was Jimmy Olsen, kid reporter from *Superman*. It was exciting—and even more so when I sold the picture to *The New York Daily News*. I was hooked.

Fast-forward more than 50 years, over 15,000 stories and more than 30,000 interviews. My life has been enriched by the people I have met and the insight I have gained. Working at local television stations for the bulk of my career has given me access to the most powerful people and opened the back doors to view the underbelly of life, the day-to-day experience of the downtrodden and the impoverished.

At the heart of every story, big and small, is a person. It is the people who make the news, and the journalist who fashions the words that communicate their stories. We are simply the storytellers. The stories I have told have been informative, educational, and enlightening. Some have been investigative exposés that have helped to bring about change. But it is my encounters with people that stand out the most to me: the mother who had just discovered that her daughter was among those dead in a fire; the 12-year-old girl who needed a heart and touched mine; the woman who married the man who blinded her, making me the cupid who brought them to the altar; the man who ran off with the bank's money and found himself.

In addition to providing me with these local encounters, my career has been an educational journey that has taken me to far-off corners of the world, and stories told on a grander scale. I have been to the launch pads at Cape Canaveral and to an opium den in war-torn Cambodia, and spent five Christmases boosting the morale of our troops in Iraq and Afghanistan. I have met with Dr. Martin Luther King Jr. along the dusty highways of America's south, and with Yasser Arafat in a smoke-filled basement in Beirut. I was there for the raucous arrival of the Beatles in America, stood face-to-face with Marilyn Monroe and poked my microphone in front of more than half a dozen American presidents.

Along the way, I have learned and re-learned a few lessons—first and foremost that I, like the people whose stories I have told, am a human being, with feelings and sensitivities. We reporters are not all cold and uncaring, as some perceive us to be. Although I have always strived to maintain my professional demeanor on-camera, there have been emotional moments when tears filled my eyes while covering a story, like when I attended the funeral of children killed by a madman on a shooting rampage, or a memorial service for the astronauts who died in the Challenger disaster. I was not embarrassed to shed a tear while on-camera during coverage of the September 11th terrorist attacks.

Through the years, I have never compromised my honesty and integrity. I have tried to stick to old-fashioned reporting, just the facts, without adding my personal views. But reliving and retelling those stories now gives me an opportunity to share some personal reflections as well.

What follows is a composite of my more memorable stories and interviews. Some are historic; others are about people you have never heard of. They are stories that were told all in a day's work, over the course of half a century.

This book is written for my grandchildren, and for all the other children of the future, who may someday see it as a time capsule of life as it once was.

And it is written in gratitude for the life and career I have been fortunate to have. After all these years, I still love what I do—telling stories. I feel blessed to be the kid from the Bronx who each day continues to fulfill his dream.

people and places

PLAYING CUPID IN THE
CRAZIEST LOVE STORY

Burt and Linda Pugach with me attending the premier of the HBO
documentary *Crazy Love.*

*i*t doesn't exactly sound like a match made in heaven. Yet the
couple that wanted to have each other knocked off ended up
in a marriage that spanned 39 years. It has been said that there
is a thin line between love and hate—but in my extensive career
I have never encountered a more bizarre example of this than in
the lifelong love affair of Burt Pugach and Linda Riis. And in the
course of reporting on it, I unwittingly became the matchmaker
who brought them together.

The story made for sensational headlines when it broke back in

1959, when 32-year-old Burt Pugach, a married lawyer, dealt with romantic rejection in a shocking way. Linda Riis, his attractive 22-year-old lover of a few years, had broken off her relationship with Burt when she learned he was married; and Burt—figuring that if he couldn't have her, no one would—paid a thug $2,000 to throw lye in her face. The assault left Linda legally blind and disfigured, and both Burt and the man he had hired were sent to prison at Attica for their cowardly act—Burt for 14 years, and the man who threw the acid, for 15. But the rancor didn't end there: while Burt was in prison, Linda tried to have him killed in retaliation.

When Burt was released in 1974, he immediately reached out to reporters to go public with his apologies to Linda, and to confess to the world that he still loved her. I was working with Channel 5, WNEW-TV, in New York at the time, and was assigned to interview him. For a reporter, even the most unusual stories can be everyday work; and for me, at the time, it was simply another assignment: a sad, strange story whose most unusual aspects were long in the past. Little did I know what was yet to unfold.

Burt and I met for a sit-down interview on a park bench in Forest Hills, Queens, and chatted about the circumstances of his crime. He related in dramatic detail how "crazy" he had been at the time, and explained his original intent of killing Linda. "What I was doing was stalking her in the deep darkness of night, waiting outside her apartment building." He was armed with a 38-caliber revolver, he said, but changed his mind after having visions of being caught and strapped into the electric chair. The death penalty was still in effect in New York back then. It certainly was a deterrent for him, he admitted. But no such fear kept him from hiring others to disfigure Linda.

The interview was more interesting than I expected it would be. But unbeknownst to me, there was yet another motive underlying Burt's request for our discussion. Under his parole agreement, Burt was forbidden from making any contact with Linda, so he had chosen the television camera as a way to get to her heart. As I signaled to my cameraman to zoom in on Burt for a close-up, Burt turned purposefully to the camera, stared into the lens and suddenly gasped, "Linda, I love you. I have always loved you! Will you marry me?" *Wow, what a moment,* I thought. *This guy gets out of prison after doing 14 years for destroying a woman's life, and now he wants to marry her! Great story—so promotable—tonight at ten!*

One of Linda's friends caught the broadcast and called her, frantically proclaiming, "You won't believe what that crazy Burt is up to now. He's proposing to you on television!" Linda tuned in to the newscast, and was quite taken by Burt's remorsefulness and amorous proposal. Because his parole stipulated that Burt have no direct contact with her, Linda called me, and we maneuvered a rendezvous at the home of one of her friends. Burt was waiting there when she showed up. Linda would admit to me months later that something had seemed to click when she reunited with Burt.

After all she had gone through, Linda confessed, "I guess I still had feelings for him."

Six months later, I received a call from Burt, inviting me to the wedding. "Yes," he exclaimed excitedly, "we're getting married!" *What a bizarre love story!* I thought. Understandably, the story quickly became fodder for the tabloids, and thousands were left shaking their heads in disbelief. Why would the victim of such a heinous crime marry the man who committed it—the very man she had tried to have killed while he was in prison?

When I asked her this question in a 1992 interview, Linda simply responded, "I felt the time was right," adding, "I had made many mistakes, and probably was partially the cause of all the problems that we had. Burt is my best friend." Was it some form of retribution or revenge, I wondered, locking Burt down as her caretaker?

"I don't think so," she shot back. "Just to be with me is revenge enough." "I'm not easy." Similarly, when I asked Burt if he had married Linda out of guilt, he was quick to answer that he hadn't.

"That I would not have done," he said. "I'm not that noble. It was that I loved Linda, and I wanted to take care of her."

We reminisced about some of the other times we had met over the years. I remembered my first visit to their apartment to interview them after they reunited, when Linda reached under the bed to reveal a box of news clippings she had saved. Yellowed with age, these were all mounted in scrapbooks, detailing every episode of their unusual love story.

At one point in the interview, Linda interrupted her husband to say, "You know, Burt, if not for Marvin Scott, and me seeing you on his broadcast, you'd still be looking for me."

Smiling, Burt turned to me and exclaimed, "Thank you, Cupid." I had been called many things in my long career, but this was the first time I was called Cupid! Still, the nickname stuck. When they presented me with a copy of their book, *A Very Different Love Story,* Burt and Linda inscribed it, "To Marvin Scott, the cupid who got us to the altar."

* * *

Getting to know the two of them over the years, I came to sense that in many ways, the Pugaches genuinely needed one another. They claimed they never talked about the past, or rehashed old wrongs. As infatuation had given rise to the embers of hatred and anger between them, in turn the same embers fed the flames of their love over the years, and the couple insisted that through everything, they remained totally devoted to one another.

"You try to hurt me," Burt hinted, "she'll kill you."

Still, it was hardly a perfect union. Though Burt once described their bond as a "fairytale marriage," they fought like crazy, constantly bickering over the most inane things. Linda would sometimes refer to Burt as "El Creepo." And although Burt has always been open with his expressions of love for Linda, "love" is a word Linda could not use.

"It's something psychological," she once confided in me. When

I asked her if she loved Burt, she replied, "Yeah—when he behaves."
This was in reference to a time when he didn't behave, and had
gotten caught with another woman whom Linda had threatened.
That story, like many others of their life together, made headline
news. Nonetheless, Linda stood by her man. "So he strayed," she
told a reporter, downplaying the incident. "He's not the only man
who's strayed. The only thing is, he was stupid to get caught."

Back in the seventies, I tried to interest a number of producers
in making a film based on the Pugach tale. Most of them considered
the story too bizarre, and passed. But in 2010, producer Dan Klores
was inspired to tell the couple's saga in the HBO documentary
Crazy Love. During a broadcast following the release of the film, I
asked the couple what it was that they thought had held their marriage together for more than three decades. Almost ten seconds of
silence elapsed before Linda prompted her partner,

"You wanna answer that, Burt?"

"I'm still obsessed with her," he proclaimed. For her part, Linda
tried to explain why many people had difficulty accepting their
twisted love story, which had endured for so many years.

"Because people don't like happy endings," she reasoned. "Our
story has a happy ending."

2

REMEMBERING JFK

JFK during a press conference in Charleston
WV, April 1960. Photo taken by author and
donated to the Library of Congress.

J ohn F. Kennedy struck me as a towering, impressive figure the
day I came face-to-face with him in front of the state capitol in
Charleston, West Virginia. He was good-looking, and as vibrant
as the afternoon sun bearing down on him. His message to the
voters in the economically distressed state in the belly of Appalachia
was one of hope. He pledged that if he was elected president, he
would work unceasingly to improve economic development and
create jobs in the poverty-stricken area. West Virginia was a battle-
ground state, and a victory there would be pivotal for Kennedy in
winning his party's nomination. Yet though his message—delivered
in his rich Boston accent—was strong, his odds of winning that

state's presidential primary just four weeks away were slim. He was a Catholic in a predominantly Protestant state, and the polls that day in April 1960 had him 20 points behind his Democratic rival, Senator Hubert Humphrey.

With his Ivy League demeanor, Kennedy was the ultimate preppy candidate, a portrait of sartorial splendor in his two-button dark suit. Yet there was a down-to-earth quality about him as he greeted the West Virginian voters, grasping their hands and encouraging them to vote for him. I followed him to the coal mines, where he sat, shoes muddied, alongside miners trying to eke out a living. After a news conference at the Kanawha Hotel, I engaged the Massachusetts senator in conversation. He told me he recognized he had a difficult battle in the weeks leading up to the May 10th primary, and that he planned to travel up and down the state encouraging voters to place their trust in him.

Adding to the candidate's appeal, of course, was that of his beautiful wife, Jacqueline. I'll never forget the night I made eye contact with her as I sat at a press table at a fund-raising dinner. She was elegant, radiant. At one point she caught me staring at her admiringly, and smiled back at me graciously.

Ultimately, Kennedy's warmth and charisma made a strong contrast to the studied, stereotypical political style of his opponent Humphrey, and triumphed over his image as a wealthy politician. He won a landslide victory, winning almost 61% of the primary vote. Unable to match Kennedy's well-financed operation, Humphrey bowed out of the race, assuring Kennedy the Presidential nomination.

Kennedy's historic victory in West Virginia remains mired in controversy. Frank Sinatra's daughter Tina has claimed that Joseph Kennedy, the patriarch of the Kennedy family, reached out to her father for a favor, to ask Chicago crime boss Sam Giancana to help deliver the union vote in the Mountain State.

Giancana reportedly agreed, telling Sinatra, "It's a couple of phone calls." But the deal Sinatra brokered, it is said, came back to haunt him when the Kennedy administration cracked down on the Mafia, an effort led by JFK's brother Robert Kennedy, who at the time was Attorney General. Over the years since President Kennedy's death, skeptics of the Warren Commission's conclusion that he was assassinated by Lee Harvey Oswald have theorized that the Mafia, acting in retribution, was in fact responsible for the murder.

* * *

For many, the assassination of our 35th president endures as a deeply personal experience: a lingering mix of heartbreak, nostalgia and the lost promise of Camelot. And they can tell you exactly where they were when the shots rang out in Dallas, that fateful day in 1963.

As a fledgling reporter, I was in the newsroom that day, and I'll always remember the relentless sounding of bells from the teletype machines—a rapid succession of ten tones accompanied by the word "Flash," alerting us that something catastrophic had happened.

It began with a teletype operator frantically breaking into a transmission—Urgent—"shots fired at President's motorcade," quickly followed by five more bells—Bulletin—"Kennedy hit." The sound was piercing; the keys kept clattering. Then came the rarely heard ten bells, and the words "Flash—President Kennedy is dead." We were numb.

Over the years, those bells have resonated in my mind at moments that seemed to bring the past into the present—as when I stood on the Grassy Knoll years later, and listened to foreigners tell me how much they had loved our young president. I will never forget the man I first met campaigning for the presidency in the coalfields of West Virginia, when he was young and full of life. And I will never forget the bells that proclaimed his death.

3

CHARLIE'S ODYSSEY

Charlie Walsh being interviewed by me on the steps of city hall.

harlie Walsh was a bank thief of sorts, but not the John
Dillinger type. The theft wasn't his idea—it was the bank's
doing. One day in 1978, in a massive computer error, the
Commercial Trust Company of New Jersey handed him more than
$100,000. Charlie gave them a few weeks to catch their mistake. But
they didn't; and so, down on his luck and destitute, the 55-year-old
former Wall Street clerk took off with the loot on what would be a
three-month, 17,000-mile cross-country odyssey.

Later, his body racked with terminal cancer, Charlie was nevertheless having a ball reliving his great adventure for me from his
hospital bed. From time to time a nurse would interrupt to take

Charlie's blood pressure or feed him some medication. But sick as he was, it was easy to see that Charlie's wild ride had made him a happy man.

Sitting beside his bed at the Jersey City Medical Center, I could see the gleam in his pale-blue eyes—sheltered behind thick bifocals—as he remembered the cold day in December when he opened his bank statement and saw a balance of $101,885.13. He knew something was wrong right away; all he actually had in his account was $1,300.

At first, "I really didn't think anything of it," he said, adding, "I knew it was a mistake and I figured I'd get a corrected statement in the mail in a day or so." I needled him a little, and brought out an infectious giggle. "Well, I did do a little daydreaming," he confessed. "I couldn't help it. What if it really *was* my money? What would I do with it?"

It would be almost a month before the quiet, unassuming man would let his daydreaming carry over into reality. The timing of the bank blunder, Charlie said, couldn't have been better. He laughed, "it was like hanging a steak in front of a hungry dog." A loner by nature, Charlie had been unemployed for four years, and lived on his own in a ramshackle old house that he was about to lose to the city because he owed more than $17,000 in taxes on it. Even so, he had waited patiently for the next bank statement to arrive; and when it did, it still showed the large balance. "Then I really started daydreaming and thinking about it," he said.

Still figuring the bank would catch the error sooner or later, Charlie walked into a local branch and asked the teller to check on his balance. To the penny, it was still $101,885.13. Four days later, Charlie decided, "What the hell," and started to withdraw the money.

"The first day, I took $11,500 in cash in the morning," he recalled, "and I went back in the afternoon and took out about $40,000 in treasury checks, in $7,000 and $8,000 denominations."

For a man who never had as much as a parking ticket to put him on the wrong side of the law, Charlie insisted he wasn't a bit nervous or scared. "That's what surprised me," he said. "I just walked in like I owned the damn bank, and drew out the money. I don't know where the hell I got the nerve. I did it very well." He stuffed the money into a beat-up old attaché case, and was so pleased with himself, he decided to take himself to a movie—*Close Encounters of the Third Kind.* Yet even in celebration of his newfound prosperity, he was hard-pressed to shake his old frugal mindset. "I was sitting there with all this money in my lap, cursing myself for wasting $3.50 on a lousy movie," he chuckled.

Over the next several days, Charlie traveled from one branch to another, withdrawing more cash and treasury checks. A couple of tellers queried why he was taking out so much cash at once; he told them he was a coin dealer, and was buying new coins for his collection—not too far off, as Charlie was in fact a coin collector. He thought it was all over during one of his last withdrawals, when the bank manager informed Charlie that they were looking into a possible error with his account. Choosing not to stick around, Charlie quickly told the manager that he was in a hurry and would come back the next day—then went to Barclays Bank in New York to purchase $23,000 in traveler's checks.

"That would be an easy way to unload the money without any questions being asked," Charlie reasoned. Charlie withdrew all the money in his account over the next few days—except for $85.13. "Why did you leave that?" I asked. "I didn't want to be a pig," he laughed. "I didn't want to close out my account."

Charlie was hardly oblivious to the fact that he had committed a crime, and could be caught.

"When I did it, I knew it was wrong," he said. "I knew the money wasn't mine." But, he reasoned, "everything was going down the tubes, and I decided, sure, I'll take a chance. What have I got to lose?" He had already sold off most of his valuable coin collection, along with his insurance policies, and was as down and out as he had ever been. "You feel like a bum when you can't even buy somebody a drink," he quipped. He figured he would try to make his newfound riches last for the rest of his life, and perhaps open a small hobby shop somewhere in the Pacific Northwest.

Now, 55, overweight and balding, Charlie set out on the journey of his life. His first major purchase was a flashy—but used—Ford LTD with racing stripes, like the one made famous by the then-popular *Starsky & Hutch* television series. He paid cash for the car, peeling off 32 hundred-dollar bills, and hit the road.

As Charlie began his drive west—heading for Las Vegas, where he figured he could easily cash all of his traveler's checks—the bank finally discovered its error, and filed grand larceny charges against him. Charlie, however, was nowhere to be found. Detectives trudged across the unshoveled snow piled up on the sidewalk in front of his dilapidated house, only to find that the house was completely vacant.

* * *

That's when I was introduced to Charlie Walsh's story. Doing a report for my nightly newscast, I listened to neighbors describe Charlie as a pillar of the community, a kind, polite man who helped others. The more I learned about Charlie and the deeper I got into his plight, the more empathy I felt for him. Here was a guy who had hit rock bottom, and was living out a fantasy to which most people could relate. And relate they did. While some locals I interviewed expressed surprise that Charlie would "steal" money from the bank, many flat-out rejoiced for him.

"Take the money and run, Charlie," exclaimed one neighbor.

Charlie did run—but cautiously. He did everything in his power not to draw attention to himself. He stayed in nice but second-rate motels, ate at "halfway decent" restaurants and limited himself to one drink at bars.

"I didn't want to get drunk and lose the money," he recalled. "I had all that money with me, and I wasn't going to take any chances." At one local bar, he was drawn into a hot discussion about a councilwoman who had given back $20,000 that a bank had erroneously credited to her account. *What would you do?* was the question among the patrons; and when it came around to Charlie—sitting on a stool with $100,000 on his lap—he said, laughingly, "Hell, I'd call the bank and tell them they made a mistake."

Though police had put out a national alert calling for his arrest, Charlie said he wasn't looking over his shoulder while he was driving. "I don't know why, but it didn't bother me. I was just enjoying the scenery, and having a good time. It was the first time I'd traveled like that." Still, he knew he could be caught if he was ever stopped and had to produce identification. His license plate, too, would be a dead giveaway. So he stopped in a few bars and tried to engage people in conversation about how to obtain false identification, once even going so far as to drive to a darkened neighborhood to meet up with "some guy"—but fear set in, and he drove off without getting his fake ID.

He had a close call with police in Oregon, where he was pulled over for going 62 miles per hour in a 55 mph zone.

"It was a speed trap, and I got caught," Charlie related. "I figured the next thing I would see were handcuffs." But instead of asking for his license, the police just handed him a ticket and told him to mail it in with $17 to the local court. With a deep sigh of relief, Charlie drove on. "It was my lucky day," he chuckled.

* * *

Charlie had been on the run for two months when I called police for a follow-up report. They told me they had traced him to Las Vegas, but he had already left by the time detectives arrived; and as I pressed for information, it became clear there was none. The national manhunt for the portly, balding man with thick glasses and no previous criminal record had gone cold. He had never changed his appearance, his license plate or his personal identification—and yet, in the vastness of America, Charlie Walsh had disappeared.

Charlie's face would later brighten with excitement as he recalled his adventure in Las Vegas, where he was dazzled by the city's neon lights—and his ability to easily unload his traveler's checks. He was right in figuring that the casinos would cash them without question, so now he went from casino to casino, ultimately cashing 42 of his 56 $250 traveler's checks. He was tempted to gamble along the way, but resisted.

"After seeing all that money being shoved down the rat-hole in the table," he mused—"no, thank you." He only gave in once, to the lure of a slot machine. He fed seven nickels into the one-armed bandit, and on the last one, lights flashed and bells rang. Charlie had won—all of $7. Meager winnings, perhaps—but the moment he won, Charlie felt a greater sense of accomplishment than he did in getting away with the bank's money.

Polite and mild-mannered as he was, Charlie wasn't particularly good-looking, and had never been a ladies' man. He couldn't remember the last time he had been out with a woman, much less had sex with one. Now, in Vegas with tens of thousands of dollars stashed away in a little vinyl bag—his attaché case had proven too big and beat-up for the journey, so he replaced it along the way with a $5 bag from Woolworth's—Charlie decided to do something he had never done before. He enlisted the services of two prostitutes for $100 an hour. At first this was far more than Charlie had bargained for: he felt inadequate and uncertain about what to do, and was embarrassed to get undressed in front of the women. But they reassured him as professionals can, and it was with a loud chuckle that Charlie later recounted his three-hour love tryst.

"I had myself some fun, and enjoyed it," he said. "Damn near killed myself, but I got my money's worth." Aside from his car, Charlie's $300 sexual encounter would prove to be the most extravagant expense of his entire adventure.

Having lived a quiet, reserved life for so many years, with no family or friends, Charlie found himself deeply changed by the risks he had taken in venturing out on his odyssey.

"For the first time, I really felt alive," he recalled. "I was coming out of my shell." Though cautious, he discovered that he enjoyed meeting and talking to people, and made many friends. In San Francisco he was attracted to a young woman at Fisherman's Wharf, and struck up a conversation with her. They talked for a while, and he invited her to dinner. The woman even invited him to join her and her family, who were charmed by the self-proclaimed "salesman" from New Jersey.

After being on the run for several weeks, Charlie began to feel more confident that he just might get away with his escapade. But he continued to fear being exposed by his New Jersey license plate and personal identification, and made several more unsuccessful attempts to get a false ID. In a number of states he tried to obtain safe-deposit boxes to hold his small fortune, but each bank he visited wanted some form of identification. Each time he would claim he had forgotten his wallet back at the hotel, and leave. He had one of the biggest scares of his adventure after one such visit, in Seattle. Charlie returned to his hotel to find it surrounded by more than a dozen police and sheriff's vehicles.

"I got the hell out of there quick," he recalled. Hours later, he was relieved to hear on the radio that there had simply been a Law Enforcement Awards luncheon at the hotel.

When Charlie arrived in Portland—where he had considered settling down and opening his hobby shop—he decided to mark the occasion by checking into a nice hotel instead of a motel. He had made it all the way across America in his quiet caper, and figured it was worth a modest celebration. Still, his habitual frugality spoke up, and rather than pay for the hotel's private garage, he decided to park his car on the street.

This proved to be Charlie's downfall. On June 26th, 1978, a couple of Portland police officers in the area were testing a new piece of equipment in their cruiser, an onboard computer linked to the National Crime Information computer system. Spotting a car with out-of-town plates, they punched in the numbers on Charlie's New Jersey license plate. A short time later, two FBI agents were rapping loudly on the door of Charlie's hotel room and asking if he was Charlie Walsh. "I said no," Charlie remembered, "but when they asked for ID, everything I had said Charlie Walsh." The agents read him his rights and told him he was under arrest, and confiscated his bag of money. Figuring he had no way out, he told the agents the whole story of his adventure. He explained how he had desperately tried to obtain false identification, but didn't know how; upon which the agents informed him, to his surprise and dismay, that there was a book in the library on the subject. They asked if he had gambled away much of the money in Las Vegas. Charlie told them he hadn't, adding that he wasn't a gambler.

"I'm not so sure about that," shot back one agent. "Seems you took a big gamble with this."

Charlie spent two weeks in a county jail in Portland, waiting for arrangements to be completed for his extradition to New Jersey. He became deeply depressed during his uncomfortable time there, reflecting on the trouble he had gotten himself into. On his way out of the local jail, when he was picking up his few belongings from the property clerk, he was asked to sign a receipt for $22.40—for a credit in the commissary—but he refused, insisting he had no credit.

"I don't want the money," he cried. "It's those damn computer records that got me into this mess in the first place!" (He was eventually sent a check—which he gave to his lawyer to return.)

Still, though handcuffed and in the custody of two Jersey City police officers, Charlie said he enjoyed the trip home. It was the first time he had ever flown, and, he would later laugh, "it was part of the adventure." Other than the criminal indictment, he had no idea what awaited him back in New Jersey.

Charlie Walsh was greeted at the airport by a cheering crowd, along with television news crews and reporters. I stood among them, shaking my head in disbelief at the mob of supporters cheering wildly for their schlubby folk hero as he stepped off the plane in the same rumpled tweed jacket and baggy pants he had on when he fled. Local papers had a great time with the story. "Good Time Charlie Returns," one bold headline screamed.

Charlie was shocked. "It surprised the hell out of me when I walked into a restaurant and people stood up and applauded me," he said. "Everybody wanted to shake my hand or pat me on the back. I couldn't believe what was happening; I thought they would boo me."

On the contrary, it was the bank that was viewed as the villain. Asserting that Charlie had been an innocent victim, newspaper editorials called for all the charges against him to be dropped. The grand jury agreed, placing the culpability with the bank's computer error and finding no evidence of criminal intent on Charlie's part. At the recommendation of the prosecutor, the bank dropped its criminal charges and settled for the money Charlie still had—$74,466 in cash, $14,300 in checks, $3,100 for his car, $2,000 from the sale of what was left of his coin collection, the last $190 from his insurance policy—and, of course, the $85.13 he had left in his bank account. Charlie had lived as frugally during his four months on the lam as he had his entire life, spending only a little over $11,000.

"I gave them everything I had in the world," Charlie recounted, "and they turned out to be nice guys after all." Along with settling, the bank let him keep a $69 television set, an electric razor and a number of other small items he had bought while on the run.

Still, Charlie was left penniless. He was also homeless: while he was gone, the city tore down the house on which he owed so many thousands of dollars in back taxes. Yet what he lacked in money, he now had in adulation. He had become a local celebrity overnight, and found friendship and support everywhere he went. He was even applauded by workers at City Hall when he showed up to apply for welfare—the cop at the security desk patted him on the back and shook his hand, and a secretary shouted, "God bless you, Charlie," while another exclaimed, "Wish ya hadn't got caught—we're rooting for you." One city official suggested that Charlie be named Grand Marshal of the next St. Patrick's Day Parade.

Later, discussing why people had lauded him as a hero, Charlie reasoned, "I lived out other people's fantasy. Others wouldn't do it because of family ties. I had no family, no friends and no job, so I could just take off." I asked him if he had any regrets. "I kinda wish I'd lived it up a little more, spent a little more of the bank's money," he responded. "But if I had it to do over again, I'd probably do it the same way." *Would* he do it again if circumstances permitted, I inquired? "Truth is, I probably would, but I wouldn't want anyone to know that," he quipped with a twinkle in his eye.

All things considered, Charlie acknowledged that his life had become far better for his caper. "My whole lifestyle changed," he said. "I'd always been a loner; now I'm in the public eye, they've made me a celebrity and everybody wants to be my friend. They want to help me." He told me he was hopeful of finding a new job—but wanted nothing to do with computers. "I've been done in by the damn technology three times," he laughed, referring to his replacement by a computer at his job on Wall Street, the bank glitch that had launched his wild ride, and the police computer system that brought it to an end. "I feel like I've been folded, stapled and mutilated!"

4

MARILYN, THE PINK ELEPHANT AND ME

Self portrait of me at 15 with camera used to photograph Marilyn Monroe riding a pink elephant at opening night benefit of the circus, 1955.

*a*mericans idolize their movie stars. They're a part of our pop culture. But few have earned the distinction Marilyn Monroe did, of becoming a timeless cultural icon. Monroe died more than half a century ago, on August 5th, 1962, but she remains very much alive in the hearts and minds of legions of fans.

For an entire generation, Marilyn Monroe was a figure of fantasy rather than flesh—but she was quite real. A product of the fifties, she was as real as hula-hoops, tail fins and the Cold War. She was the woman every woman wanted to be and every man wanted to be with. Lois Banner, who taught classes on Marilyn Monroe at the University of Southern California, characterized her as "the greatest enchantress in Western history since Cleopatra."

The Hollywood star glowed with baby-doll innocence, but her walk and expressions radiated sexuality. Born Norma Jeane Mortensen and brought up in foster homes, Marilyn Monroe cultivated a public image that belied the way she saw herself. According to those who knew her, Monroe considered herself introverted, shy and oftentimes unintelligent. While she had difficult relationships with men, she had a relationship with the camera that has never been matched.

In the words of photographer Eve Arnold, "She was the animal trainer and the photographers the beast."

* * *

I will never forget the night America's Sex Goddess toyed with my camera as a kitten toys with a spool of wool, generating an electric charge with each click of my shutter. The year was 1955, and Marilyn was the star attraction at the opening night of the Ringling Brothers Barnum and Bailey Circus at Madison Square Garden. It was a benefit for the Leukemia Society, and Marilyn rode into the arena atop a pink elephant, drop-dead gorgeous in her form-fitting black-and-white costume sparkling with sequins.

I was a kid of 15 at the time, and managed to maneuver my way into the event with my high-school press pass. A week earlier, I told the press agents I was doing a story for my high-school newspaper—a little white lie that got me the chance to meet Marilyn Monroe up close and take her picture. That night I put on a sport jacket and nice shirt, loaded my Rolleiflex camera with Tri-X black-and-white film and slung the heavy strobe-flash unit over my shoulder, and entered the side entrance to Madison Square Garden, where I positioned myself in the middle of the pack of newspaper photographers like I belonged there. Unlike many competitive paparazzi today, the photogs back then were nice guys, and didn't think to bother a kid with a camera.

Suddenly I saw a flash go off, and turned to see Marilyn walking toward us, strutting past the clowns and circus animals. Wiggling and jiggling just the way she did across the silver screen, she was statuesque, her long legs covered in fishnet stockings, her breasts plump above a skimpy costume, her blonde hair swept back. This was her first public appearance since her divorce from Joe DiMaggio, and I positioned myself in a spot where I knew I could have a clear shot of her walking with her friend and photographer Milton Green, at whose home she had been staying since the split.

My finger was frozen on the shutter as I snapped away, grabbing several frames as she walked toward the pink elephant that she would ride into the arena. She was radiant and gracious, frequently stopping to the chorus of shouts from photographers exclaiming, "Marilyn, this way—one more." At one point, she turned from the rest of the pack and looked right at me. I sensed a slight smile as she threw back her head, raised an arm and asked, in a faint voice, "Is this all right?" I couldn't believe it—Marilyn Monroe had actually spoken to me! As a teenager with raging hormones, I couldn't help but think, *Wow! Wait'll I tell my buddies!*

There was a magical quality about this beautiful woman in front of my camera. Her smile was real, though her pose seemed studied; she was as large as life. She mounted the elephant, giving me another great shot, and rode triumphantly into the arena to the thunderous cheers and applause of adoring fans. She appeared to be loving every moment of it.

* * *

To be loved—for the 36 years of her life, that was Marilyn Monroe's fantasy. While her lasting love affair was with the camera, millions of fans had their own love affairs with this mystical blonde, the visible Venus of her time. She played the sensuous blonde, a role she came to personify, in such unforgettable films as *Gentlemen Prefer Blondes, The Seven Year Itch* and *Some Like it Hot,* and over the last ten years of her life, her movies earned more than $200 million.

Monroe wanted to be taken seriously as an actress, and desperately sought affection from others.

"She wanted a home, a family, children," Lois Banner wrote of her. "Above all, she wanted love." Yet her marriages—including one to Yankee great DiMaggio, and another to author Arthur Miller—failed, and she fell into deep depression. Her death in 1962 was officially declared a suicide, but with the passage of time, rumors and conspiracy theories have suggested that the Mafia or her purported affairs with President John F. Kennedy and Senator Robert Kennedy were somehow related to her untimely death.

The mystery of her death has added to the mystique that still surrounds her. Monroe's name has appeared on so many products and establishments that *Forbes* magazine once listed her as third in its annual billing of top deceased celebrity earners, with her heirs earning in excess of $27 million in one year alone. Even today, so many years after her death, the American public still can't get enough of Marilyn Monroe. Just look on social media—she has tens of thousands of followers on Twitter, and more than three million fans on Facebook.

Although she was idolized as America's number-one sex queen, Marilyn Monroe always wanted more. And she never forgot who her friends were.

"People made me a star," she said in one of her last interviews. "No studio, no person, but the people." And it is the people who carry on her legacy. A columnist once observed that "Marilyn Monroe was the stuff dreams are made of. Her legacy to us is that we are still dreaming."

5

AMITYVILLE—
HORROR OR HOAX?

I joined a midnight séance where a psychic said there was something dark and evil in
the "Amityville Horror" house. March 1976.

i felt a mix of trepidation and excitement as I pulled up to the
Dutch Colonial house at 112 Ocean Avenue. The adventurer
in me was eager to join in a scheduled séance with a group of
demonologists, psychics and parapsychologists. But being one who
can get queasy during horror movies, I wasn't quite sure if I was
ready for what I might experience here.

I was about to enter America's most notorious haunted house,
from which a family claimed it was driven by demonic forces—and
where, 16 months earlier, a young man murdered his parents and

four siblings. This combination of the diabolical murder of one family and the purported occult hauntings of another would later inspire the book and iconic motion picture *The Amityville Horror,* a purportedly true story that terrified a global audience, unceremoniously shoved a quiet suburban community into the international spotlight, and spawned a cottage industry that would make it one of the most lucrative ghost stories of all time.

My assignment, on that chilly March night in 1976, was to determine if there was any credibility to the tales of George and Kathy Lutz that their house was possessed by demons. Three months earlier they had complained of inexplicable, weird occurrences throughout their spacious home. They reported extreme fluctuations in temperature, loud scrapes and banging sounds from rooms, green slime oozing from the walls, swarms of devilish flies gathering in the dead of winter, the appearance of a mysterious red room in the basement, and strange vibrations and the sound of voices at all hours of the day and night. The Lutzes' youngest child, Missy, described speaking to an "angel" named Jodie who lived in her room, and who Missy said would present herself in the room as a large pig able to change shape and form at will. The family claimed the unnerving events began almost immediately after they had moved in, and the subsequent blessing of the house by Father Ralph Pecoraro, a Roman Catholic priest who said he heard a voice demanding that he get out, seemed to initiate a chain reaction of events that sent the Lutzes and their three children running for their lives a mere 28 days after they had moved in. The family never returned.

Now I arrived for the midnight gathering, a séance arranged by my producer and colleague Laura Di Dio. The rest of the group, already assembled, invited me to join them at a long kitchen table, in the center of which a crucifix and blessed candles were placed. This was done, they told me, with hopes of provoking the overpowering force believed to be in the house, and drawing it out. Noted demonologist Lorraine Warren exclaimed, "There's no doubt that something of a demonic nature has haunted this house."

An air of anticipation took over as the room became silent. Psychic Alberta Riley pursed her lips and closed her eyes in concentration. Her hands rose to her face as she spoke up in a frightened voice. "Whatever is here—" she began, then faltered. "Is it trying to hurt you?" asked one of the other participants. "Yeah," Riley managed, then continued, "Something comes at you and makes your heart speed up." Mary Pascarella, another psychic, described her vision of whatever it was that was demonizing the house as being "like some kind of a black shadow that forms a head, and it moves. And as it moves, I feel personally threatened."

Everyone at the table was riveted by these declarations of the psychics. And yet, intense and entertaining as they were, I admit I was skeptical, and experienced little that challenged that skepticism. The only sensation I felt during the entire séance was a slight chill behind my left ear—which nevertheless would prompt author Jay Anson to suggest, in the epilogue to *The Amityville Horror,* that I had been "touched" by something supernatural in the house that night.

After the séance, a parapsychologist from the Psychical Research Foundation set up cameras and sensitive monitoring equipment, which the group expected would detect any unusual movement in the house. As Saturday night turned into the early hours of Sunday morning, I curled up under blankets on a sofa in the living room, awaiting any supernatural occurrence. We heard none of the noises or voices the Lutzes claimed to have heard. The only voices I heard that night were those of my crew, wanting to know when we were going to have the sandwiches we had brought along.

Still, looking up at the large moose head jutting from the wall above us, I did feel a bit eerie being in a house where six people had been murdered a little over a year earlier.

* * *

It didn't take police long to determine that 23-year-old Ronald DeFeo Jr. had murdered his mother, father, two brothers and two sisters as they slept. DeFeo himself, in fact, confessed to the murders almost immediately. At the time, some suggested he was simply crazy, or high on drugs; others, however, saw something more sinister in his sudden murderous rampage.

"Ron was into some very dark things," Lorraine Warren told me. "He was into occult practices." Her husband, famed demonologist Ed Warren, agreed, adding, "Ronnie told me there was a dark black mask or shadow that was obsessing his thoughts and telling him to kill everybody."

DeFeo had indeed claimed that he had heard voices. But his defense attorney, William Weber, never believed his client was possessed, declaring instead that DeFeo was insane. Weber attempted to use that alleged insanity as a defense at DeFeo's trial, but a jury found DeFeo guilty on all counts, and he was sentenced to six life terms. Despite his initial confession, DeFeo's story has wavered over the years, accusing various others, including the mob, of having committed the murders while he was in the basement smoking marijuana. In correspondence with me, he suggested that it was his sister Allison who killed everyone, and that he killed her while wrestling for the gun.

There were a few longstanding mysteries in the case, one of them being the fact that none of the family members or neighbors had been awakened by the initial blasts of DeFeo's carbine. Ed Warren theorized that this was because the family had been under psychic paralysis at the time.

"That's why they didn't run," he said. "That's why they didn't yell out." Many more such theories arose after the Lutzes' story came out. Some believers in the occult suggested that the infamous negative force in the house came from the angry spirit of a Native American entombed in an old burial ground beneath the house.

For her part, Lorraine Warren believed DeFeo's actions had been influenced by demonic forces within the house, and claimed she felt them directly.

"Whatever is here is, in my estimation, most definitely of a negative nature," she told me. "It is right from the bowels of the earth."

* * *

It was just before three in the morning when Lorraine nudged me off the sofa to join her upstairs in the sewing room. This had been the bedroom of two of the murdered DeFeo children, and the place that supposedly held the strongest demonic force. At 3:15 a.m., the exact time DeFeo had begun executing his family, we sat on the floor in front of candles and a crucifix, and another séance was conducted. This second séance was as uneventful for me as the first; again I felt nothing unusual. Yet a trembling Lorraine Warren did.

"I hope this is as close to hell as I ever get," she exclaimed. "It's like evil personified."

If there was a demonic force in the Amityville house that night, it certainly didn't manifest itself to me. To be frank, I didn't experience *anything* I considered unusual throughout my whole experience there. My cameraman, Steve Petropolis, claimed he felt a rash of heart palpitations and shortness of breath while climbing up to the second floor, in the same spot where Lorraine Warren had previously said she became ill—and Petropolis, an avid runner who was in good health, said he had never experienced anything like this before. But I felt nothing like that. The parapsychologists suggested that this was because the house had been neutralized, or that the atmosphere wasn't right at the moment, or that perhaps the demons had been scared off by all the people and television cameras.

The question often arises of whether the Lutzes' tale meets muster. To this day, DeFeo's attorney William Weber remains convinced it doesn't.

"It's a fraudulent story," he told me. "The Lutzes took advantage of an unfortunate incident in that house, and built a supernatural story around it." Ronald DeFeo himself, in letters to me from prison, also claimed the story was a hoax.

"It's all about money, an industry," he asserted. Yet he claimed that his attorney had been in on it as well, and took advantage of him. DeFeo showed me documents that indicated that Weber had been looking for lucrative book and movie deals, and accused the lawyer of starting the Amityville hoax. Weber confessed that he had played a part in the story's creation.

"I contributed, absolutely," he said. He explained to me that he had met with George and Kathy Lutz to discuss a book idea. "We sat down and talked over some wine—I think three bottles of wine," he confided, going on to admit that "the story grew with each bottle of wine...each bottle it became a better story." The Lutzes acknowledged the meetings with Weber, but until their dying days stuck to their story of demonic happenings in their house. However, at one point they did admit to my colleague Laura Di Dio that many aspects of the story were exaggerated.

Weber offered more plausible explanations for every unusual incident in the house. Speaking about the mysterious swarm of flies, Weber said he had told the Lutzes the insects were in the house where the bodies had been, and that the couple "took those flies and created a complete supernatural scene around them." He explained that the green slime they reported seeing oozing from the walls was actually fingerprint powder and other substances used by police in their forensic investigation. As for the mysterious red room found behind a door in the basement, a boyhood friend of DeFeo's remembered the senior DeFeo giving the kids a can of red paint to add a splash of color to what had been a toy closet.

Others, too, have taken pains to debunk the story. While the Warrens never recanted their belief that it was demonic forces that drove the Lutzes from their house at 112 Ocean Avenue, four families who have lived there since have reported no strange occurrences. One of the subsequent owners, Barbara Cromarty, tried to put an end to the frenzy surrounding the house, and called a news conference to proclaim the whole Amityville frenzy an unequivocal hoax.

Of course, none of this has stopped the curious from driving by for a look-see at the house, which has since undergone a transformation. Gone are the eerie eye-shaped windows in the attic; the dark shingled siding has been replaced with a much lighter shade; and the address has been changed from 112 to 108 Ocean Avenue, in hopes of deterring onlookers.

* * *

For four decades, the Amityville story has terrified, captivated and thrilled millions around the world. Americans love a good ghost story, and are endlessly intrigued by the occult. A Gallup poll once showed that three out of four Americans believe in the paranormal, which explains why the Amityville story has generated millions of dollars in revenue for half a dozen films, a dozen books and numerous television shows—even though, for all they claim to have endured, the Lutzes reportedly received only $300,000 from it.

Because of my one-night experience in the house, and because I was referred to in the epilogue of Jay Anson's book, albeit inaccurately, I myself have been enlisted for appearances on half a dozen documentaries and films about Amityville. At least once a year, a letter from somewhere in the world—incorrectly addressed—will find me, sent from an Amityville believer who wants to hear my take on it all. Understandably, most often I'm asked if I was scared the night I spent in the house. Quite honestly, the two hours I spent watching the film with a rowdy, pot-smoking audience was much more of a horror than the six hours I spent in that house in Amityville.

6

THE BRAVEST PERSON
I EVER MET

Stephanie Collado was vibrant and spiritual at the age of 12 when she appeared on one of my broadcasts just months after surviving a heart transplant.

*C*ourage is a seven-letter word synonymous with Stephanie Collado. She embodied the very definition of courage as the quality of mind or spirit that enables a person to face difficulty, danger and pain without fear. Hers is the uplifting tale of a brave young girl who needed a heart, and touched mine.

Of the more than 35,000 people I have interviewed during my career, Stephanie stands out as the most inspirational. Through most of her young life, even in the face of adversity and on the threshold of death, she held onto her faith in God, and it was this spiritual positivity that sustained all of those around her.

I first met Stephanie's family in 1998, when they reached out publicly to find a donor heart for their 11-year-old daughter. The girl's own heart was failing due to a complex medical condition, and they needed to find a donor fast. The family had been waiting for months; they needed a miracle.

The miracle was answered. Stephanie received her new heart, from the young victim of an automobile accident; and on her 12th birthday she was wheeled out of the intensive-care ward at Babies and Children's Hospital at Columbia Presbyterian in New York. Her room was filled with flowers, balloons and birthday cards—and lots of loving relatives.

Still weak and hooked up to numerous tubes and medical equipment, Stephanie managed a slight smile, and in a faint voice told me, "I want to thank God for my new life." Too often such stories end tragically early, and it was a joyous moment to see this young girl beat the odds and find a new beginning, with a new heart beating in her chest. She could barely speak, but when I asked her what she thought had enabled her to survive, she managed an answer. "Everybody has to have a lot of faith in God," she declared.

As she left the hospital, her new life looked bright and full of promise. "I'll miss you," she joked with the nurses, "not the building." She bubbled over with joy outside as she released her balloons into the air, telling us, "I feel happy. I feel good. I feel like jumping."

In surviving as she did, Stephanie touched many hearts, and raised an awareness of the pressing need for organ donors. At her elementary-school graduation in Brooklyn, the sixth-grader told me that "God has organ donors in a special place, for when he needs them." Tears filled her eyes as teachers praised her for her "will to face something terrifying with courage and strength."

"You faced your greatest fear, and you triumphed," they told her, and added, "Miracles do happen."

Given her own turn to speak, Stephanie looked into the

crowded auditorium and told her teachers and classmates about her will to survive. "I fought with love, because that's what I felt helped me get through this," she said, giving special thanks to all of those who had prayed for her.

As she resumed her normal life, Stephanie was like a flower in the wind, blossoming from childhood to young womanhood and always looking toward the brightness of tomorrow. We stayed in touch over the years. Stephanie had been far more than just another news story for me. She was someone special, someone I greatly admired for her strength, her courage, her wisdom and her dogged determination to stay alive and stay positive.

Though Stephanie and her mother moved to Florida, we never lost contact with one another. I made it a point to call Stephanie on her birthday each year, and she and her mother Juana would occasionally exchange letters and calls with me at other times. It's unusual for reporters to strike up such a bond with the subjects of their reports, but Stephanie was different; she and her family were true friends of mine, and a constant source of inspiration.

Stephanie appeared to be doing well. Eight years after her initial surgery, she had a job, a steady boyfriend and a full life ahead of her when her donor heart began to fail. Again, she needed a new heart. I called her on a Friday night to let her know I would be flying down to the hospital at the University of Florida with a crew the following week, to tell her story once again. Though she sounded weak and in pain, I could still hear the smile in her voice; more than anything she sounded upbeat, confident that her faith and prayers would once again help her beat the odds.

But it was not to be. The heart she needed never came, and in the end Stephanie's pain and illness overpowered her. Her distraught mother called in the morning to inform me that Stephanie had passed during the night. "She was so happy you were coming to visit," she told me. "She even picked out the dress she wanted to wear."

Mark Twain wrote, "Courage is resistance to fear, mastery of fear, not absence of fear." Stephanie Collado faced her fear stoically and bravely. She wanted to live, but faced the alternative with faith and resolution. To her own mother she insisted that if she died, it would be the will of God. And in her final days, she was ready.

"I don't want to stay in this world no more," she cried, "because I feel the suffering is too much, and I don't feel God wants that from me anymore." Prophetically, she added, "I hear His voice every night. He doesn't want me here anymore; He wants me with Him."

At the funeral service, I delivered the eulogy in celebration of the life of a young girl who was now one of God's angels. Stephanie was only 20 years old.

crime and punishment

7

"GOING TO HUNT HUMANS"

Filing my report from the scene of bloody McDonald's massacre in San Ysidro, CA, July 1984. Crazed gunman James Oliver Huberty told his wife he was going to "hunt humans."

i had just finished interviewing a delegate on the floor of the 1984 Democratic National Convention in San Francisco, when I was frantically summoned by my news director. There had been a horrific mass shooting in southern California, and he wanted me on the next plane to San Diego to cover the story. By the time I arrived, the shooting had stopped, leaving 21 people dead—five of them children—and 19 others wounded at a McDonald's restaurant in suburban San Ysidro, a border community just north of Tijuana, Mexico.

On arrival I hooked up with a colleague from a local TV station, who took me to the scene of the shooting. It was chaos there, with bodies scattered inside and around the fast-food restaurant. Dozens of people had gone to that McDonald's for a late-afternoon snack, only to encounter a madman who was armed to the hilt and determined to kill as many people as he could before he was stopped. The restaurant's plate-glass windows were riddled with bullet holes, a testament to the 245 rounds the murderer had fired from three different weapons over the course of his rampage.

As he walked out of his house that sunny afternoon, 41-year-old James Oliver Huberty—a man others had described as angry at the whole world—told his wife, "I'm going hunting for humans, and I won't be back." Etna Huberty didn't take him seriously. Minutes later, he strode into the McDonald's two blocks from his home, wearing army fatigues, a black T-shirt and glasses. It was four o'clock in the afternoon, and dozens of customers were there, having burgers and fries or ice cream.

Suddenly, the tall, gaunt man screamed the chilling words, "Everybody get down, or I'll kill somebody." All of the restaurant's patrons complied, but he began to kill them anyway. Armed with an Uzi submachine gun, a 12-gauge shotgun and a nine-millimeter Browning semiautomatic pistol, Huberty opened fire on men, women and children, strolling among the tables and shooting anyone who moved. Witnesses said that at one point he blurted, "I killed a thousand in Vietnam. I'll kill a thousand more." Despite his claim, it was later learned that Huberty had never served in the military.

As Huberty continued his killing spree, his 12-year-old daughter Zelia watched the deadly saga unfold from a neighbor's nearby apartment, unaware that it was her father who was doing the shooting. After losing precious minutes by being dispatched to a wrong McDonald's location, the local SWAT team arrived and set their sights on taking down the gunman. But they were initially unable to get a clear shot at him. The cries of frightened children and people begging for their lives were heard as the carnage continued. At one point Huberty took aim at an 11-year-old girl, but her aunt, 18-year-old Jackie Reyes, jumped in front of his Uzi and took all 48 of the bullets he fired. Beside her body, her 8-month-old son Carlos sat up crying, and Huberty shot him dead.

As three boys approached on their BMX bikes for an afternoon fix of ice cream, Huberty fired through the window, killing David Flores and Omar Hernandez, both 11. The third boy, Joshua Coleman, played dead and survived. He later told me from his hospital bed, "I kept thinking he was going to come and shoot me. I kept looking back at my two friends who were lying behind me." A McDonald's employee, 17-year-old Wendy Flanagan, heard the burst of gunfire, grabbed a coworker's hand and shouted, "Run, Maggie, run!" As they ran, Maggie let go of Wendy's hand and fell to the floor. She was dead. Several others survived the rampage by taking refuge in a closet near the kitchen.

On hearing a wounded teenager moaning in a booth, Huberty turned to him and shot him in the head, then fired on several others before pausing again. By now a sea of blood covered the floor, and the restaurant grew silent. Huberty had killed everybody there, or thought he had. The siege had gone on for 78 minutes when a police sharpshooter, perched on a building across the street, finally had a clear shot at Huberty and took it, killing the gunman with a single bullet to the chest.

The aftermath of Huberty's rampage was ghastly. Even from a distance, I knew I hadn't seen carnage like this before—so many bodies were visible at the scene. At the time, it was the deadliest mass shooting in U.S. history. As a reporter covering it, it was impossible for me not to feel all the overpowering emotions of that moment. As quickly as I could, I scripted my story and edited the tape to feed back to the Independent Network News in New York. The events of the day were weighing heavily on me and I needed a momentary break. My colleague and I crossed the border into Tijuana and had tequila shots and dinner as we watched the vibrant sun slowly sink into the clear blue Pacific Ocean. It was a much-needed moment of tranquility to cap an otherwise dark day.

* * *

A new day dawned with flags flying at half-staff. Workers had already arrived at the ravaged McDonald's to replace the shattered windows and hose away the bloodstains. But the scars left by the gunman's fury would leave San Ysidro's tight-knit community traumatized. As the many funerals were being arranged, family crisis centers were opened for residents coping with the events of the day before, and special psychologists were brought in for the town's children, who complained of sleeplessness and nightmares.

The McDonald's massacre, as the shooting came to be called, touched the collective consciousness of an entire nation, and brought new urgency to the debate over gun control. Yet according to authorities close to the investigation, even more restrictive gun laws could have done nothing to divert the murderous intent of James Oliver Huberty, a man they called a "walking time bomb."

"It's obvious he wanted to die," one authority noted, "and he wanted to take a lot of people with him."

In the wake of the tragedy, investigators set out to learn more about Huberty and what triggered his murderous rampage. People who knew him claimed that Huberty had become unhinged at an early age, after having been abandoned by his mother and suffering from the effects of polio. After working for years as a welder, he had been laid off and eventually moved to San Ysidro, where he had trouble landing a job. When he finally got one, he was fired shortly thereafter. In a rambling letter, Huberty's widow revealed that her husband, who had long resisted any therapeutic treatment for his anger, had called the county mental health office two days before his murderous spree.

Failing to get an appointment, Huberty proclaimed to his wife, "Society had their chance." Etna Huberty also revealed that her despondent husband had tried to commit suicide a year earlier, but she had managed to pry the gun out of his hand.

Among the theories concerning what had driven Huberty to

the brink was one suggesting that he had inhaled toxic fumes while working as a welder. After leaving that job, he complained that the fumes made him crazy, and the autopsy performed on his body did indeed show high levels of metal cadmium in Huberty's blood. Months after the massacre, Etna Huberty tried to use the autopsy report in a bizarre attempt to claim that McDonald's itself was responsible for the bloodbath. In an unsuccessful $5 million legal suit, she argued that the preservatives in the company's burgers had reacted with the chemicals in her husband's body to set off his murderous actions.

Joan Kroc, widow of McDonald's founder Ray Kroc, permanently closed the fast-food restaurant that had been attacked, and converted the site into a memorial park. She also established a $1 million survivors' fund for those who lived through Huberty's attack, and to assist with the victims' funerals.

I attended the first of many funerals for the twenty one victims. In the shadow of the Mexican hillside, where many of the victims were born, mourners came by the hundreds to Our Lady of Mt. Carmel Church. Among them was Mrs. Kroc, who came to comfort the families. So did the widow of the man responsible for it all: Etna Huberty, dressed in black, stood somberly in the crowd. The air was heavy, the humidity oppressive, the sky gray. Emotions were high as five caskets were lined up, one of them containing the bodies of Jackie Reyes and her infant son Carlos. The caskets were blessed with holy water, and prayers were recited.

I was in the second pew during the mass, my eyes fixed on the five white caskets in front of me. When congregants were asked to join hands in a sign of peace, I pressed my hand into that of a teary-eyed woman next to me. A chill came over my body and my eyes became watery. At that moment, I wasn't simply a reporter covering a tragic story. I had become one of the mourners.

8

THE GREENWICH MURDERS

Kim Klein and Jim Klein.

*i*t had all the earmarks of a mob execution: two women shot in the head at close range, no signs of forced entry, no fingerprints found. However, while the evidence uncovered potential ties to organized crime or drug trafficking, police ended up pinning the murders on the estranged husband of one of the victims.

38-year-old James Michael Klein was the most expedient suspect in the murders of his ex-wife Joanne Kim Klein, a 31-year-old former model, and her 28-year-old live-in Colombian maid, Martha Lema. The bodies of the two women were found in the master bedroom of Kim Klein's five-bedroom split-level house, in the affluent suburban community of Greenwich, Connecticut—a community whose residents abhorred scandal and seeing their tony town in the news.

Though it was only the third murder case in Greenwich over the past quarter-century, the sensational double homicide of Klein and Lema was big news back in June of 1976. This was due in part to the fact that the community was already in the national crosshairs for another headline murder case. The bludgeoning death of 16-year-old Martha Moxley just eight months earlier had garnered national attention when the murder was linked to two nephews of Ethel Skakel Kennedy, widow of the late Senator Robert Kennedy. (One of these suspects, Michael Skakel, was later convicted of the crime.) Already under criticism for their poor handling of the Moxley investigation, Greenwich police now faced another national-level murder challenge—for which they knew they needed an open-and-shut case, and a suspect quickly in custody.

They found their man in Jim Klein. The evidence against Klein was circumstantial—his only link to the crime scene was his acknowledgement that he had visited the house hours before the murders—but police built their entire case around Klein's admission, to pin the murders solely on him.

* * *

After an almost three-month-long investigation in which my colleagues and I (at then-WNEW-TV Channel 5 in New York) collaborated with newspaper reporter Doug Williams of the *Portchester Daily Item*, we uncovered faulty police work on the part of the Greenwich Police Department in their case against Jim Klein. We found that some of the evidence against Klein had been outright falsified, and that there were inaccurate reports of criminal forensic tests, erroneous statements in evidence reporting, and inconsistencies in statements and reports by Greenwich's Captain of Detectives—and later Chief—Thomas Keegan.

It had begun with the initial discovery of the bodies of Kim

Klein and Martha Lema. Police showed up at Kim Klein's Perkins Road home after Kim failed to pick up her six-year-old son Jay from school. When nobody answered the door, police entered through a second-floor window, where they discovered the fully clothed bodies of the two women. Kim had been shot in the head and mouth, and Martha twice in the head. Blood was spattered everywhere. Untouched on the dresser were three $50 bills.

Though four shots had been fired, police recovered only one shell casing, from a nine-millimeter weapon. It was theorized that the killer had retrieved the other casings but was unable to find the fourth, which was later found under Kim's body. Despite the appearance that this may have been the work of a professional killer, the theory was vociferously denied by Captain Keegan, who already had his sights on Jim Klein.

Klein told police he had gone to the house to discuss financial issues with Kim, from whom he had been divorced for a year and a half. He said they'd had coffee together, and quarreled when Kim asked for $200 beyond her usual alimony. Jim gave her $150 and left in a huff, cutting a finger as he slammed the trunk of his rented car. "Fuck you, lady" were his final words to his ex-wife. Hours later, she was dead.

A private investigator found witnesses who put Jim back at his Manhattan East Side apartment around 4 p.m. Afterward, he had gone out partying with friends. Police had no evidence that he was in the house at the time of the murders, but an affidavit to the grand jury implied that he didn't get back to New York from Connecticut until 4 a.m., when he was informed of Kim's murder and questioned by detectives. Because whoever committed the murders would likely have been splattered with blood, detectives subsequently obtained a warrant to take some of Jim's clothing to be tested. They also drew blood from him for forensic testing.

In the hours and days that followed, a clearer and darker image emerged of the murder victims, suggesting that they could have been targeted by someone other than Jim Klein. Kim was born in Calumet City, Illinois, a town with a wide-open, sleazy reputation quite different from the affluent suburban world of Greenwich. In telephone conversations I had with her mother, I learned that Kim had somewhat of a checkered past. She had been a prostitute and go-go dancer, and was married previously to a Mafia lawyer connected to Chicago mob kingpin Sam Giancana. She had friendships with several organized-crime figures, and at one point had been interviewed by an Illinois crime commission.

Captain Keegan was curt with me when I called to query him about what I had learned from Kim's mother.

He had no response to the information and sounded annoyed, snapping at me, "We're already aware of that." He suggested I stay out of his investigation. He didn't like that I appeared to be jumping ahead of him, and at one point, if I understood him correctly, he threatened to run me out of town. A couple of days later, I learned that after my conversation with him, Keegan personally placed a call to Kim's mother.

The deeper my colleagues and I probed, the more we learned about the victims and the man suspected of killing them. Kim, we were told, had boasted about her relationships with mobsters, and informed a former employer that she had written an autobiography that she claimed to be an exposé, in which she would name names. She reportedly kept the manuscript in a bedside table—but the manuscript was never found. Jim said she had once confided in him that she was blackmailing an executive she met on a train. He didn't ask for specifics. When my colleague John Parsons asked Keegan about the blackmail account, Keegan admitted that the police had never considered it.

Kim was also an aspiring photographer, and liked to take nature pictures. Among the personal effects the Klein family turned over to us for our investigation, however, we found a number of nude photos of an unknown woman sitting by the indoor pool, and we received an unsubstantiated report that on the day she was murdered, Kim had an appointment to photograph a man in the nude. We wanted to know why police didn't have these photos or follow up on this report. But we never got our answer.

While Jim Klein was no saint—he was said to be into extra-marital relationships and drugs, and had quite a temper—Kim, we learned, had her own secrets to keep. She was a swinger who had relationships with men and women, and, according to her stepdaughter Debbie, "was involved with drugs, with cocaine and marijuana, and she took pills." She threw parties in her Perkins Road home that often included drug-fests around the indoor pool. Her live-in maid, Martha Lema, was reportedly the coke connection fueling these parties. Martha had once boasted to Jim that she knew the biggest coke dealer on Long Island; and a couple of days before the murders, she had returned from Medellín, Colombia. Was Martha a drug courier in a deal gone bad? Was she the real target of the murder, and Kim simply collateral damage? Police rejected this theory as well, claiming that their investigation found no connection with either woman to drugs or organized crime. Keegan exploded in anger over reports that his department wasn't doing an adequate investigation. He called a news conference to refute these assertions, in which he continued to deny that Kim Klein had ever had any Mafia connections, and defended the character of Martha Lema.

* * *

A possible break in the case came when I received a tip that an international hit man had been arrested by New York police on a weapons charge. Frank Aranio was from Medellin, Colombia, Martha Lema's hometown, and lived in the same Queens neighborhood where she had once lived. Based on other information I had received, I reported that it was very likely that Aranio was the drug dealer Martha said she knew. On the broadcast, we called on police to run ballistic tests on Aranio's guns to determine whether any of them could have been the weapon used to kill the two women. The Walther P38 in his possession was a nine-millimeter, the same caliber as the murder weapon. Forensic tests showed no match to the shell casing found at the murder scene, but being that a few months had passed since the murders, I noted that a professional killer could easily have changed the barrel of the gun.

Aranio was also reported to have a green car with a black top. Curiously, on the day of the murders, witnesses reported seeing a car of that description in the driveway. Captain Keegan initially denied these reports, but the following day he admitted to me that there had been a car in witnesses' accounts. It belonged, he said, to a contractor working at a neighbor's home, some 200 yards away; though he offered no explanation as to why someone would park so far away—the length of two football fields—from a house where he was working.

Three and a half months after the murders, Jim Klein traveled to Florida to visit his son Jay, who was living with Jim's parents. Detectives followed him there, and showed up with a sealed indictment and warrant for his arrest. His bail was set at a quarter of a million dollars. Unable to pay it, Jim remained locked up for 69 days before his attorney got the bail reduced to $150,000, which his family put up. Though Jim insisted he informed police of his whereabouts when he traveled to Florida, Captain Keegan suggested he was attempting to escape prosecution.

Now out on bail, Jim fell deeper and deeper into depression. His legal team and private investigator Walter Smith found inconsistencies and false information in police affidavits, which they claimed constituted an attempt by the police to solidify their case against Jim. In one police document it was stated that, "Based on the way the women were shot, it is likely and probable that the murderer would have been splattered with blood." There was no such mention of that in the affidavit signed by Keegan. He would later admit that the statement was "an unfortunate choice of words." Unfortunate indeed, argued Klein's legal team—particularly after the FBI lab in Washington only found *traces* of blood on a pair of Jim's trousers, and in an amount so minute, they couldn't determine whose blood it was. The report was inconclusive; it could well have been from the finger Jim had cut while slamming the trunk of his car.

Other tests also failed to prove any guilt. Most notable was the test meant to determine if Jim Klein had recently fired a gun. The U.S. Bureau of Alcohol, Tobacco and Firearms did a chemical analysis of swabs taken from the suspect's hand, and reported that chemists found 3.5 micrograms of barium on one of the swabs. This seemed like positive news for the case police were building against him, until Walter Smith and Jim's attorney David Wise studied the findings and found that the amount wasn't 3.5 micrograms, but 0.325 micrograms, an amount of barium too miniscule to have been the result of gunfire.

In yet another discrepancy, Detective Stephen Carroll showed Jim's daughter a sketch of a gun that could have been similar to the murder weapon, and asked her if it resembled any of the three weapons legally owned by her father.

"It looked like nothing I described," she told me. Yet in Captain Keegan's report, he stated that she concurred that one of Jim's guns did resemble an automatic or semi-automatic pistol.

* * *

Seventeen detectives and investigators were assigned to the Greenwich murder case, but in the end the case against Jim Klein was full of discrepancies, mistakes and, according to witnesses themselves, complete reversals of fact. No murder weapon was ever found; no fingerprints were discovered; not a single witness placed Jim Klein at the scene at the time of the murders. The only solid evidence police had was Jim's own acknowledgement that he had been in the house that day. Despite these negatives, however, Captain Keegan was ready to go to trial.

"At this point," he declared, expressing his confidence that Jim would be found guilty, "we have no evidence that anyone else is responsible."

But he would never have the opportunity to prosecute his case to the fullest. Jim Klein, believing he was being framed and would die in prison, became so despondent that he committed suicide, leaving two notes beside an empty bottle of sleeping pills.

"I hope everyone will forgive me for taking this drastic step," he began. "The only ones who are going to be happy about this are the Greenwich Police and the State of Connecticut. If I can be granted a last wish," he added, "it is that they do not get off lightly. I just can't take the pressure anymore. Knowing that a state is dedicated to putting me away for life...has driven me crazy."

In a bizarre turn of events, within weeks after the suicide, Jim's uncle, Stanley Adler, who had just given a lawyer $10,000 to help clear his nephew's name, was found shot to death in his mattress store. Police called the murder an attempted robbery, though almost $200 was found in his wallet.

John Parsons, Doug Williams and I felt we had built a strong case showing that people other than Jim Klein had committed the murders in Greenwich. The criminologists and legal experts with whom we conferred were of the opinion that the state's case against Jim Klein was weak at best, and called the case's police work "sloppy." Investigator Walter Smith, who had worked on 43 murder cases, said he was confident that, had Jim gone to trial, he would have been found innocent. As an added element, I called psychic Dorothy Allison, who had previously worked with police in helping to solve crimes. My conversation with her was uncanny. Dorothy was not at all familiar with the case, but as we were speaking on the phone, she began to rattle off tidbits of descriptive information of which she could not have had any direct knowledge. She agreed to meet with Kim Klein's stepdaughter Debbie, who held a personal belonging of her stepmother's during their conversation. Dorothy came up with more of the dark background of both Jim and Kim Klein. She had visions of Kim talking with a man on a train about collaborating on a book, and claimed to see a tall, dark figure in the room where the women were murdered. Interesting stuff—but nothing conclusive as to who might have committed the crime. The segment, which we filmed, was dramatic and would have made for good television—but I chose not to use it on the air, for fear that police would claim that a psychic had been our source for information, and dismiss our conclusions. What we uncovered in our investigation was substantial and stood alone.

In the end, our investigation concluded that Jim Klein was likely the victim of a grave injustice, and that superficial police work had failed to determine the real killer of Kim Klein and Martha Lema. Nevertheless, up until his retirement Thomas Keegan remained steadfast in his contention that the evidence he had compiled still stands. "Case closed!"

9

THE FBI BEAT ME
TO THE RANSOM

 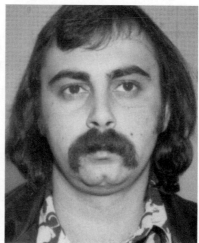

Left: Cesar Augusto Ortega. Right: Richard Louis Ventola.

*i*t was a kidnapping that ended in a matter of hours with the safe return of an 8-year-old boy and the quick arrest of his abductors. But it would be weeks before the FBI would recover the ransom money—and I came close to being the person who returned it.

Young John Calzadilla was kidnapped while returning from school in the exclusive Dix Hills section of Long Island, New York. It was the latest in a dozen kidnappings that had taken place across the country in 1974, including the abduction just six weeks earlier of newspaper heiress Patty Hearst. His father Michael Calzadilla, a local tire-company executive, was terrified, and feared the worst. A Cuban exile, he believed his son's abduction was politically motivated.

It wasn't. The kidnappers' motives became clear early that evening, when the phone rang and a male voice on the other end claimed to have the boy, and demanded $50,000 for his return. Calzadilla spent the next 24 hours raising the cash. As instructed, he had it collected in tens, twenties, fifties and hundreds, all carefully marked by the FBI, before he headed out to the drop point in North Bergen, New Jersey. He was sweaty and trembling during the one-hour drive, filled with uncertainty about his son as he listened to reports of the kidnapping on the radio. He prayed that John was still alive, and that the kidnappers would release him unharmed after he delivered the money.

It was 2 a.m. when Calzadilla approached a remote railroad overpass at the end of a darkened road. His eyes strained to cut through the blackness. No one was in sight. He climbed up to the tracks, stood for a moment and tossed the small black attaché case with the loot into a ravine. Having met the kidnappers' demands, he raced home to await their next call. It came shortly after 4 a.m. Anger and threats filled the male caller's voice as he claimed the ransom was not where it should have been. In a panic, the father raced frantically back to the drop point. The money was gone.

With their ransom unpaid, and fearful that police were on their trail, the kidnappers panicked and decided to release young John Calzadilla, who walked into a motel near the Holland Tunnel and asked a clerk to call police and his family. He was unharmed, and the 32-hour ordeal was over—but the whereabouts of the kidnappers and the $50,000 ransom remained unknown.

Within days, seven people— two adults and five teens—were arrested in connection with the crime, and charged with kidnapping and extortion. The prosecutor described the case as "a bungled kidnapping that became a comedy of errors." Under intense questioning by the FBI, corroborated by a lie-detector test, all of the suspects denied receiving the ransom, prompting then–U.S. Attorney for New Jersey Jonathan Goldstein to declare that anyone who had the money would be held just as culpable for the kidnapping as those who had already been charged.

That sent shivers through the spine of Richard Louis Ventola, a conductor, and Cesar Augusto Ortega, a brakeman for Penn Central Railroad. The two had been assembling a freight train the night Calzadilla made his drop, and after seeing something being thrown from the tracks, they went to explore and were stunned when they found the case stacked with thousands of dollars. "Finders keepers" was their immediate thought, as they fantasized about what they could do with all that cash. Ventola was heavily in debt, and Ortega's wife was expecting another baby in a matter of weeks. They argued over whether or not to tell authorities about their find—but they figured that since someone had thrown it away, it was probably Mafia money, so they decided to keep it.

Sitting alongside the track, they stuffed the cash into their coveralls and lunch boxes, later stashing it in their work lockers for safekeeping until they could make an equal split. But the story of the missing ransom was all over the news, and it wasn't long before the two railmen realized that it was the money they found. Ortega was frightened, and suggested to his coworker that they call the police and turn the money in. But they didn't immediately, out of fear that they would be implicated in the kidnapping.

With no idea how to unload their loot, Ventola, who was 26, and Ortega, 23, went into panic mode. They were convinced that the bills had been marked, and by now their fingerprints were all over them. So they decided to wash each bill with soap and water, and hung them up to dry on a clothesline in Ortega's kitchen. Afterwards, they stacked all the bills into a box and hid it in Ortega's freezer, behind the ice cubes. (Well, not exactly all of it—they each peeled off a few hundred dollars for themselves, with which Ventola took a quick trip home to Santo Domingo, and Ortega bought a crib and other furniture for his new baby.)

The FBI, which had over 200 agents working on the case, focused its search for the ransom on the railroad yard after one agent discovered a money wrapper near the ransom drop point. Penn Central workers, including Ventola and Ortega, were questioned. After being brought before a grand jury, where they perjured themselves, the duo decided they had gotten deeper into this than they had expected, and felt it was time to get rid of the money. They contacted an attorney, who tried to cut a deal with the U.S. Attorney whereby the money would be returned in exchange for a guarantee that no criminal charges would be filed. Jonathan Goldstein rejected the offer, declaring, "We will not be blackmailed."

Meanwhile, the situation was taking its toll on Ortega and Ventola. Ortega's wife threatened to leave him unless he surrendered the money—and both men were petrified of going to jail if they were caught. They figured that if they dumped the money somewhere with a note, the heat would be off of them. Someone suggested they use a reporter as an intermediary, somebody who could be led to the money at a predetermined location, to turn it over to the police without giving them any knowledge who it came from. Ortega's attorney, Dennis Salerno, asked me if I would be interested in such a covert mission. "Absolutely," I replied. He took my card, and told me one of the men would call me to discuss details.

The call never came. Ortega and Ventola were arrested while they were in the process of "laundering" the money a second time, trying to remove any remaining fingerprints. When FBI agents recovered the money, the bills were still moist. Their attorney later told me that Ortega informed him he was putting the money through the cleansing process one more time, in preparation to call me.

The two were charged with illegal possession of ransom money and perjury for lying to the grand jury. At their arraignment, defense attorney Kevin Prongay pleaded for leniency, describing his clients as "just two Joe Schmoes who were standing there doing their jobs when, all of a sudden, the money fell down." Going further, he pleaded with the judge, "We're all human, we're all mortals, we all act irrationally at times." Prongay went on to argue that his clients "had not acted with criminal intent," and said that once they had the money, fearful that police had marked the bills, they simply didn't know how to do anything with it without incriminating themselves.

Ventola pleaded guilty to the charges, and received a suspended sentence. Ortega decided to fight and went to trial. He was found guilty and sentenced to six months in jail. The court was lenient with both men, because neither had been in trouble before. Authorities recovered all but $3,900 of the $50,000 ransom, which the rail workers pledged to repay.

Shortly after they were arrested, I received a call from J. Wallace LaPrade, special agent in charge of the FBI in New Jersey. He was curious to know why my business card was found in the possession of one of the defendants! I explained to him that I was supposed to be the guy they were going to lead to the ransom money, adding, "But you guys beat me to it."

10

THE FUGITIVES AND ME

Fugitive Kent Laning revealing plans to surrender during live broadcast.

*i*n 1972, it was the best reality television of the time—a fugitive from justice walking into a TV studio to talk about his escape from prison and announce his intentions to surrender. And I had the scoop. It would be the first in a number of similar cases, in which my reputation as a trustworthy local reporter would bring me into close contact with men on the run from the law.

33-year-old Kent Laning had been on the lam for two months from the minimum-security prison farm in New Jersey where he had been serving a one-to-three-year sentence for burglary. Police had long since put out a national alert for his arrest by Friday, April 14, 1972, when he walked into the studios of WNEW-TV in New

York and agreed to join me during our live 10 o'clock newscast to announce that he was ready to give himself up.

Wearing a light zippered jacket, brown shirt and tan slacks, Laning appeared a little nervous as he looked over my shoulder into the camera to tell us, "I can't live like I'm living now." He declined to say where and how he had been living since going AWOL, saying, "I'd be letting friends down."

There was sadness in his deep-set eyes as Laning justified his escape. He claimed that corrections officers had refused to allow him to phone home after he learned that his wife and two of his children were sick. When he didn't hear from his wife, he became alarmed.

"I felt there was something serious at home, and I wanted to be there," he explained.

As we continued our live interview—which ran over eight minutes, unprecedented for local newscasts at the time—the station's switchboard began to light up with dozens of calls from viewers. Some callers complained that we were glorifying fugitives. Others were sympathetic, and offered to help Laning.

The lanky fugitive said he had decided to tell his story on the air in order to dramatize the need for prison reform.

"Something needs to be done," he said. "There's a lot of people there that want help, but they're just not getting to them." Among the reforms he said he would like to see implemented were better rehabilitation programs, extended furloughs and work-release details, and "getting some of those guards off our backs."

Though I, and others, had expected Laning to turn himself over to police after the broadcast, it wasn't until we were on the air that I learned of his intention to surrender on Monday, after spending the weekend with his family to celebrate his sixth wedding anniversary and his daughter's fifth birthday. Joe Grant, publisher of Penal Press International, accompanied Laning to the studio, and said that before the broadcast he had informed New Jersey Director of Corrections and Parole Al Wagner of Laning's plan, and was told it wouldn't be a problem—a claim Wagner later denied.

After the interview, Laning stopped to accept handshakes and good wishes from members of the studio crew, and to take a couple of calls from viewers. There was a sudden burst of anxiety throughout the studio when the news desk informed us that they had received a call from police, inquiring about the fugitive we had on the air live. As I escorted Laning and Grant out through the garage, I observed a couple of detectives entering the main entrance to the building, just a few yards away. I didn't want to know where Laning was heading, but asked him to call me on Monday so I could be with him when he surrendered. As the two drove off, they passed other detectives from the precinct just a block away, who were now descending on the studio.

The next morning I called the Americana Hotel, where I knew Joe Grant was staying. To my surprise, it was Laning who answered the phone. I told him of the uproar his appearance had created, and that it had made headlines in all of the city's newspapers. New York police and New Jersey corrections authorities were red-faced with embarrassment over the fact that Laning had managed to elude them after his shocking appearance on television, and the pressure was on to find him. I encouraged him to turn himself in immediately. We agreed to do a follow-up interview, but when I arrived at the hotel, only Grant was in the room. He agreed that Laning shouldn't delay his surrender any longer—but it was too late. A telephone call from my news desk informed us that Laning had been arrested and taken to the 14th police precinct.

We arrived as he was being led toward a police car for booking in lower Manhattan. With his hands cuffed behind his back, Laning managed just a few words, saying he had hoped it would not end this way, and that he had in fact intended to keep his promise, and surrender in two days.

Laning was extradited back to New Jersey, where a grand jury promptly indicted him for escape. Initially, Laning pleaded not guilty, and I was subpoenaed to testify at his trial. But it never came to that. Laning ultimately changed his plea to guilty, and the judge added one year to the sentence he had already been serving.

* * *

Two years later, newspaper reporter Lawrence Babich and I were contacted by another fugitive, a New Jersey mechanic who wanted to surrender to us. The suspect told us he was concerned for his safety, and feared that police would physically harm him.

35-year-old Peter Crandall was wanted for the murder of two-year-old Lorraine Hoffman and the physical abuse of her three-year-old sister Kelly Ann, who was found with multiple bruises on her body. The children's mother, Kathleen Pearl Hoffman, had already been charged with murder and child abuse.

Dressed in light-blue slacks and a brown sport shirt with the sleeves rolled halfway up his arms, Crandall drove his blue station wagon into the parking lot near the Holland Tunnel where we had arranged to meet. Joined by his wife Kathy and attorney Peter Willis, Crandall insisted he was innocent, claiming he was the victim of a "grudge act" by the children's mother, who was in love with him. The Crandalls took Kathleen Hoffman into their home because she had no place to stay with her children, and months later asked her to leave after she came home intoxicated and angry. Mrs. Crandall said that when Kathleen left she threatened "she would get revenge on me, and that's why she has implicated my husband in this crime." As we sat in a nearby diner over hot cups of coffee, Crandall claimed he first heard of the crime when he read in the newspaper that there was a warrant out for his arrest.

"I was so scared," he said. "I was just driving around, trying to get myself together. I haven't slept or eaten."

His voice faltered for a moment as he spoke emotionally about the crime he was accused of committing. "I'd sooner kill myself than kill a child," he declared. "I don't beat my own kids. Why should

I beat someone else's child?"

We escorted Crandall to police headquarters, where he kissed his wife goodbye and was taken into custody by Lieutenant Thomas Fitzpatrick, commander of the homicide squad, who vowed to take personal responsibility for his safety.

A grand jury subsequently indicted Crandall for murder and child abuse. Unable to post bail, he was held in the county jail for almost a year before his trial. His distraught wife Kathy corresponded with me, hoping I could be of some help, "because maybe a newsman has more power with people than just a person on the street." Assuring me that Peter was a good man, she added,

"He has three children with me, and he has never hurt them," and she expressed the fear that "if they put him away he'll die not only inside, but physically as well. He didn't do it, he couldn't do it. He doesn't have it in him."

In letters to me from the county jail, Crandall kept me updated on the progress of his case as he awaited trial. In one hand-scrawled letter, he expressed his desire to donate one of his kidneys. "Believe me, this is not a con game and has nothing to do with my case," he wrote. "Someday my three kids may have kidney trouble, and they will need help. I feel it's my place to help somebody."

Crandall was so determined that his offer to donate a kidney resulted in a court hearing, where I was subpoenaed to testify about my correspondence with him. Prosecutors said that while Crandall's gesture was noble and magnanimous, they feared the medical procedure would further delay the trial. New Jersey Superior Court Judge Joseph Hanrahan agreed and denied Crandall's request, noting that Crandall could be just as gracious after his trial.

In the end, Crandall never donated his kidney—nor did he go to prison. A jury found him not guilty after his attorney presented apologetic letters from the dead girl's mother, exonerating her co-defendant from any involvement in the child's murder.

After his ordeal, Crandall moved to Florida, got a job and stayed out of trouble. He returned to New Jersey ten years later to see his attorney one more time—to present him with a check for $5000, a debt he simply couldn't afford to pay a decade earlier.

* * *

My reputation among the inmates at Trenton State Penitentiary was what prompted Charlie Potter to reach out to me. Potter was a fast-talking con artist who jolted me out of bed one morning with a phone call.

"You Marvin Scott?" he asked. Barely waiting for my answer, he blurted, "If you want a story, get your ass down to Trenton." He proceeded to tell me that he was a fugitive who had escaped from nearby Trenton State, and was ready to turn himself in, but wanted a reporter to arrange his surrender to someone from the New Jersey Attorney General's office. Potter told me he had been serving time for murder.

I informed my news director, Ted Kavanau, about the call, and asked him to make contact with New Jersey authorities and arrange for a camera crew to meet me at the Holiday Inn across the street from the statehouse. With a kiss and "Have a good day" sendoff from my wife, I got into my car and raced down the turnpike to Trenton, where I rendezvoused with Potter in front of the bus terminal. Bristling with bravado, he got into the car and immediately let me know he was armed with a .38-caliber revolver and that police wouldn't take him alive.

That rattled me a bit! Here I was in a moving car, sitting next to an armed escaped convict with no visual signs that I was a reporter. With no specific destination in mind, he told me to drive on. There being no cell phones back then, I stopped periodically at pay phones to call the news desk to determine whether the Attorney General's office had been contacted, and if the crew was on the way.

With at least two hours to kill, I continued to drive around the streets of Trenton, listening to Potter's ramblings about the injustices of the prison system and its need for reform. A couple of times, he had me stop so he could have a drink at a local bar. At one, he boasted to the bartender that he was a convict who had escaped from Trenton State, then downed another drink as the bartender chuckled nervously. On several occasions Potter reminded me that he was armed, and would not be taken alive if confronted by police; he never showed me the weapon, but I wasn't about to challenge him.

After another call to New York, I learned that the crew had arrived at the Holiday Inn, and was waiting for us. By the time Potter and I entered the room on the second floor, he was clearly inebriated, but remained coherent as he rattled off his grievances during a brief on-camera interview.

Minutes later came a knock at the door, and two burly State Police detectives, sent by the New Jersey Attorney General, entered. Standing face-to-face with the fugitive, they asked, "Are you Charlie Potter?"

When he responded in the affirmative, they asked if he was armed, and he declared, "No." If only I had known that six hours earlier! He was then frisked, placed in handcuffs and led away to face escape charges. Only after he was gone did I learn that Potter wasn't an escaped murderer from Trenton State, but someone serving time for vehicular homicide at the state's minimum-security prison farm, where he had been out on furlough but failed to return at his prescribed time.

Nevertheless, it made for a good lead story for our 10 o'clock newscast. The next day I learned that News Director Kavanau had given the crew a bonus in hazard pay, for taking on an assignment with a fugitive believed to be armed. As for me, I got a gold star with a two-word note: "Good job."

11

THE WRONG MAN

Isidore Zimmerman.

*i*t's been said that sometimes life just deals you a bad hand—that things happen in our lives that just aren't fair. No one knew that better than Isidore Zimmerman, who came within two hours of dying in New York's electric chair for a crime he didn't commit.

His is just one of the multitude of stories I've covered that point to the flaws in our criminal justice system, a system so inherently problematic that it routinely allows evidence to slip through the cracks, and wrongfully sends innocent people to prison. Zimmerman was a 19-year-old aspiring lawyer, hoping for a football scholarship to Columbia University when he was implicated in the murder of a police detective during a botched robbery on April 10,

1937. Six men were arrested in connection with the crime, and one of them—in an apparent effort to conceal his own involvement—falsely accused Zimmerman of supplying the murder weapon. Despite Zimmerman's protestations of innocence—he had merely picked up a coat for one of his friends, he said, and didn't know the gun was in the coat pocket—he and the six others were all convicted of first-degree murder, and sentenced to death in New York's infamous Sing Sing prison.

Five of them were executed in the electric chair, and the sixth died in prison. Zimmerman himself came within two hours of his own meeting with the grim reaper. After almost two years on death row, he was given his last meal, his head was shaved, and slits were cut in his trousers for the electrodes. Zimmerman was praying with a rabbi when they were interrupted by the deputy warden, who proclaimed, "Zimmerman, you're not dying tonight!" After reviewing evidence of irregularities in the original testimony that led to Zimmerman's conviction, Governor Herbert Lehman, at the last minute, commuted his sentence to life in prison. It took another 23 years of legal battles before a state court reviewed the case and overturned his conviction. His life spared, the 45-year-old Zimmerman finally walked free.

Following his release, however, Zimmerman was haunted by the trauma of the experience.

"I haven't had a good night's sleep, because of too many nightmares interfering with my mind," he would later tell me in an interview. He claimed he had been brutalized in prison by anti-Semitic guards, who put him through mental torture and beatings. He also complained of long periods spent in solitary confinement, during which he was forced to live solely on bread and water. "This was the most degrading experience a man can endure," he said, his voice cracking at the memory. "You're at the whims and fancies of guards who abhor convicts." He claimed they used the least excuse "to beat you senseless."

What got Zimmerman through the ordeal of prison—made doubly torturous to him by the knowledge that he didn't belong there—was helping others. He became a jailhouse lawyer during his time inside, and helped turn out 700 fellow inmates. "Helping them out with their problems," he reflected, "helped me forget my own." This work led him to become one of the founders of the Fortune Society, an organization devoted to the rights of prisoners.

After his release, Zimmerman felt he should be compensated by the State of New York for the life it had unjustly taken from him, and petitioned to have a bill passed in the state legislature that would allow him to sue the state. It took him 20 years to get the bill passed, after which he brought his lawsuit, seeking $10 million in compensation. The judge, however, settled on $1 million as "fair and reasonable." After legal fees and other expenses, Zimmerman had a balance of about $660,000. "Once I paid off my debts, I was left with $300,000," he remembered sadly. "I felt I should have been compensated to the point that I could live comfortably, and establish the dreams I have," he added haltingly. "Now they have destroyed my dreams." The paltry payout, he emphasized, was only the second miscarriage of justice he suffered. "People never think that this could ever happen to them," he declared. "But it does. I'm living proof of that." His attorney would later agree, telling me that Zimmerman "always said he had this black cloud over him."

All the anguish and despair took its toll on Zimmerman's life. Now balding, wearing glasses and walking with a cane, he looked older than his 66 years. I asked him about his future plans, and how he planned to spend the settlement money he had just received. He had already bought a new car and taken a trip to an upstate New York resort for a few days.

"I want to rest and relax, and I don't want to worry about tomorrow. The only way to defeat the recurring nightmare is to rest and relax." He bubbled with excitement as he described his marriage. "I have a beautiful woman who waited 25 years for me.

She's like my second warden—I must admit that." With a twinkle in his eye, he declared, "I adore her."

Isidore Zimmerman never got to live his dream. Two weeks after our interview—a mere four months after he received his disappointing settlement from the state—he suffered a fatal heart attack at the age of 66. He was the opposite side to the grand, dramatic story of redemption with which our culture is familiar: an ordinary man, to whom life had simply dealt a bad hand.

the times

12

THE TRIUMPH AND TRAGEDY OF SPACE

Space Shuttle Challenger explodes minutes after launch. January 28, 1986.

"We choose to go to the moon in this decade and do other things, not because they are easy but because they are hard."
—PRESIDENT JOHN F. KENNEDY, MAY 1961

*t*he national commitment made by President Kennedy, one month after the Russians made history by placing the first human in earth orbit, captured the imagination of people everywhere, setting in motion one of the greatest challenges ever to face mankind. After all, placing a man on the moon was the stuff science fiction was made of.

The Space Center at Cape Canaveral on the east coast of Florida became the focal point of America's space operations. It was here that seven intrepid astronauts, known as the Mercury 7, blazed the trail for the country's future missions to the moon. John Glenn, Alan Shepard, Wally Schirra, Virgil "Gus" Grissom, Scott Carpenter, Donald "Deke" Slayton and Gordon Cooper were the first Americans to ride into orbit, aboard cramped space capsules the size of a telephone booth.

The Mercury program had advanced to another phase when I arrived in the space-frenzied town of Cocoa Beach on my first assignment in 1966. Once a quiet vacation town, Cocoa Beach had become a boomtown in the sixties when the John F. Kennedy Space Center, 15 miles to the north, became a mecca for jobs. As a result, the town quickly grew to a population of 250,000. Now it was Moonport, USA, with thousands of its residents employed by the space program. Pristine white beaches were lined with hotels bearing names like Sea Missile, Polaris and Apollo; there was even a Celestial Trailer Court. Restaurants like the Moon Hut offered "moon burgers" and "three stage martinis." Restrooms accommodated "Astronauts" and "Astronettes."

This was an enclave for the media covering the space missions, and there was always somewhat of a party atmosphere before each launch. Tom Wolfe's men with the "right stuff" would hang out with reporters around the pool at the Holiday Inn, and hundreds of contractors would host cocktail receptions and hand out token presents on which their companies' names were emblazoned. Almost every day before a launch was a day to celebrate. Walter Cronkite, Jules Bergman and other network anchors would host breakfasts at their hotels before venturing off to the Space Center on the morning of a launch. As pool producer for network radio, I would host a breakfast for my colleagues as well.

Hours before the launch, a long caravan of vehicles meandered 15 miles down the highway to Merritt Island and the main gate.

It wasn't quite dawn as we approached the press site about three miles from Launch Complex 19, which was bathed in lights and surrounded by the lifting morning fog. There, visible atop a Titan II rocket, was the cone-shaped Gemini 9, a space capsule that would carry astronauts Eugene Cernan and Tom Stafford on a three-day mission, including a docking maneuver and a spacewalk. A huge countdown clock ticked down the minutes before launch.

Soon the voice from mission control was narrating the final countdown sequence. Then a huge flame gushed from the launch complex, and slowly the rocket lifted off. As Gemini slipped into the sky, the sound waves from the launch rumbled through the ground at the press site. It was quite an exhilarating experience to view a launch firsthand, from so close.

*　*　*

Aside from a few glitches and setbacks, the space program moved along quite well in the beginning. Launches were soon being scheduled every few months, and development of the Apollo program—which would ultimately carry Americans to the moon—was well underway. Things were running smoothly—until January 27th, 1967.

As radio pool producer for the upcoming mission of Apollo 1, I was working out of the CBS Broadcast Center in New York on that rain-swept Friday. I was making arrangements for my trip to Cape Canaveral the following Monday, just three weeks before the mission's scheduled liftoff. It was early evening when I heard a CBS producer running through the building, screaming out for Walter Cronkite. There was something urgent and ominous in his voice. Moments later, Cronkite was on the air with the bulletin that three astronauts were dead in a launch-pad fire at the Space Center.

I gasped in disbelieving horror as I raced to the UPI teletype for more details. It was an awful disaster. Astronauts Virgil "Gus" Grissom, Roger Chaffee and Edward White were undergoing a routine test inside a pressurized space capsule when one of them was heard to exclaim, "Fire in the cockpit." Rescue workers rushed to try to save the astronauts, but the fire spread too quickly; the atmosphere in the cabin was pure, 100 percent oxygen, and under extreme pressure. The three men never had a chance. I felt overwhelming sadness for the astronauts, whom I had met the previous year. They were three of the most valued, courageous men in the space program, and their loss was devastating.

With the aborting of the Apollo mission, the pool operation was immediately disbanded. I reached out to my colleagues in Fajardo, Puerto Rico, who were there checking out the recovery ship for the mission. They too were overwhelmed with shock and sadness when I informed them of what had happened. My news director at Mutual Broadcasting directed me to get on the next plane to Florida. Eastern Airlines added a special flight there, stopping first in New York for members of the media, then in Washington to pick up officials of the space program. I arrived at the Space Center shortly after 5 a.m., in time to file a report for our 6 a.m. national newscast. Flags were flying at half-staff and the lights were shining brightly at Launch Complex 34—but NASA officials were still in the dark over what caused the flash fire.

A space agency official escorted a group of reporters to the 250-foot-high steel gantry, around which the space capsule was wrapped. The spacecraft itself was not visible, but we were told the heat had been so intense that its steel exterior was blackened. Inside, we learned, the astronauts' bodies were charred; the heat had melted their nylon space suits. Investigators would later trace the flash fire to a damaged wire under Grissom's seat. It was theorized that the wire had contacted metal, creating sparks that ignited the nylon netting that lined the cabin; the cabin's pure oxygen atmosphere fueled the resulting inferno.

The city of Houston, where the astronauts had lived and worked, was numbed by the tragedy. The entire country, and people the world over, mourned the loss of the three men of courage who had lived on the edge of the future.

Grissom and Chaffee were laid to rest with full military honors at Arlington National Cemetery. Ed White had an austere military burial at West Point. I attended the astronauts' memorial services. Martha Chaffee, dressed in a black suit with fur collar, clutched her small children's hands as she entered the Presbyterian church where the family had worshipped. Her swollen eyes hidden behind sunglasses, she listened as Roger Chaffee was eulogized as "a man who dreamed dreams and had gone out to fulfill the high calling of God." Virgil Grissom, America's second man in space, was remembered for his greatness and devotion to duty. Edward White, the first man to walk in space, was praised as a man who gave deeply of himself. The Reverend Conrad Winborn told a capacity-filled chapel, "We have all been the recipients of a priceless and eternal treasure."

The melodious tones of the church choir were overridden by the sound of three NASA T-38 jets, which flew low over the church in formation with one space left empty—a pilot's salute to a fallen comrade.

* * *

The accident was a major setback in President Kennedy's mission to put a man on the moon before the end of the decade; the Apollo program was put on hold for two years. Then Apollo 8 made a historic Christmas journey around the moon in 1968, followed by Apollo 10 six months later. Finally, on July 16, 1969, a new day dawned. Man was ready to journey to the moon.

It was a beautiful morning at Launch Complex 39—bright sunshine, a few fleecy clouds and temperatures nearing 90. A light breeze off the nearby Atlantic ruffled flags fluttering behind the wooden bleachers at the viewing site. 5,000 invited guests were there, including Vice President Spiro Agnew, former President and Mrs. Lyndon B. Johnson and aviation pioneer Charles Lindbergh. I was among 3,500 members of the press corps from 56 nations.

And miles away, jamming the riverfronts, beaches and highway approaches to the Space Center, were an estimated one million people who had come to witness the most daring voyage of exploration ever attempted.

And it couldn't have come at a better time. America needed a morale boost. The war was raging in Vietnam, anti-war protests were tearing our cities apart, and the nation was still mourning the assassinations of Martin Luther King Jr. and Robert Kennedy. We needed a diversion.

At Launch Complex 39, Astronauts Neil Armstrong, Buzz Aldrin and Mike Collins were sitting atop the 36-story Saturn V rocket, making last-minute checks. The huge countdown clock, was ticking down. Nine seconds before liftoff, the five first-stage engines of the Saturn rocket erupted like inverted volcanoes.

Jack King in mission control bellowed the final count: "five... four...three...two...one...liftoff, we have liftoff!" Building to seven-and-a-half million pounds of thrust—the equivalent of 180 million horsepower—the Saturn V slowly lifted off the pad in a brilliant fireball. I'll never forget the roar of the rocket and the rumble of the ground, or the chill that consumed my body in the 90-degree heat as I watched the rocket climb deeper into the almost cloudless sky. I was awestruck. As I shouted my excitement into a microphone, I found myself joining in the chant of the crowd: "Go, baby, go...*go, baby, go!*" Everyone was in a state of euphoria. Many cried tears of joy and pride. America was on the way to the moon.

Four days later, on July 20th, Neil Armstrong became the first human to set foot on the moon. "That's one small step for man, one giant leap for mankind," were his words that echoed around the world. It was a historic moment, forever frozen in time.

There would be five more manned landings on the moon before the Apollo program disbanded in 1973. It would be eight years before the U.S. would resume manned flights aboard a new reusable spacecraft, known as the Shuttle.

* * *

Space flight was quite routine by the time I returned to the Space Center on April 21, 1981. Blight had overcome the once booming towns that once made up America's thriving moon port. Gone were the moon burgers and motels with heavenly names. Businesses were closed, and buildings boarded. One thing hadn't changed, however: the long line of cars crawling toward the Space Center. At 4:30 in the morning, it took more than two hours to clear security checkpoints to finally arrive at the press site. Off in the distance, under the bright lights of the launch pad, we could see the gleaming-white space shuttle Columbia, poised for a mission that would lead her into the pages of space-exploration history.

A few setbacks had delayed the flight, but this looked like the morning Columbia would finally blast off into the heavens. The shuttle program was already two-and-a-half years behind schedule and $10 billion over budget. The astronauts, John Young and Bob Crippen, were ready, as were the spectators. Clouds of moist smoke encircled the shuttle, which was being fueled with half a million gallons of liquid oxygen and hydrogen.

The sun peered out from behind scattered clouds as the countdown clock transitioned from hours to minutes. At liftoff, flames gushed from the solid rocket boosters as the shuttle, with its external fuel tanks strapped to its side, inched off the pad. *Is it going to make it?*—I hesitated in thought; but then the mighty Saturn V edged upward, all 36 stories and four-and-a-half million pounds of it. A crescendo of cheers roared from the crowd. With the engines generating 1300 tons of thrust, Columbia began to clear the launch complex. She rolled on her side during the initial climb, and for a moment I feared she was going to tip over—but then I realized it was the way it was supposed to be. As I watched Columbia thunder into the deep-blue sky, I felt a tremendous sense of pride; once again America had triumphed, and I was an eyewitness to history.

Minutes after launch, the shuttle had diminished to a flaming speck in the sky. A little over two minutes into the flight, at 25 miles up, the solid rocket boosters, their fuel consumed, separated from the shuttle and fell 160 miles downrange into the Atlantic, to be recovered for future missions. Columbia herself broke the bonds of gravity, and orbited the Earth 37 times before landing two days later at Edwards Air Force Base in California. It was the first time a spacecraft would land on Earth by gliding down a runway, instead of splashing into the ocean. Like the first moon landing, the first space-shuttle launch still stands as a testament to the brilliance of American technology and human accomplishment.

* * *

But along with these triumphs came other tragedies. The euphoria of Columbia's feat was violently shattered 22 years later in 2003, when, on its 28th mission, the shuttle broke apart and disintegrated while reentering Earth's atmosphere, killing the entire seven-member crew. The Columbia disaster ended nearly two decades of accident-free shuttle missions and signaled the end of the shuttle program, which was formally scrubbed in 2011.

For me, it brought back memories of the program's only other catastrophe, 17 years previous. January 28, 1986, was the date set to record a new chapter in the history of manned space flight. The Space Shuttle Challenger was about to be launched, carrying its first civilian crewmember. Christa McAuliffe, an elementary-school teacher from New Hampshire, was going to conduct two lessons from outer space. Her third-grade class had been invited to view the launch from the VIP bleachers, along with her husband, children and parents.

I wanted to be there for the launch, but my news director decided not to send me on this one—shuttle flights had become so routine, he didn't see a need to have a reporter there. We still broadcast the launch, using video provided by NASA. We were riveted to the TV screen as Challenger surged flawlessly into the sky. But 73 seconds into the flight, cheers of joy suddenly turned to gasps of panic as the white contrail in the sky became erratic, jutting out in different directions. A fiery explosion seconds later left no doubt that the shuttle had exploded. Wreckage rained over the ocean as NASA declared the shuttle and its crew lost.

My news director didn't hesitate when I suggested I get on the next plane to cover this devastating story, and I arrived in time to file a telephone report for our 7:30 newscast. Temperatures dropped sharply in the night air, down to somewhere in the 40s. I hadn't brought clothing warm enough and I started to shiver, my teeth still chattering minutes before I was to go live. Someone brought me a hot cup of coffee, and I rolled the cup in my hands to warm them. I wondered how they could have planned on launching a shuttle in such cold conditions. Engineers had worried before about cold conditions impacting the integrity of the spacecraft, and after an exhaustive investigation, it was determined that these adverse conditions had indeed contributed to the disaster. The cold had caused the failure of the rubber O-rings that were used to prevent fuel from escaping during initial propulsion of the rocket boosters, eventually causing the boosters to rupture and explode.

A pall of grief and disbelief had fallen over the Space Center and its surrounding communities. Space-agency workers appeared dazed as they walked along the complex. Many were so distraught they had difficulty speaking, their voices choked with emotion. Once again, flags were draped at half-staff, and marquees around town bore the names of the seven lost astronauts along with the words, "You are heroes." America's loss felt like a personal loss to each and every one of us. It was impossible not to be touched by the loss of these seven young souls, particularly the crusading teacher who had volunteered to teach kids everywhere a lesson from space. What a moment that would have been.

It made me reflect on my own fantasy to venture into space, and the risks involved. I had already made the initial cut as a candidate for the Journalist-in-Space program, which was to follow these early civilian ventures. I was not deterred by the Challenger disaster, and felt more eager than ever to make such a pioneering journey; it would have been the ultimate assignment. But it wasn't to be. In the aftermath of the tragedy, the program was scrubbed, along with many other ambitious projects. It would be two years, in fact, before America's space program would resume, with the launch of the space shuttle Discovery.

* * *

Astronauts, like all explorers, understand that with the spirit and reward of exploration come risks. Our astronauts continued to take them as they forged ahead with their conquest of space.

A few weeks before he was killed in the Apollo 1's launch pad accident, Gus Grissom said, "We hope if anything happens to us, it will not delay the program." And though there were setbacks, the space program did continue, with 11 subsequent Apollo missions and 136 space shuttle missions. In the process, we helped build a space station, sent telescopes to probe the vastness of the universe and landed unmanned spacecraft on distant planets like Mars. And back on Earth, decades of space research have benefited our lives in so many ways, leading to the development of innovations from microchips, cell phones and GPS technology to solar panels and implantable heart monitors. The rewards of our exploration have been far more than ideological; they have been real human triumphs, and every day redeem the tragic sacrifices that made them possible. As Grissom said, again so prophetically, "The conquest of space is worth the risk."

13

THE ALCOHOLIC WHO
SAVED MY LIFE

The devastating scene on Sterling Place, Brooklyn, where the United Airlines jet fell after colliding with a TWA plane over New York. Photo Courtesy: New York Fire Department.

*t*he bells on the teletype were ringing incessantly, alerting us to a major breaking story. Bulletins morphed into newsflashes, with developing details of a mid-air collision between two commercial airliners over New York City. It was Friday, December 16th, 1960, and I was working the tail end of my overnight shift at radio station WCOL in Columbus, Ohio. I interrupted regular programming with our first bulletin of the disaster.

My pulse quickened as the story unfolded. A seven-alarm inferno was raging in the streets of Brooklyn, where a United Airlines jetliner had just plunged from the sky. Groping its way through snow and fog, and off-course by 11 miles, the jet broadsided a smaller prop-driven plane, sending it spinning wildly through the air before crashing on Staten Island. In all, 134 people died that day, including six people on the ground. In addition to being a national tragedy, this was a devastating local story for our Ohio listeners: the smaller of the two planes, TWA Flight 266, originated in Columbus and had many Ohio residents aboard. And as the bulletins came through, I was shocked to realize that I could very well have been one of the passengers aboard that ill-fated flight.

* * *

It had seemed the perfect weekend to visit home in New York. It was just before Christmas and my mother's birthday, and it provided the ideal opportunity for me to get to the Israeli Consulate to pick up the credentials they had approved for me to cover the trial of Nazi war criminal Adolf Eichmann. My initial plan was to begin a long weekend that Friday, and the TWA flight out of Columbus looked like my best bet.

As it turned out, a colleague's irresponsible behavior saved my life. A few days before my scheduled trip, News Director Allen Jeffries called me into his office to tell me he needed me to stay a day longer to work the overnight shift. One of my fellow news anchors, who regularly worked that shift, had been suspended after a third incident of being too intoxicated to go on the air. "Just leave on Saturday," Jeffries advised me, "and take an extra day on Monday."

By staying on the job, I found myself working past my shift to continue reporting the story and conducting telephone interviews with local airport officials and people who'd had loved ones on the doomed plane. Later, exhausted after working overnight, I headed back to my apartment for some much-needed sleep. I returned a few hours later for the station's annual Christmas party, which quickly turned into a celebration of me, with colleagues hugging and toasting me for not having been on Flight 266 that day.

* * *

Less than 24 hours later, I boarded another TWA plane bearing the same flight number as the one that had crashed the day before. I could sense the tension among my fellow passengers, many of whom gripped newspapers emblazoned with headlines of the disaster. The notes I scribbled during that flight are now yellowed, and tattered from age. But my memories of the disaster remain quite vivid.

After they picked me up at LaGuardia Airport, my parents drove me to the scene of the crash on Sterling Place in Brooklyn. I had a note from my news director, identifying me as a reporter and requesting that I be given access to the crash site. What I saw was like a scene from the worst disaster movie. Twisted and mangled chunks of a once-sleek airliner littered the street. The jet's right wing could be seen sliced into a four-story brownstone, the nose resting amid the charred remains of the Pillar of Fire Church. Somehow I managed to walk across the water-soaked carpet covering a portion of the fuselage that lay across the street. The seats had been torn from their mountings. Parts of the twisted landing gear were scattered beside a tree. An overturned car lay crushed under the plane, parts of which had fallen into a nearby funeral home with the passengers still strapped in their seats. Bloodstains were slowly vanishing in the melting snow.

Out of all the carnage there was life, if only briefly—a lone survivor who touched the consciousness and entered the prayers of people worldwide. 11-year-old Stephen Baltz, who had been on the United flight on his way to spend Christmas with his grandparents, was thrown clear of the crash and into a snow bank. When rescuers found him, he was in shock and had burns over 80% of his body, along with scorched lungs and broken bones. Through all his pain, he managed to joke with a hospital attendant, telling her, "The next time, I want my private plane." He asked his rescuers if he was going to die, and they tried to reassure him that he would not. But 26 hours later, Stephen succumbed to his injuries.

A permanent memorial to what was, at the time, the nation's worst aviation disaster is today located a dozen blocks from the crash site. On the back wall of the chapel at New York's Methodist Hospital, where the courageous young Stephen Baltz was treated, is a bronze plaque with the words: "Our tribute to a brave little boy." Attached to the plaque are nine burned nickels and dimes—the 65 cents rescuers found in Stephen's pocket when they pulled him out of the snow bank in Brooklyn.

Each anniversary of that disaster serves as a reminder of the fragility and preciousness of life. Every year, I give thanks to my drunken colleague who gave me reason to work that fateful day. And missing Flight 266 has had another impact on me. As silly as it may sound, I make every effort not to fly on the 16th of December.

14

ADDING A VOICE TO HISTORY

Frame 237 from Abraham Zapruder's film of JFK's assassination. Photo Courtesy: Zapruder Film © 1967. Renewed 1995 The Sixth Floor Museum at Dealey Plaza.

*i*t is arguably the most graphic and chilling visual record of a murder ever filmed, and surely the most controversial. The Zapruder film—the 26.6 seconds of silent imagery that captured the instant on November 22nd, 1963, when President John F. Kennedy was assassinated—served as the centerpiece of the investigation that led the Warren Commission to conclude that Lee Harvey Oswald was the lone shooter. Yet intense scrutiny of the film also gave rise to numerous conspiracy theories, including theories that the film had been created by the CIA using special effects.

In the fall of 1966, I went to Dallas to produce a documentary for the Mutual Broadcasting System, on the third anniversary of the

Kennedy assassination. I was determined to interview dress manu-facturer Abraham Zapruder about how he had come to be at the right place at the right time to record one of the darkest moments in American history.

It was to be a challenge. A quiet, unassuming man, Zapruder consistently shied away from public attention, and did not like to do interviews. When I called him from a motel near his office, he accepted my call, but—very graciously—declined to meet with me. Though I assured him that the interview would be brief, he would not relent. Not willing to give up so quickly, however, I engaged him in further conversation, talking with him about New York, particularly Brooklyn, where he had lived until he was 15 with his Jewish parents, who had emigrated from Russia.

With a subtle hint of an immigrant's accent, he seemed to enjoy talking with me about the New York yesterdays. About ten minutes into our conversation, he became interested in knowing more about me. As we chatted, it became apparent that we had something in common: we were both Jewish. We shared a few Yiddish words, and he wanted to know if I had been Bar Mitzvahed. That did it! Before I knew it, we had bonded, and the doors to his office suddenly parted.

"Can you be here at 2 o'clock?" he asked.

"Absolutely," I replied, buoyant to have snagged the prized interview. I would later learn that it was one of only a handful of broadcast interviews Zapruder had ever done.

A short, balding man, "Mr. Z," as his employees called him, welcomed me into his office that afternoon. Right away he explained his usual reticence, telling me how difficult it was for him to talk about that fateful day three years earlier. He had broken into uncon-trollable tears after witnessing the murder, and reliving the event always brought those intense feelings back. I promised to respect his sensitivity.

He was agreeable to joining me downstairs, just across the street, to conduct the interview on the grassy knoll where he had stood on November 22, 1963. His assistant, Marilyn Sitzman, 20 years his junior, joined us. Mr. Z told me how he had forgotten to bring his camera that day, and was encouraged by his secretary, Lillian Rogers, to go back home to get it.

"How many times will you have a crack at getting color movies of the president?" she reasoned. He said he loved President Kennedy, and was looking forward to seeing him and his beautiful First Lady up close.

Zapruder's voice dropped into the back of his throat as the dreadful moment went into rewind, and he began to bring it all back.

"I saw the motorcycles, then the car approached and Jacqueline and the president were waving," he said, his voice growing haltingly slower. "As it came in line with my camera, I heard a shot. I saw the president lean over to Jacqueline, then the second shot came; and then I realized I saw his head open up, and I started yelling, 'They killed him, they killed him,' and I continued shooting until they went under the underpass. It's left in my mind like a wound that heals up, yet there is some pain left as to what had happened." Zapruder removed his glasses to dab a tear from his eye. Sitzman recalled that her boss had become "hysterical" in the minutes after the assassination, which led us to an interesting revelation. Contrary to the findings of the Warren Commission, which determined that Lee Harvey Oswald had fired three shots from the sixth-floor window of the Texas School Book Depository, Zapruder said that he and Sitzman only heard two shots from behind and over their left shoulder, where the building was located. He explained that he did not dispute the Commission's conclusion, expressing his belief that he may not have heard the third shot because he was so traumatized by witnessing the murder of the president.

My interview with Zapruder and Sitzman lasted about 20 minutes. I was so appreciative, I invited both of them to join me for dinner; but Mr. Z would hear nothing of it.

"I want my wife to meet you," he insisted, smiling warmly.

That evening Zapruder brought me to his home, where we shot pool and his charming wife Lillian served us cocktails. He reached into a cabinet to show me the unopened camera that Bell & Howell had sent him in exchange for his B&H Zoomatic, which he had given to the company for their archives. He said he could never look through a viewfinder again, because it brought back all the awful images. He also told me he never wanted to have a copy of the historic film at home, for fear that someone would break in and steal it.

The Zapruders then hosted me at dinner, in a magnificent restaurant overlooking Dallas. With the lights of the city twinkling below, we kept the conversation light and entertaining. Mrs. Zapruder teasingly wanted to know why "a nice Jewish boy" like me wasn't married.

* * *

The 8-millimeter Zapruder film runs 26.6 seconds. The audio portion of my interview, in which he described just what he saw, runs 33 seconds. The first time I saw a full screening of the shocking film, I had the idea to synchronize that portion of the interview with the video to make it sound like Zapruder was actually narrating it. All I needed was the film. No easy task! It took me 40 years to make it happen; for decades, I was unable to get permission to use the film without paying an exorbitant fee.

On the 40th anniversary of the assassination, however, I learned that the Sixth Floor Museum in Dealey Plaza had been given the licensing rights by the Zapruder family.

I called the museum's curator, and basically told them, "Let's make a deal. You have something I want, and I have something I believe you will want." I told them of my interview decades earlier, and explained my idea. He was enthusiastic to learn about my rare interview with the man who recorded one of the darkest moments in American history. The museum overnighted me a copy of the film, along with permission to use it in my report. In exchange I donated my original cassette recording of the 1966 interview to them, as well as a copy of the letter sent to me afterward by Zapruder, thanking me and saying he thought the radio program turned out better than he had expected.

With some careful editing, removing a pause here and there, I made the idea work. In the new edit, Abraham Zapruder is heard describing the images unfolding on the screen in his own words. My original recording of the 1966 interview, as well as the newly edited videotape with Zapruder's narrative, are now part of the "Marvin Scott Collection," among the permanent assassination archives at the Sixth Floor Museum in Dealey Plaza. Gary Mack, the museum's curator, said he was amazed such an informative interview still existed, claiming that it added "significant information to Zapruder's testimony before the Warren Commission and in the Clay Shaw trial."

Time-Life bought Zapruder's film from him in 1963, for $150,000—the equivalent of $1 million in today's currency. Zapruder donated a portion of that to the widow of J.D. Tippit, the police officer shot by Lee Harvey Oswald. Though he never wanted to see a profit from his film, in 1999 the U.S. government paid the Zapruder family $16 million for it. According to the Guinness Book of World Records, that's a record $615,383 per second, for 26.6 seconds of film.

Abe Zapruder died of cancer in 1970, at the age of 62—a quiet but dignified man, who never expected to be immortalized by the moment in history his images have frozen in time.

15

THE NIGHT THE
MARTIANS LANDED

"Awesome Orson" By Hulton Archive, Getty Images.

g rover's Mill, New Jersey, is perhaps the only historical site in the world made famous by an event that never happened. The story of a terrifying night that put the tiny hamlet on the map and had more than one million people across the country running for the hills, fearful of being annihilated by an invading army of aliens from Mars, has endured for almost 80 years. For decades, a bullet-riddled water tower has stood on flimsy metal legs, serving as a mute reminder of the great "battle" that was waged here on a foggy night on October 30th, 1938.

The town of Grover's Mill—named for an old grist mill that once provided feed and flour for farmers—was the imaginary landing site for the Martians that Sunday night. Cigar-shaped spaceships 30 yards long were said to be dropping like locusts, first into the rich New Jersey farmland, then into dozens of other towns and cities across the nation. Strange-looking creatures carrying death-ray guns were reported to be destroying everything in sight. In the minds of hundreds of thousands of people, these events were terrifyingly real.

In reality, of course, there was no danger at all. The "invasion" originated in a New York studio, where Orson Welles and a group of actors were dramatizing a devilishly convincing adaptation of H.G. Welles's 1898 science-fiction thriller, *The War of the Worlds*. The program was produced to be the night-before-Halloween presentation of the Mercury Theatre on the Air. An estimated six million people were listening to the program when it aired over 100 stations affiliated with the Columbia Broadcasting System.

With anxieties already high over the imminent threat of war in Europe and the United States becoming involved, people were fixated on their radios, and had become accustomed to news bulletins interrupting their regular programs. Listeners' anxieties heightened when they heard the radio announcer interrupt a live music broadcast to declare: "A bulletin from Trenton, New Jersey. At least 40 people, including six state troopers, lie dead in a field east of the village of Grover's Mill."

Paul Moran was ten back then, and heard the report with terror. He said his mother and aunt had taken their rosary beads, got down on their knees and started praying.

"They thought the world was coming to an end."

* * *

During my four visits to Grover's Mill to re-tell the story of the night America panicked, I found it incredible to think that people actually believed Martians had invaded the New Jersey farmland. The broadcasters had in fact announced that they were presenting a dramatization—but few listeners paid attention amid the clamor of "breaking news" bulletins.

To give the story greater authenticity, the producers had directed their $75-a-week scriptwriter to make it sound like a news program, with frequent bulletins. The beginning of the program seemed plausible enough: a weather report, followed by dance music. This, however, was soon interrupted with frequent "bulletin updates" from the fictitious Intercontinental Radio News. First it was revealed that astronomers had detected unusual gas explosions on Mars. A few minutes later, listeners were informed that a shock of almost earthquake-level intensity had been registered near Grover's Mill, a small town six miles east of Princeton.

Don Perrine told me that his father had found the reports of what was supposedly happening a mile and a half from his home so believable, that he hurriedly packed his wife and three sons into his car and driven them to relatives' homes in Trenton. He wasn't the only one—there was a mass exodus out of town. One terrified farmer pulled up to a gas station, filled up his tank, got back in the car and drove off, forgetting to remove the hose from the tank. 76-year-old Willie Dock raced home to grab his shotgun and sat out the night on his porch, determined to keep the Martians off his property. Though he never fired a shot, it took some doing to convince him there were no Martians. Others, however, did fire shots that night—at a high water tower, shrouded in dense fog, which they thought was an alien spaceship.

Further panic ensued when the broadcast was again interrupted with an update and the announcer intoned, "Those strange beings who landed in the Jersey farmlands tonight are the vanguard of an invading army from the planet Mars. The battle that took place tonight in Grover's Mill has ended in one of the most startling defeats ever suffered by an army in modern times. 7,000 armed men with rifles and machine guns, pitted against a single fighting machine of the invaders from Mars...120 known survivors."

The actor playing the role of an on-scene reporter brought credibility to the ridiculous. Excitedly but authoritatively, he described how the creatures from the spaceship were advancing with mirror-like devices in their hands, from which shot jets of flame. "Now the whole field has caught fire—the woods, the barns. It's spreading everywhere. It's coming this way...about 20 yards to my right..." Then there was a thunderous crash...then silence.

The reaction to all of this was as incredible as the yarn itself. As the actors continued their hour-long dramatization, they remained oblivious to the panic gripping the nation. In Indianapolis, a husband came home to find his wife attempting suicide, screaming that she would rather die by poison than by Martian death rays. Another woman was reported to have screamed out in church, "It's the end of the world!" As additional Martian cylinders were reported falling in New York City, Buffalo, Chicago, St. Louis and other cities, police switchboards were flooded with calls from hysterical people who wanted to know what to do to protect themselves. Some demanded gas masks; others huddled in closets and attics in hopes of eluding the alien creatures.

Eddie Kemp remembered: "A lot of people heading for the hills of Pennsylvania in an attempt to escape the aliens from the red planet." All the roads into and out of Grover's Mill were clogged. As residents escaped, curiosity-seekers flooded in, hoping to see the aliens for themselves. Hundreds of strangers trampled across the cornfield on David Wilson's farm; unable to find the Wilmuth farm, the fictional location where the broadcasters pinpointed all the action, they figured the announcer had meant to say *Wilson*. One local entrepreneur took advantage of the chaos, charging motorists 50 cents to park near the so-called Martian landing spot.

It wasn't until Orson Welles came out of character on the program to allay the fears of the nation that the panic abated that

Halloween eve. He assured his listeners that the broadcast was simply a "radio version of dressing up in a sheet and jumping out of a bush and saying 'boo!'"

"We couldn't soap all your windows and steal your garden gates," Welles continued, "so we did the next best thing: we annihilated the entire world before your very ears."

The explanation did little to stem the tide of lawsuits that were then filed against Welles and CBS for injuries and damage caused by the panic their broadcast had created. These claims ran into the millions, though without precedent for any of them, none ever came to trial. CBS apologized for the hoax, and said it would never happen again. The chairman of the Federal Communication Commission called the whole episode "regrettable," and subsequently tightened regulations on broadcasters.

* * *

Years later, a full moon illuminating the night sky, I walked across the cornfield of the former Wilson farm, pushing aside giant stalks of corn while I tried to visualize what people had been feeling that Halloween eve, and why they reacted the way they did. Holding a recording of the broadcast to my ear, I couldn't but find it all incomprehensible.

Grover's Mill had become the focal point of the fictional drama entirely by chance. Scriptwriter Howard Koch had picked it by closing his eyes and dropping a pencil onto a New Jersey road map.

"I liked the sound," he recalled. "It had an authentic ring to it." In the whole sleepy hamlet, I managed to find only a few survivors of the night the Martians "invaded" their town. Some were too embarrassed to admit that they had been among those who were caught up in the mass hysteria. Others spoke reluctantly about the events that had brought such notoriety to their peaceful town.

So how could more than a million people have been led to believe that such an outlandish story was true?

Paul Moran told me, "Unlike television, where you see all the action, on radio you imagine things based on the sounds you hear," and he remembered that the program had been very realistic. Princeton University undertook a two-year research project to determine the causes behind the mass hysteria, and concluded that the panic had not been the result of nationwide stupidity, but rather a reflection on America's jitters in a warring, chaotic world.

Despite the widespread belief that such an event could never happen again, it did—11 years later in Quito, Ecuador, when radio station HCQRX ran its own version of the invasion-from-Mars program. The station's listeners reacted much the way their North American counterparts did, and there was panic in the streets. But this time, when the people learned the truth, far greater tragedy ensued: an enraged mob stormed the three-story building that housed the radio station and burned it down, killing 15 people trapped inside.

Although Orson Welles's broadcast on the invasion at Grover's Mill is now part of American folklore, there are no annual parades or celebrations in the town to observe it. However, there is an eight-foot-high bronze monument to the unique event that rests near a pond in the tiny hamlet's Van Nest Park. In bold, raised letters, it says "Martian Landing Site," and reads, "This was to become a landmark in broadcast history, provoking continuing thought about media responsibility, social psychology and civil defense."

The residents of Grover's Mill, however, would eventually find themselves in a much closer connection to Mars than even they would have imagined. In a development tinged with irony, 38 years after the fictional Mars landing, the RCA Space Center—located just down the road from Grover's Mill—built the sophisticated communications system for the two Viking spacecraft that would land on Mars in 1976. The news prompted one resident to declare, "It's about time we returned the visit."

16

THE BEATLES—
COMING TO AMERICA

Ringo Starr, during The Beatles first US visit in 1964, telling me how excited the group was over their American reception.

*i*t wasn't the biggest story of 1964, but it was one that transformed the music culture of an entire generation.

I was one of 200 reporters and photographers who were at Kennedy Airport that cold Friday afternoon in February, awaiting the arrival of four working-class lads from Liverpool who were about to "invade" the very country that first inspired them to become musicians. The piercing screams of more than 5,000 adoring, wide-eyed fans standing on the observation deck overpowered the whine of the jet engines as Pan Am flight 101 landed at 1:35 p.m.

I had never witnessed such hysteria before, and I had no idea how significant the day would become in music history. There was a crescendo of shouts—"We want the Beatles! We love the Beatles!"—and deafening shrieks when the doors of the plane opened and Paul McCartney, Ringo Starr, George Harrison and John Lennon emerged, waving to the crowd. *A strange-looking lot,* I thought. What with those funny-looking mod suits and pudding-bowl haircuts, they could have been aliens from another planet. Little did I know, Beatlemania had come to America.

One would have thought these guys would be accustomed to the hysteria that had previously greeted them in Sweden, France, Germany and their native Britain. But they'd been nervous about their visit to the U.S. On the flight over, Lennon was concerned because Americans had been indifferent to the release of two of their records a year earlier, and he was reported to have quipped fearfully at one point, "We won't make it." To the contrary, they arrived as conquering heroes just six days after the release of their latest recording, "I Want To Hold Your Hand." The record sold a quarter of a million copies in just three days, and immediately became the number-one single in the nation.

There was pandemonium at the airport, a near-riot, as thousands of fans pressed forward, trying to catch a closer glimpse of their heartthrob musical quartet. All these years later, I can almost hear those screams ringing in my ears—they were electrifying. I had previously seen bobbysoxers screeching for Frank Sinatra and fans howling for Elvis Presley. But this was a different time, and a different crowd. The Beatles represented a diversion that the nation desperately needed, just 77 days after the assassination of President Kennedy. Beatlemania was also a welcome respite from news of the Vietnam War and the Civil Rights struggles in the South.

Disc jockey Bruce Murrow remembered, "Young people were trying to find one another. We weren't smiling anymore. These guys made us smile." Another part of the Beatles phenomenon was their pop-cultural timing. American rock-and-roll of the fifties had become tired, bland and in need of revitalization, and the Beatles, who were inspired by the beat of rock-and-roll, were able to blaze a new trail. Their music was vibrant. It was different, and it was new.

Now a frenzy grew among the reporters trying to ask questions of the band during a news conference inside the airport terminal. Some of the questions were inane, like, "Are you a little embarrassed by the lunacy you cause?"

"We love it," Harrison shot back.

Another reporter said, "A psychiatrist recently said you're nothing but a bunch of British Elvis Presleys," to which Lennon responded, "He must be blind." But it was Ringo who got the biggest laugh. "How do you find America?" a reporter asked. Without missing a beat, Ringo declared, "Turn left at Greenland." They were upbeat, they were poised, they were charming—and they endeared themselves to the hardcore New York press corps. They were the Beatles.

I followed them into Manhattan, where they were staying at the Plaza Hotel. Police had set up barricades to hold back the crowds. As adults looked on in astonishment, kids screamed at the top of their lungs as limousines pulled up and, one by one, the Beatles got out.

I managed to get in the path of the arriving entourage, close enough to thrust my microphone in front of Ringo.

"How's the reception?" I shouted as he raced past me.

"Marvelous, fantastic," was his breathless response. Some adults who said they'd never heard of the Beatles were stunned by it all.

"Who are they?" exclaimed one woman, who said she was just there because she had seen a crowd and was curious. A waiter in the hotel, who I later interviewed, described the boys as "strange, but polite." He said they had a taste for unusual cocktails, like Scotch and Coca-Cola.

Two days after their arrival, the Beatles made their first appearance on *The Ed Sullivan Show*. 73 million people tuned in to the broadcast—about 40% of the U.S. population. The Beatles were paid a mere $10,000 for three appearances on the show, a seminal moment in music history. But a couple of days later, the group gave its first concert in the U.S. at the Coliseum in Washington, D.C.—and 20,000 fans went wild. The next day they gave back-to-back performances at New York's Carnegie Hall, and police had to close the streets around the area because of the frenzy created by thousands of fans. Their talent agent, Sid Bernstein, was a true visionary. He told me that he had booked Carnegie Hall a year earlier, long before most Americans had even heard of the band, purely "on gut instinct."

In a matter of days, the Beatles had truly conquered America. I met them again later that year, when they returned to the States for a 32-city tour. I greeted Ringo and George Harrison as they got off the plane in New York. The two graciously stopped for a brief interview, and told me how overwhelmed they were by the way they were received in our country. It was understandable; but not everyone was enamored by the band. One reviewer panned their performance on *The Ed Sullivan Show,* writing, "Musically, they were a near-disaster." *Newsweek* magazine concurred, stating, "Visually they were a disaster." Even Ed Sullivan's musical director Ray Bloc saw them as a fad, and declared, "I give them a year." Odds-makers at the time also doubted that they would ever amount to anything big. Years later, McCartney would confess that the group thought they would be good for a couple of years at most.

"We never thought it would last at all," he told an interviewer.

Boy, was he wrong. Within months of their arrival, the Beatles had five number-one songs on Billboard's Hot 100 Singles chart, and soon after, they had 14—an incredible achievement never equaled since. By the time the group disbanded and went their separate ways in 1970, they had produced an unprecedented 30 top singles and 18 albums, which have sold more than 600 million copies worldwide to date.

The band's music remains as relevant and popular today as it was that cold day in February, when I stood on the tarmac to witness the arrival of the four mop-heads from Liverpool who would trigger a cultural revolution. As their music proclaims, they came to hold our hand—but they ended up capturing the heart and soul of an entire nation.

* * *

Like me, the legions of Beatles fans in America will always remember that special moment when they came to our shores. And they will never forget the moment 16 years later, when the music died—the night John Lennon was murdered. We lost more than a brilliant musician that awful December night in 1980. For many young people who were embraced by his music and love, Lennon's death meant the loss of part of their childhood.

It was just before 11 p.m. when we learned that Lennon had been shot. My colleague Tim Malloy and I charged out of the newsroom, but by the time we arrived at Roosevelt Hospital, Lennon was gone, unable to survive the four bullet wounds to his back and chest. The hospital's declaration of death came at 11:15. Lennon had turned 40 just weeks earlier. Near collapse, his wife, Yoko Ono, cried hysterically, "It's not true, it's not true!"

Less than an hour earlier, Lennon and Ono had returned to their residence at the Dakota, the massive Victorian apartment building on Central Park West, after an arduous day that included a photo shoot with photographer Annie Leibovitz and a lengthy recording session. Instead of driving through the front gate into the private courtyard entrance, Lennon decided to get out of the limo to greet some fans who had gathered in front of the building. Among them was Mark David Chapman, a 25-year-old loner who had earlier gotten Lennon to autograph a copy of his newest album, *Double Fantasy*. As Lennon chatted with fans, some of whom had waited all day to catch a glimpse of their idol, Chapman pulled a .38-caliber revolver from his black trench coat and shouted, "Mr. Lennon."

Lennon had barely turned when Chapman fired five shots at him, four of which tore through the musician's body.

Lennon was rushed to Roosevelt Hospital, where doctors worked feverishly in an effort to save him. They pumped his heart over and over, but to no avail—and the man who had once said, "I really thought love would save us all" was pronounced dead. One man's hatred and paranoia had betrayed his prophecy.

Handcuffed in the rear of a police car, Chapman reportedly told the arresting officers, "Sorry I ruined your night."

Shock gave way to universal numbness as fans gathered by the thousands in front of the Dakota. They stood and stared at the building where the most famous Beatle had lived, and cried openly.

One man, tears streaming down his cheeks, turned to my microphone to declare, "I don't know why someone would kill such a beautiful person."

A young woman told me, "He's a part of my childhood," and a middle-aged man, choked with emotion, said, "He helped us find ourselves."

Mourners placed flowers everywhere. There were bouquets, a rose here and there, and carnations, along with personal notes expressing love and sadness. It was as though a member of everyone's family had died. The fans gathered at the Dakota sang individually, and together in groups; "All you need is love" became their anthem, filtering constantly through the air.

For days, people kept vigil in front of the famed building where Lennon had lived and died. It seemed so surreal, so unreal, that the inspiration behind the Beatles was actually gone. On the Sunday following his murder, more than 50,000 people, young and old, staged a memorial tribute to him, in what was to become the Strawberry Fields section of Central Park. Some perched themselves on the limbs of trees. They carried candles and flowers—and they sang. The music of the Beatles, much of which Lennon had composed, resonated across the fields on the cold December afternoon. It was all so moving; and as I reported on the emotional memorial, my mind flashed back to that special day 16 years earlier, when I stood at Kennedy Airport reporting on the arrival of the Beatles in America.

We can all only imagine what might have been, had that gun misfired on December 8, 1980. John Lennon would have written more iconic music, and we would be celebrating his birthday each year instead of mourning the anniversary of his death. His killer remains in prison to this day, his multiple appeals for parole denied.

Each day, visitors return to Strawberry Fields in Central Park, where there is now a beautiful mosaic of the word "IMAGINE." They stand in reverence and sing Lennon's songs of love and peace, which remain as relevant today as they were the day he wrote them. "Imagine all the people/Living life in peace"—these are such poignant lyrics, the words of a dreamer who is gone, and whose dream is yet to be realized.

* * *

More than half a century after they became a household name, the Beatles' star still shines brightly. Ringo Starr and now-Sir Paul McCartney, the only surviving members of the group, are sought after constantly for concerts and public appearances. I was there for one of them, the night McCartney dazzled 15,000 fans crammed into Brooklyn's Barclays Center. For me it was like a time warp, flashing back to younger days when we were carefree and innocent, and found pure escape in the music of those four lovable lads from Liverpool. McCartney was playing solo this time, performing nonstop for fans who wouldn't let him leave the stage.

"So you want more?" he asked, a glint in his eye. To the roaring approval of the crowd, he responded with a simple, "Okay," delivering such Beatles classics as "Yesterday" and "Lovely Rita," along with some songs he had never performed on any previous tour.

I marveled as my eyes scanned the crowd, seeing the once-reckless teens now baby boomers in their sixties, many paunchy and gray, mouthing lyrics and waving their arms to the sound of McCartney's music. Fans held up signs with messages like "All You Need Is Paul." I caught myself swaying with the crowd, my arms locked in my wife's to the left and a friend's to the right as McCartney led us through the melodic strains of "Hey Jude." We were thousands of strangers standing under one roof, bonded for an evening as one, and McCartney's concert was a rejuvenation of our youth, if only for a few hours.

McCartney, now in his 70s, showed boundless energy as he waltzed across the huge stage for two and a half hours without a break, his voice never faltering. Projected on jumbo screens, the musical genius alternated between guitar and piano, dedicating songs to his current and former wives. Throughout the concert he had the audience in the palm of his hand, and he seemed to love it as much as we did. When the show ended McCartney left the stage to the deafening roar of a grateful audience stomping their feet—then returned once more for a final reprise of his ever-popular "Yesterday."

It is the yesterdays that we cling to; and it is memories of concerts like this one and the many that came before it, uniting and reuniting us with these beloved musicians, that will remain with us and future generations through the many tomorrows.

17

MARCHING WITH MARTIN LUTHER KING, IN LIFE AND DEATH

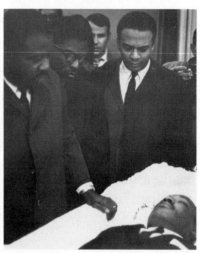

Keeping in step with Dr. Martin Luther King during march through Mississippi, June 1966 and observing an emotional moment in Memphis funeral home in April 1968.

*t*here are few figures in American history iconic enough to have endured the test of time and woven themselves permanently into the very fabric of America's consciousness. Dr. Martin Luther King Jr. was one of those figures. As a young reporter, I covered part of his journey as he traversed the highways and streets of the South, effectively using non-violence as a weapon against hatred and injustice. And years later, I was there when thousands mourned the death of Dr. King—a victim of the violence he tried to eradicate.

At just over five-and-a-half feet, Dr. King turned out to be much shorter than I had envisioned, when we shook hands that warm June day in 1966 in Hernando, Mississippi. A stocky man with broad shoulders and skin the color of burnished mahogany, he was there to continue the March Against Fear after its organizer, James Meredith, the man who broke the color barrier at the University of Mississippi, was shot and wounded by a white gunman.

What Dr. King lacked in physical height, he exhibited in the stature of his character. As he interacted with his fellow marchers, I saw a powerful personality who knew how to electrify and inspire others. He was a master wordsmith who articulated his message clearly and strikingly, as was evidenced by his response to a question I asked about the Meredith shooting. "It is indicative of the fact that we still live in a morally inclement climate, filled with torrents of hatred and jostling winds of violence," he said, adding, "and I think many levels of our society must take responsibility for this."

As other leaders of the civil rights movement gathered—including James Farmer from the Congress of Racial Equality and Stokely Carmichael of the Student Nonviolent Coordinating Committee—I looked for a telephone to file a report for the Mutual Broadcasting System. I finally found a telephone booth, only to discover that the receiver had been cut from the phone. Several other locations had undergone similar acts of vandalism; authorities believed it was the work of the Ku Klux Klan, in a coordinated effort to prevent reporters from getting their stories out. It was clear that reporters were not welcome here; the hostility was palpable in other ways as well. The locals didn't like that we were showing ugly images of them to the world, and responded with rage and threats to reporters.

Determined to get my report out, I drove to a nearby junkyard and engaged the owner with a poor imitation of a Southern accent. "Mornin'," I drawled, telling him that I was a local reporter and asking to use his phone. It worked, and the bigoted geezer sat down next to me to listen in. Wary of arousing his suspicions, I soon had my colleagues on the other end of the line in New York thinking that I had lost my mind as I used language entirely uncharacteristic of me. (Yes, I used the "N" word several times.) It worked. When I asked the old fellow if he would retrieve something from my car for me, he complied without hesitation, giving me a moment of privacy to explain myself to my editors and record my exclusive about the KKK's interference.

As a young reporter, I was experiencing my first foray into the Deep South. It was a place of contradictions—most strikingly the overwhelming beauty and serenity of the red clay country contrasted with the ugly behavior of the rednecks out to stir trouble and try to deny the Negroes—as even politely they were called back then—the right to march through their state. Toward evening I would witness groups of these hatemongers in pickup trucks, circling like locusts menacingly around the campsite where the marchers were bedded down for the night. The locals didn't like how we reporters were portraying them in the media, and I could feel the hostility everywhere. "May I ask you a question?" I remember asking one man, who promptly gritted his teeth and barked, "No, ya can't—now git out of my face!"

Fortunately, there were other exchanges less fraught with tension. For the first few days of the assignment, I was based out of a Holiday Inn Junior in Sardis, Mississippi, where I met a little angel named Donna Nead. Donna, the daughter of the hotel manager, was an inquisitive, smart and very impressionable eight-year-old. She approached me one morning during breakfast, while I was writing notes and listening to my tape recorder, and asked if I was a reporter and what I was doing there. When she learned I was from New York, she told me she had never met a Yankee, and looked at me curiously. On further conversation, she revealed that she always thought that Yankees had horns! I was delighted to change her impression, and for years afterward we remained pen pals.

As we walked south along Highway 51—the tar, molten from

the hot afternoon sun, clutching at my feet—I kept pace with Dr. King, keeping my microphone pointed at him to pick up his words. He kept up a stream of speech; he was motivational, inspirational, hopeful. As we passed a cotton field in Senatobia, he waved into the distance, exclaiming, "Come on, children, come on!" I watched in amazement as small dark figures emerged from afar: first 10, then 20 and more, coming from behind the tree line to join the march.

The interaction among the civil rights leaders themselves was something to observe. Each had a distinctly different approach and style. Dr. King eloquently preached his message of non-violence— the unwavering principle of his leadership—and uncompromising demand for justice.

"We don't want some of our rights, not token handouts," I remember him declaring. "We want *all* of our rights." Alongside him, with fire in his voice, the radical Stokely Carmichael spoke to the incipient Black Power movement.

"The way we're going to stop black people from being shoved out is when we get black sheriffs," he bellowed. "What we need is Black Power!"

James Farmer, founder of the Congress of Racial Equality and one of the most articulate civil-rights leaders I've ever met, intoned, "We're tired of people telling us we have to go someplace else for our rights."

The vanguard of marchers grew in number as they made their way ever so slowly along the 220-mile journey to Jackson, sweltering under the oppressive June heat. The chant of "We Shall Overcome" echoed through the hills and valleys, as agitated locals honked their horns and shouted obscenities.

"All they want is attention," one gawker insisted. Another shouted, "Tell them to go home." One man told me he believed Dr. King was "in this for the money."

Already overpowered by the heat, I found myself consumed with emotion when I saw hundreds of marchers clustered in the shade under a giant pin oak tree. They were standing over the body of a 58-year-old sharecropper who, against the will of his family, had joined the march to speak out for freedom. Armistead Phipps had a heart condition, and the first day out, he collapsed and died in the 94-degree heat. In death, Phipps's sacrifice gained him the recognition he never had in life, as King and the other leaders of the Civil Rights movement recited the 23rd Psalm and sang Negro spirituals.

During a break in the march, I dashed into a motel along Highway 51 to phone in a report. On my way out I chatted with a couple of employees, who voiced their disdain over "the n*ggers trespassing through our town." I grabbed a couple of Cokes from the vending machine, and joined Dr. King where he sat on a dirt mound just off the highway. I offered him one of the drinks, looking around at the glares of dagger hostility directed at me by the folks at the motel across the road. Dr. King and I chatted pleasantly for a few minutes. I asked him why he was doing this, why was he putting his life on the line. (By that time he had already withstood several attempts on his life, including being stabbed with a letter opener.) His answer was short and to the point.

"For the children," he said, his voice trailing off as he repeated, "for the children." He was optimistic but grounded in the difficult realities of the movement; while he felt that great strides had been made, he saw clearly the long road still ahead. He expressed concern about "Negroes losing motivation," because so many aspects of their lives consistently made them feel as though they didn't count. To him, the civil rights movement was an issue of self-worth among blacks, as well as tolerance among whites. That evening, I would hear him speak directly in answer to this feeling, proclaiming to the gathering of marchers, "I came to Mississippi to tell you that you are somebody."

* * *

22 months later, Dr. King came to Memphis, Tennessee, to support sanitation workers looking to unionize. His visit was cut short,

and once again I would come face-to-face with him—this time as he lay in an open casket at the R.S. Lewis and Sons Funeral Home. He had been murdered the day before on April 4th, 1968, by lone assassin James Earl Ray.

Riots were already rocking cities across the nation as my plane made its final approach to Memphis. Suddenly we felt a severe jolt, and my first thought was that we had been hit by something fired from below. It was also the first impression of my neighbor in the next seat, veteran CBS reporter Ike Pappas, who had seen his share of violence during his coverage of the Vietnam War. He bolted from a deep sleep, fear emanating from his eyes, and together we were relieved to hear the captain's announcement that it had been nothing more than bad turbulence. It seemed a fitting introduction to the political turmoil to come.

There was a chill in the air as daylight filtered through the early-morning clouds outside the Lorraine Motel, where Dr. King had been shot hours earlier as he stood on the balcony of his second-floor room. It was the dawning of one of the darkest days in American history, and for me, it was surreal to stand there, looking at stone-faced police officers overseeing an active crime scene against the backdrop of disbelieving mourners gathered in the parking lot, their eyes swollen from tears. A young Jesse Jackson first emerged that day, as the self-declared spokesman for the King family. He spoke of the civil rights leader's greatness, and the impact of his loss. Jackson was with King when he was shot, and claimed, "I cradled him in my arms."

As I interviewed people who had been close to Dr. King, I learned that King might have prophesied his own death. In a speech delivered the night before his murder, he spoke at a Mason temple about threats that had been made on his life. My notes are fading now, but his words remain indelibly clear.

"We've got some difficult days ahead," he said, "but it really doesn't matter with me now, because I've been to the mountaintop.

And I don't mind. Like anybody, I would like to live a long life. Longevity has its place. But I'm not concerned about that now. I just want to do God's will. I'm happy tonight," he concluded. "I'm not worried about anything." 24 hours later, Dr. Martin Luther King was dead at the age of 39.

It was quickly determined that the assassin's bullet came from a dilapidated rooming house on Main Street, in plain sight of the Lorraine Motel some 200 yards away. Once police finished their investigation there, I managed to sneak inside. Bessie Brewer's boarding house was a two-story building—run-down, with paint peeling from the walls and ceiling. The steps were broken and creaky. I'll never forget the awful stench permeating the place; rather than walk down the hall to the community bathroom, some residents chose to use large metal pretzel cans to collect their urine and feces. One resident told me he heard a single shot and saw a man, later identified as James Earl Ray, running from the bathroom.

When no one was looking, I walked into the bathroom for a look at the assassin's lair. Investigators would later determine that Ray had to have had his feet firmly planted in the ceramic bathtub to take his deadly shot. With one foot on the edge of that bathtub, and the other on the toilet, I leaned on the ledge of the window facing the Lorraine Motel. I spoke into my tape recorder, describing just what the assassin would have seen. I realized that one did not have to be a marksman to hit such a target as King; at 200 yards away, with a high-powered rifle and a scope, the killer's vantage was dreadfully clear.

Riots erupted in about 60 American cities in the aftermath of Dr. King's murder, including Memphis. Its famed Beale Street, the birthplace of the blues, was off-limits to civilians, due to a curfew. As a reporter, I sensed an eerie silence as I walked along the desolate street, usually aglitter with flickering neon lights and music emanating from the dozens of clubs along the street. In contrast, all I could hear was the sound of broken glass beneath my shuffling feet, and the occasional rumble of military vehicles patrolling the area.

A local National Guard unit invited me to join them on patrol, looking for looters and snipers roaming the debris-littered streets. This was a bit disconcerting, as they placed me on the highest point at the rear of the Jeep without a protective helmet, pointedly calling me "the Yankee reporter." The guardsmen with me were young: one was 19, a couple of others 20. They showed a lot of bravado, waving their carbines in the air. I was appalled when one of them swung his weapon around viciously, declaring, "I want to get me a nigger head tonight." But eventually—and irresponsibly—they abandoned their patrol, and the young guardsmen rolled the Jeep into an apartment complex where one of their girlfriends was having a party.

After Dr. King's body was released by the medical examiner, it was taken to the R.S. Lewis and Sons Funeral Home, where staff worked for 13 hours to prepare it for the funeral. The right side of his jaw had been shattered by the assassin's bullet, as had his spinal cord. Before the wake, I was one of three reporters who managed to get inside the chapel where King's body was laid out in an open casket. The tearful cries of a dozen women in black dresses occupying the front row of seats were piercing. It was hot and humid, and overwhelmingly emotional when Reverend Ralph David Abernathy—who assumed leadership of King's Southern Christian Leadership Conference—Andrew Young and two others stood over the casket. King was dressed in a black suit, and aside from a slight mark on his jaw, bore no visible signs of his traumatic wound. I was standing close enough to hear Abernathy murmur, "Martin, Martin," as he reached out to gently touch the body of his friend and colleague. The grief and magnitude of the loss were evident in the somber faces of those standing over the casket. They stood a few moments in silence, and then Reverend Abernathy led the group in a recitation of the 23rd Psalm.

During this entire emotional experience, I was recording the sounds of grief as I whispered a descriptive narrative of what I was seeing. I felt I was bearing witness to something truly extraordinary, and was fortunate to be in a position to share it with my listeners. But that moment turned out to be one of the greatest frustrations of my career. The audiotape jammed in the recorder, and I discovered afterwards that everything I thought I had recorded wasn't there. The two other reporters who were there offered to share their recordings with me, but it wasn't the same. Some things just can't be replicated.

Before the funeral in Atlanta, King's widow Coretta Scott King agreed to lead a march through Memphis in support of the city's striking sanitation workers. The police department set rules for journalists covering the march, but these rules were too restrictive, and a meeting was requested with the police director. I was selected as a pool representative to join with two reporters from Tennessee in a meeting with the director. There, he bluntly threatened to arrest any reporter who failed to abide by his rules. I appealed that reporters be given reasonable access to the line of march, and gave assurances that we would not approach Mrs. King. Finally, the director relented, and said he would ease the terms for coverage if they were approved by civil rights leader Bayard Rustin. They were; but on the day of the march, this deal was not honored and I was threatened with arrest. Days later, I was told that the word was out: if I or another outspoken reporter got in the way, we were "to be taken care of"—whatever that meant.

Arriving in Atlanta to report on the funeral, I got into a taxi with a "Negro" driver, who told me what an inspiration Dr. King was to him. He was overwhelmed with emotion when he learned that I had met and spoken with the fallen civil-rights leader. When we arrived at my hotel, he wouldn't take any money from me. He was so thrilled, he said, to meet someone who actually knew Dr. King, and abruptly began to cry. Through his tears, voicing what would be the sentiment of history, he muttered, "I loved him."

18

SEPTEMBER 11, 2001–
A REMEMBRANCE

One of the most difficult reporting days after terrorists brought down the World Trade Center on Sept. 11, 2001.

*t*he blackout shades in my bedroom shielded me from the brilliance of the sun in the early morning hours of that second Tuesday in September. I had no idea what darkness lay at the other end of the telephone, as the incessant ringing jolted me from a deep sleep. This was primary election day in New York, and I was scheduled to work nightside. I had gotten to sleep late. It was 18 minutes after nine when I brought the phone to my ear and heard my daughter Jill on the other end.

"Dad, do you have the TV on?" she screamed. "They crashed two planes into the World Trade Center!"

"What?" I shrieked, darting toward the TV.

I heard her words, but the reality of what my daughter was saying didn't register until I saw the images filling my television screen. "Oh my God," I thought aloud, grabbing the phone again to call the news assignment desk at WPIX. I couldn't get through. I dialed every conceivable number at the office, along with the personal cell phones of the editors there, to no avail. An attempt to send a fax—*Just heard news…unable to get through to you on phone…trying to come in immediately…understand tunnels and bridges are closed… trying to get ferry…where would you like me to go?*—also proved futile. Television sets and radios were now on in every room of my home as I prepared to get myself into the city. My home is in New Jersey, just six and a half miles from my office in Manhattan, but with the bridges and tunnels closed I had to figure out another way to get across the river. I hoped my police-issued press credentials and honorary shields from law-enforcement groups would be my passport.

Those first images unfolding on the TV screen were devastating, and have haunted me ever since—particularly the video replay of the planes flying into the skyscrapers and exploding in balls of flame. I was frozen in horror and disbelief; as I watched and listened, it felt as though I was going through those moments in slow motion. Despite these feelings, I hadn't yet connected emotionally to what was happening the way I had when I watched Jack Ruby shoot Lee Harvey Oswald on live TV, or when the Challenger space shuttle exploded across my television screen. In this case, I was overwhelmed with thoughts of getting to the story—it felt like no other event I had ever covered. I had to get to the city.

My frustration grew with each failed attempt to reach the news desk and my inability to contact my fiancée, Lorri Gorman, who was working in the city that morning. She finally got through to me on her cell phone to say she was safe, and she managed to connect me via conference call with my editors. Initially it was suggested that since I already was in New Jersey, I go to the Jersey City Medical

Center, where it was thought that some of the injured might be brought; but I was determined to be closer to the story, and told them I would get into the city somehow.

It all hit me as I approached my parking lot. My eyes were drawn to the south, just across the river, where I was accustomed to seeing the Twin Towers defining the skyline of New York. They were no longer there. Ominous, thick clouds of smoke rose up in place of their gleaming presence. An awful chill seized my body. The number of casualties had to be staggering.

Traffic stood at a standstill as I began the one-mile drive to the ferry, which I expected would get me to Manhattan. My press card and familiar face helped get me past the first roadblock, where I claimed I was meeting a camera crew at the marina in nearby Weehawken. The scene at the ferry terminal was chaotic, with police, fire and medical personnel attempting to set up a triage area for the injured they were expecting to soon be ferried across. Thousands of others were there too—commuters who, hours earlier, had gone to work on the warm late-summer day, taking the seven-minute ferry ride across the Hudson River. Now they were returning, evacuating a city under siege. Their faces were ashen, horror clearly etched on their expressions. There were hugs and tears as friends and family embraced one another against the backdrop of the darkening clouds across the river.

I jotted down what observations I could in my notepad, but the anxiety of not being able to get to the story was making me crazy. Despite my pleas and protestations, however, neither the police nor the ferry-terminal managers would allow me to get aboard any of the ferries making return runs to Manhattan; they were all going back empty.

"New York is closed," bellowed one police sergeant.

As I plotted my next move, I began taking video of the scene with my digital camera. I figured I could use it as part of a report on the city's mass exodus. A sea of people coming off the boats flooded the terminal. Cops and doctors stood everywhere, awaiting something to do while, visible on the other side, that ever-present cloud of terror rose high into the air, blocking the clear blue sky with a layer of ominous gray dust.

From the corner of my eye, I spotted a small powerboat at the nearby marina's gas dock, about 60 yards away. I made a mad dash for it, and appealed for a ride to the other side. I flashed my press card at the boat's owner.

"I know who you are," he shot back.

"Will you take me across?" I pleaded.

"I'll pay you anything." He agreed to take me, graciously declining any money; and after we persuaded the dock master to fill our tank, I jumped aboard.

A crowd quickly gathered on the dock. Claiming they had loved ones at the World Trade Center, they appealed for a ride.

"Please," screamed one woman in tears, "my daughter is there—I have to be with her!" Her cries, and those of the others clamoring to get aboard, were disturbing, but with six people already on the small boat, there simply was not enough room.

Pointing at a *New York Post* reporter and me, another woman demanded to know, "Why are you taking them?" The explanation that we were reporters accredited by police, and therefore more likely to get through a Coast Guard blockade, was of little comfort. As we left the dock, I felt guilty that we had abandoned these people at a moment of such grief and fear. But there was little else we could do. I still had to get to the story. As the white wake grew behind our boat, the dark cloud ahead loomed even larger as we neared the Manhattan side.

At the pier, more than a thousand people were standing in line to board a charter boat that would shuttle them back across the river. My heart began palpitating and my breathing became more difficult as I ran in search of a taxi. There were none to be found. I stopped for a seemingly endless moment to look toward the devastation. Less than a mile away, I could see the cloud of smoke rising hundreds of feet into the air. In front of me sat an ambulance, its engine idling, and in front of that, there were at least 80 other vehicles of mercy, all waiting in anticipation of a mission that would never come.

Shortly after noon, more than three hours after the terrorists had struck, I finally reached the newsroom, where News Director Karen Scott directed me to relieve anchor Jim Watkins, who had been on the air for hours without a break. Initially, I was disappointed that I wasn't being sent to the scene, as foreboding as conditions were—some had likened downtown Manhattan to a nuclear winter—I felt I should be at Ground Zero with the other reporters. Instead, the studio became my isolation chamber, where I spent untold hours. The anchor desk was a clutter of notes and news copy. A cold slice of pizza sat neglected on a table behind it. The images and sounds from the television monitors that surrounded us formed an incongruous tapestry of calamity. An ancillary impact of the World Trade Center attack was immediately evident in our studio. The colorful Duratron panorama of the New York skyline that formed the backdrop of our news set had already been altered: the Twin Towers, which had been framed in the center of the photograph, had been hastily removed, and the two remaining sections of the backdrop were now stapled together.

As I joined my solemn-faced co-anchor Mary Murphy, I knew I had a daunting responsibility to an audience craving to know more. I wasn't reading from a script or teleprompter this time, but speaking extemporaneously, relaying information as it became available and tossing to our reporters near Ground Zero and at hospitals and other locations. Authority and credibility are important requisites for any reporter, but telling this story called for more: I had to be sensitive, calming and reassuring as well, in view of the fact that many of our viewers had loved ones who worked in the buildings, and at this point didn't know whether they were dead or alive. This wasn't a terror attack in some distant part of the world, but rather in our own city. Though the tone of my voice reflected the sadness I felt, I avoided talking about the anticipated death toll in those early hours, and focused on the number of survivors and the countless others we all hoped would be found alive in the rubble. Meanwhile, we kept eyes on what was happening through our reporters in the field, including our traffic reporter, Melinda Murphy, who remained aloft in the only news helicopter still allowed in the air. Our cameramen, their own lives in danger, captured some of the most graphic images imaginable of the planes slamming into the buildings, the horror of people jumping from the upper floors, the buildings crashing to the ground, people running for their lives—images that would be indelibly seared into the memory of the city and the nation.

It was a story that put us all to the test, because it was like nothing we had ever been through before. As reporters, we're not supposed to show our emotions on the air. But this time, it was all but impossible not to. Unlike the case with Herb Morrison, who was criticized for his tearful outburst on live radio when the Hindenburg blew up in front of his eyes in 1937, no one was putting us down now for sharing our feelings with the rest of America. I had no qualms telling viewers that I was feeling exactly what they were feeling. You could hear it in my voice; you could sense it in my demeanor. A couple of times, I unconsciously found myself dabbing tears from my eyes on-camera. How could I not feel something after hearing the woman in an in-studio interview professing her love for her husband—who, she informed us, had been working on the 102nd floor of the North Tower when it went down—and expressing her confidence that he was safe and would be home for dinner? It was those interviews that were most difficult for me—coming face-to-face with people in their hour of grief. As difficult as these moments were for them, they needed to talk, and to show photos of their loved ones, in hopes that they would learn that they had gotten out alive. I listened to their heart-wrenching stories one after another, and on occasion my voice faltered in response. Following an interview with another woman whose father and brother were among the missing, I got choked up on-camera; and afterwards, when we cut away for a report from the White House, I reached for the phone behind me to call my fiancée, my daughter and my son, to tell them all how much I loved them, and how glad I was that they were safe.

Most of us knew someone who worked in the buildings. My friend John O'Neil had just left his position with the FBI to become Chief of Security at the World Trade Center. He began his new job the day before the attack. We were supposed to have lunch that week, and from the studio I kept calling his cell phone, hoping to get some direct information from him. I left several messages, but he never returned my calls. John's body was recovered a week later. I would later learn that he had initially managed to get out safely, but dashed back inside to help others. Kaity Tong, who soon joined me at the anchor desk, was concerned that she was still unable to make contact with her 14-year-old son Philip, who attended Stuyvesant High School just four blocks north of Ground Zero. She shared her personal story with our viewers and then, despite her own worries, gazed steadily into the camera and related the latest news developments.

It never ceases to amaze me how insensitive some people can be at times like this. One of our producers informed me in my earpiece that he had a man on the phone who claimed to have just crawled out from the rubble. I was skeptical. I voiced my misgivings, and suggested that the producer pre-screen the caller. Kaity agreed. But the producer demanded we take the call immediately. With some trepidation, Kaity and I greeted the man on the other end of the line. His voice was young and halting; right away, we could sense a fake cough in his voice.

He assured us he was okay, but when Kaity asked him for details on just how he had gotten out from beneath the rubble, he blurted, "Ah, ah, Howard Stern helped me." The shock jock fan then laughed, and quickly hung up.

Kaity Tong's lips tightened angrily as she glared into the camera and said, "You're an idiot."

As though caught in a bad dream, we kept replaying those awful images of passenger planes turning into fireballs, and clouds of dust replacing once-majestic buildings. My voice had become strained and heavy. In contrast, the sound bites from our public officials were strong. New York Senator Charles Schumer referred to the terror attack as "the 21st-century Pearl Harbor." Mayor Rudy Giuliani emerged as a towering figure early on. Almost a casualty of the buildings' collapse himself, he was reassuring as he told reporters,

"The city will survive...it's going to be a difficult time, but we're not going to let terrorists stop us." In the almost 20 years I had known Giuliani, I had never seen him quite like this before. He certainly had his moments of arrogance as a politician—and sure, he was combative with the media—but now, in the midst of crisis, we were seeing a different side of him. He was compassionate, comforting and reassuring, all while grieving with the rest of us. His leadership during the calamity would later be likened to the manner in which Winston Churchill had guided the city of London through its darkest hour during the Nazi bombardment in World War II.

There were so many haunting images that day. One of the more subtly powerful images struck me after nightfall. It was from a remote camera facing toward lower Manhattan, where on any clear night we would ordinarily have seen the twinkling lights of the Twin Towers. On this night, however, there was a void in the darkness, like a gaping hole in the heart of New York. My voice cracked as I observed to my viewers, "Hard as it is to believe, they are no longer there." A cloud of white smoke, brightened by the powerful lights of emergency crews, now filled the space where the towers had once stood.

* * *

That first day was intense. I spent almost 14 hours on the job, including more than six hours live in the studio as WPIX canceled all other programming for continuous coverage of the calamity. On the way to the hotel where I would stay for the next four days, I could smell the smoke that permeated the air throughout the city. In my hotel room, I became fixated on the television; it was the first time I had seen news coverage of the day's events without actually delivering it. Now alone, I could let out some of the emotion I had been holding back all day. I grabbed two small bottles of vodka and a bag of chips from the minibar, and drifted off to sleep.

In the days ahead, I was compelled to get to Ground Zero. To report it, I felt I had to see it for myself. Reaching out to every contact I had nurtured over the course of almost 40 years as a reporter in New York City, I finally reached a friend in the city's Office of Emergency Management, who hooked me up with a pool group of reporters. As our motorcade headed downtown, we passed clusters of people applauding rescue workers and waving American flags and supportive placards. They were standing in front of makeshift shrines. Pictures of missing loved ones clung to metal fences; candles flickered with hope; flowers wilted in the wind.

We had to go through several security checkpoints, showing our picture identification at each one. The environment changed as we got closer to Ground Zero. Colors on the street morphed slowly into an eerie grayness that covered the facades of buildings and the faces of beleaguered rescue workers. I stood in frozen disbelief at my first glance at the blackened, jagged remnants of the façade of the North Tower. Fires were still burning. It was all so surreal. I feared the scent of death, but there was none. There was just the choking smell of fire…and calamity. *It must be part of the disaster ride at a movie theme park,* I mused for a fleeting moment. If only! There was no way our television viewers could truly grasp the horror of it all. Being there and seeing the magnitude of the destruction was incomprehensible.

We were given hardhats and facemasks, and were instructed not to photograph any bodies if any were found during our visit. "Point your lens to the sky," our escort decreed. In small groups of six, we were led into what had once been the magnificent plaza between the two towering structures. Now it looked like the crater of a volcano. I stood on a concrete precipice overlooking the scene. Hundreds of workers in hardhats swarmed over the debris. Acetylene torches were cutting through steel, jackhammers cracking through concrete. Remnants of the buildings' façade jutted from the ashes like bits of modern sculpture. Columns of steel that had held up two of the tallest buildings in the world were outstretched like Pick-Up Stix. I was astounded to see very little concrete or glass in the rubble—these, I was told, had been completely pulverized. The stench of toxic smoke and ash was choking, but again to my surprise, there was no scent of death, though upwards of 5,000 people were still missing.

As I eyed the devastation, my mind flashed back to the many times I had been in those buildings before—when I had lunch with my children at the Windows on the World restaurant on the 107th floor, when I had covered news conferences in the towers' spacious offices and conference rooms. And there were all those pictures I had taken of the Twin Towers over the years—from helicopters and a blimp high overhead, from my powerboat in the harbor, from Ellis Island at night. From every angle the buildings were a photographer's delight; at night, their thousand lights had sparkled like jewels. Those bold, majestic buildings that defined the skyline of New York took on different personalities at different seasons and times of day. They stood tall as monumental symbols of our nation's financial power—truly among the manmade wonders of the world.

The last time I had worn a hardhat to the World Trade Center as a reporter was in 1970, as I stood on the incomplete 92nd floor of the North Tower, gazing in awe at the progress of its construction. It was a clear day, and I could see for miles from the open space around the steel and concrete in which another floor was taking shape of what was to be the tallest building in New York and, at that time, the world.

The buildings were architectural masterpieces in their time, built to the highest construction standards. Engineers had declared that the towering edifices could withstand severe winds, extreme weather— even a crash of the largest airliner at the time, a Boeing 707.

Now, once again in a hardhat, standing on the ground where the towers once stood and surveying the unbelievable devastation, I felt an emptiness inside, and was enraged that terrorists could do this to us. Instinctively, I bowed my head in a moment of silence.

* * *

Arising from all this horror, there came an uplifting fervor of patriotism that would consume the country for some time after the attack. At Ground Zero, there were American flags everywhere. I saw a tattered flag flying in front of one damaged building, and a sea of small flags protruding from the hardhats of workers. They were on bulldozers and cranes, and drapings of red, white and blue brought color to the gray façades of the mortally wounded buildings. Through the smoke, a banner could be seen stretching across the American Express Building, which declared, "We Shall Never Forget."

One news executive responded to this outpouring of patriotic sentiment by ordering his staff not to display the American flag in their programming. I was so incensed by this, I had to say something about it at the end of my weekly PIX11 *News Closeup* program.

"In my journalistic career," I said, "I have never seen such a period of intense patriotic fervor sweep our nation. We display our flag as a symbol of solidarity and determination to overcome a cowardly act of terror." Glancing at the red, white and blue ribbon blossoming from my lapel, I went on: "We display our flag as a symbol of who we are—one nation, under God, indivisible, with liberty and justice for all. This week, terrorists succeeded in destroying our buildings, but they failed to destroy our spirit."

Often I return to the site of the attacks, hallowed ground that has since undergone a rebirth. A glistening new edifice now fills the void where two majestic buildings once stood. Rising a symbolic 1776 feet, the new World Trade Center symbolizes America's resilience and resolve to never be defeated by those who want to destroy us. A beacon on top is designed to shine as brightly as the American spirit itself.

war

19

JOURNEY TO SUEZ

Suez Canal 1970, during a lull in artillery exchanges.

*f*or a reporter, there is no work more challenging and dangerous than covering global conflicts: traveling to combat zones and joining the military on the front lines to tell the human stories of war. Over the course of my career, I've witnessed the ravages of war in the Middle East, Cambodia, Iraq and Afghanistan. In 1967 I cut my teeth in war reporting long-distance, by covering the six-day war between Israel and Egypt by telephone. As Assistant Bureau Chief for the Mutual Broadcasting System, I took in the early-morning feeds from our foreign correspondents. Len Whartman in Jerusalem, in addition to filing his reports, would regularly put me in touch with key military sources in the country. On the fourth day of the conflict, an Israeli operator was having difficulty reaching one of my sources. She tried repeatedly to call several numbers I had given her, then finally gave up in frustration, advising me, "Call back tomorrow. It'll all be over." The war was over two days later.

The optimism, confidence and determination of the Israelis that I observed over the phone during those tense days, I witnessed firsthand when I visited Israel in 1970 on a media tour. The tour had been arranged by an American Zionist organization, and as might have been expected, its principal goal was to promote a positive image of the tiny nation among foreign journalists. We met with many government leaders, businesspeople and natural-born Israelis—including settlers living on a kibbutz. One of our standout meetings was with Prime Minister Golda Meir. My lasting impression of this powerful leader was that of a grandmother on steroids. She exuded endless homebody charm and charisma at our meeting, welcoming us into her office and warmly embracing each of us. Along with her sweet familiarity, she left no doubt that she was the imperious "Iron Lady" of Israel. Her voice was strong, and her message stronger.

When asked what it would take to bring peace to the region, she replied, "Peace will come when the Arabs love their children more than they hate us."

After several days, I decided I had heard enough of the official Israeli story. As a journalist I felt it was imperative that we hear the other side as well—the point of view of the Arabs. Venturing out on my own, I visited the Arab sector of Jerusalem, where I engaged a few Palestinians in conversation. They accused the Israelis of being the war's real aggressors, by "throwing them out" of their own country. The country's policy of discrimination against the Arab people, they claimed, was intolerable; they wanted their own land on which to settle their homes. Our benign tour continued through the relatively peaceful part of the country, while to the south, the battle between Israel and Egypt continued to rage. I wanted to visit the Suez Canal.

"Impossible," I was told. Not one to easily accept no for an answer, I reached out to some of the military contacts I had nurtured three years earlier. I finally coerced an Israeli general to fly a pool group of journalists—representatives of print, radio and television—to Suez.

The next day, a television producer from NBC, an editorial cartoonist from an upstate New York newspaper and I flew in a cramped six-seat, non-military aircraft across the barren Sinai desert. Flying at a low altitude, we watched the wind whip across the sand dunes, spreading fine granules of sand across a two-lane black paved highway that stretched south into the distance. Occasionally, sand would whisk away to reveal remnants of the steel rails of the old Palestine-to-Egypt railway. From the air, it was easy to spot groups of Bedouin nomads crossing the foreboding landscape.

Our plane touched down on an old Egyptian airstrip, on the outskirts of the abandoned city of Kantara. The runway was short, and the plane overshot it by about 20 feet, coming to a dramatic stop when the prop tipped over into a sand dune. We were a little shaken, but managed to get out safely. We were told that another plane would be sent for the return trip.

Now 12 miles from the front lines, we sat uncomfortably in a military vehicle, tightly encased in our flak jackets and steel helmets. The air was dry and hot as we rode along. The desert was barren, except for mysterious black patches just visible on the dunes in the distance. A great haze of dust kicked up from the roadway as a caravan of tanks and trucks passed. The young soldiers aboard were in full battle gear. They carried Uzi automatic carbines and held transistor radios to their ears. The sound of rock 'n' roll was muted by the clatter of tank treads pounding over the concrete.

The afternoon sun was blinding, its brilliance casting deep shadows across the dunes and littered debris of war. The charred and rusting remnants of Egyptian tanks and trucks from the 1967 war struck our eyes like pieces of some avant-garde metallic sculpture. Off in the distance, the sound of shells whizzing through the air could be heard. Our anxieties built as we learned that the Israelis and Egyptians were engaged in a heavy artillery exchange across the canal. We observed gaping pockets in the sand where freshly delivered shells had been swallowed. Our military escort informed us that the shells were falling short; the Egyptians were trying to knock out the road we were currently racing across. The dunes drew closer and we discovered that the black patches we had seen along the way were in fact Israeli howitzers and anti-aircraft guns, protruding from the white, sloping sand. They were covered in tarps to camouflage them from the air.

The roadway narrowed as we approached the war-ravaged city of Kantara, the only major city on the banks of the Suez Canal to fall into Israeli hands. All of its residents had fled and now it was a ghost town, desolate and silent. Hardly a building had escaped the wrath of the Egyptian firepower. The walls of collapsed buildings and the minarets of wrecked mosques formed a jagged silhouette against the deep-blue Mediterranean sky. Window shutters flapped back and forth in the wind.

Our vehicle pulled up alongside the rubble of a villa. "Keep low and out of sight," our escort bellowed to us. "You're in Egyptian sniper range." He pointed to a house mere yards away across the narrow stretch of the canal, its roof sagging from the many strikes of Israeli shells. "That's enemy territory," he told us. It was our first realization of just how close the lines actually were: the Egyptian and Israeli positions were separated by about 125 yards—little more than the length of a football field.

The air was beginning to cool as we advanced into the afternoon, but the heat under our flak jackets was intense. My palms were clammy. With our escort covering with his Uzi, we dashed across a dirt road one at a time, our backs humped forward in the running dance we had been taught to avoid becoming a sniper's target. The half-block run felt like miles. We reached the other side, breathless.

We were now in a nameless Israeli fire base, where we entered a trench. The trench was narrow, only two-and-a-half feet wide. The sides were shored up with wooden planks and topped by a mountain of sandbags. With our knees digging into our chins, we began to move slowly toward a periscope. Without warning, we heard a crack like a thousand claps of thunder and felt the ground shake under the impact of falling Egyptian shells. Minutes later, another shell came flying across. I dove deeper into the trench, picking up splinters of wood in my flak jacket. I scribbled notes and recorded the sounds swirling around me; a cold sweat consumed me, but I was too overwhelmed by all that was happening to think about being frightened.

The soldiers on the front lines were a mix of young draftees and slightly older reservists. Manning a nearby gunnery position was David, an 18-year-old draftee from Tel Aviv who had been here three months. He told me that time passed quickly on the base.

"Everyone has a job to do," he said, "and what little time remains is spent sleeping." As for the constant shelling, he conceded, "It's not one of the easy things in life, but we learn to live with it."

The artillery fire soon ceased for a few minutes, and it felt safe enough for me to make my way to the periscope. This, as it turned out, was a modified pair of binoculars with two sighting extensions, poking out above the sandbags and covered with parts of burlap bags. Pressing my eyes against the scope, I could just barely see the edge of the canal in the foreground. I saw no signs of life on the other side, but as I panned I focused on a house that I was told was a sniper's nest. As I scanned the area all around, it was clear that the Egyptians had sustained heavy damage from all the shelling.

Another explosion ripped through the air as we made a mad dash for the nearest bunker. There we followed a narrow, darkened passageway deep belowground to meet the base commander, a rugged, good-looking man who was introduced to us as "Deddy." This was his nickname; journalists were not permitted to identify Israeli officers by their legal name or rank. As the base's senior officer, Deddy assured us that we were safe in his bunker. He boasted that in more than three years of shelling, it had not been penetrated once. The facility, he explained, was reinforced with concrete and fortified with rails—again from the defunct Palestine-to-Egypt railway—which crisscrossed the top of the bunker, making it virtually impenetrable.

The underground quarters were cramped, but livable. The morale of the soldiers seemed to be good. "They have good backing from their people, and military backing as well," Deddy told us. The soldiers certainly ate well—the food was plentiful, and the menu varied. I was particularly surprised to learn that here, in the throes of battle, the soldiers even managed to keep kosher: following the strictures of the Jewish religion, they kept separate dishes for meat and dairy, and maintained two sinks outside the bunker to clean them. As another part of the effort to maintain high morale, the Israeli army also permitted homesick soldiers to call home once a week; we saw miles of telephone cables strung across the combat zone. But there was nothing like a letter from home. The gunner, David, shared one with us that he had just received from his mother.

"She just wants to know if I'm all right," he related. "Somehow, mothers and girlfriends don't believe you when you write that all is well. They're not prepared to believe you until they see you." He told us that military censors limited what he was allowed to write, so he kept it simple. "When I write to my family," he said, "I write that in this day I am still alive."

The hour was growing late. The front lines were secured after 5 p.m., with no traffic in or out aside from military patrols. We said our shaloms and raced against a red-setting desert sun toward our awaiting plane. Two Israeli Mirage jets swooped over our heads as we drove to the landing strip, returning to the base after the day's sorties against Egyptian targets. In 90 minutes, we were back in Tel Aviv. The sounds and vibrancy of the modern Israeli city, its lights glittering below us, gave no hint that we were in a country in the midst of war. My muscles were fatigued, tense from the day's experiences, but I wasn't so much tired as I was stimulated. It had been my first live taste of warfare.

20

BEWARE THE SILENCE

Interviewing Col. Lon Non, the charismatic brother of then Premier Lon Nol. 1971.

*m*y wife kept insisting I had a death wish as she tried to deter me from venturing off for another brief endeavor as a war correspondent. It was 1971, a year after my visit to Israel, and the war was raging in Vietnam while violent anti-war protests at home were creating havoc in our cities. As a journalist, I wanted to see firsthand what this war was all about, and better understand why it was so unpopular.

Ted Kavanau, the news director of then–WNEW-TV, agreed to broadcast my reports, but he wanted to join me on the trip. Japan Airlines agreed to fly us to Tokyo, in return for coverage of a golf tournament they were sponsoring in Fugu, Japan. Once we arrived in Tokyo we promptly visited the Vietnamese Consulate, only to learn that it would take days, perhaps a week, before we could receive a visa to Vietnam. Kavanau was disappointed; because of our time constraints, we couldn't wait.

"Let's try Cambodia," he exclaimed. The Cambodian diplomats turned out to be eager for us to tell how their military forces were engaged in repelling the insurgency by North Vietnamese forces and local Khmer Rouge Communists, and without hesitation gave us the documents we needed to fly to Phnom Penh.

From what we observed in a few short days, the Cambodian government forces were underequipped and ill-prepared to counter the onslaught they faced. When the government ordered the North Vietnamese and Viet Cong to leave the sanctuaries and supply corridors they had established inside Cambodia for launching their attacks on South Vietnam, the rebellious anti-government Khmer Rouge took their side, and together they proved to be a formidable fighting force. When we arrived, the conflict had already claimed the lives of 4,000 Cambodians, 1,000 of them civilians. But the worst was yet to come.

The capitol city of Phnom Penh was a bustling metropolis of one-and-a-half million people, still untouched by the war that was already underway in the rural countryside. The city, with its grand boulevards and striking French architecture intermixed with age-old pagodas, stupas and temples along the banks of the Mekong River, had the distinction of being known as "the Pearl of Asia."

But being well within mortar range of the insurgents, it was a city holding its breath on the threshold of war. Roads were barricaded with barbed-wire fences. Armed guards stood watch in front of public buildings. Mirrors were used to look under vehicles, to ensure no explosives were planted there. Because of gas rationing, there were very few cars, and the streets were a perennial traffic jam of bicycles and pedicabs. The guard in military fatigues who stood watch in front of the Monoram Hotel, where we stayed, was 12 years old, and the rifle he carried was as long as he was tall. There were lots of kids in the army, he told me, many of them orphans.

My room in the hotel was dark; we kept the shades drawn. An overhead fan circulated the stagnant air from a noisy air conditioner. At night I would be lulled to sleep by the sound of aircraft circling the perimeter of the city. I was told these were "shadows" or "snoopies"—converted transport planes with heat-seeking devices and armaments protruding from the underbelly, that flew in search of enemy troop concentrations. One morning, a sudden burst of gunfire jostled me out of bed. It was two Cambodian soldiers playfully firing their carbines into the air—not an uncommon practice, I would later learn.

At a military briefing, we were informed of the potential hazards we faced as journalists going to where the fighting was. We would have to travel along Highway 3 to get to our destination of Tram Knar, where a military operation dubbed "Burning Eyes of Revolution" had begun just days earlier. The military did not provide helicopters, or any other means of transportation to get journalists to the front lines—we had to get there on our own. The bureau chief from NBC News offered us sage advice: hire an experienced driver we could trust, who had a well-maintained car. He warned us to be particularly cautious as we traveled along Highways 2 and 3, sometimes referred to as Ambush Alley, because that was where enemy troops often lay in wait. He cautioned us to be alert, and especially to "beware the silence," explaining that if we passed an area that was unusually quiet, with no signs of life—not even the sounds of creatures of the jungle—it could be an indication that enemy troops were lurking nearby. It was sobering to learn that more than 20 reporters had been killed or captured while heading to cover a battle here. Journalists captured by the Viet Cong or North Vietnamese, we were informed, were held prisoner; those taken by the merciless Khmer Rouge were immediately executed.

As risky as it was, Kavanau and I knew we had to make the

journey. My stomach was in knots and my mouth dry as I got dressed on the morning of our trip. I recognized that there was a real possibility that I could be killed that day. Before leaving the hotel, I decided to write a letter to my wife of three years, letting her know that I loved her and offering my apologies for not listening to her efforts to deter me from the trip. Trying to avoid being overly dramatic, I nevertheless encouraged her to go on with her life, and to always treasure the memories we had shared together. "While you will grieve over my death," I wrote, "I want you to understand that I was doing something I loved. Being a reporter was always my dream, and once again, I was in pursuit of a story." I left the sealed envelope on the nightstand in my room, to be found if I failed to return.

I joined Kavanau for breakfast at the nearby Le Rule Hotel, a popular refuge for foreign journalists. Noting that I had a young wife at home and was attempting to start a family, he tried to discourage me from going. There was no way I was backing down, but my nerves were rattled enough for me to order a Scotch and soda—the first time I ever had a drink in the morning.

Our driver, Ou Seng Hor, showed up in an air-conditioned Mercedes-Benz, his radio blaring with rock-and-roll music from the military radio station in South Vietnam. The drive along the dangerous Highway 3 seemed pleasant enough, as we passed rice fields ready for harvest, small patches of jungle and villages of thatched houses on stilts. There was heavy troop movement along the highway at this point, which was fairly well controlled by the army between 8:30 a.m. and 3:30 p.m. These were the safest hours for journalists to cover the war; later in the day, the Viet Cong were likely to seize control.

We stopped to photograph a homeless family sitting on a mat beneath a mango tree. They had been displaced from their home by the Communist invaders. The mother cradled an infant in her arms, her eyes filled with fear, while three other children sat nearby. A military unit pulled up alongside us to offer them some food rations. Such signs of life diminished after we passed a fork in the road. Suddenly there were no trucks, no cars, no bicycles—just oxen and horses. Our driver stopped at a military checkpoint, where he requested an escort to get us around a blown-up bridge. In their efforts to get to the front, reporters often had to make crossings like these on foot, on plank walkways supported by bamboo poles. On the other side waited a band of war profiteers, small boys with bicycles who offered to ride the correspondents the remaining two miles to the front for the equivalent of 20 cents.

When we reached the forward position at Tram Knar, we were surprised to find a picnic atmosphere in the war zone. Dozens of soldiers were casually stretched across a field—some sitting and having lunch, others sleeping under armored vehicles—while a few yards away, an artillery unit fired mortar rounds at enemy positions. An all-volunteer force, the Cambodian army's ranks had swelled in one year from 35,000 to 170,000. The soldiers had to buy their own uniforms, but were otherwise provided for by the army and, by Cambodian standards at the time, paid well—$30 a month.

Still, the troops at this forward base appeared to be unde-requipped, and often used vintage American, French and Chinese weapons. Given the shortage of military vehicles, they were often transported to the front in old Pepsi-Cola trucks and Chinese-made buses. Recruits included women, and children as young as 10.

One officer quipped, "We have to let the children in the army or they'll cry." Many of the kids were members of so-called "Orphan Platoons," whose families had been killed in the war. The commander of the unit was called "Papa" by his troops, and he called his young soldiers "my sons."

One boy told me, "We don't mind living like this. We have no families and no place to go. The general is the only one who cares for us."

The 15th Brigade ran the show at Tram Knar. A foppish group of artists and actors, they were part of the only brigade in the Cambodian army that had its own dance band. Kavanau and I were ushered into a jeep for a short ride down the road to meet the colorful commander of the military operation. 40-year-old Colonel Lon Non, the younger brother of Cambodian Premier Lon Nol, was a stocky, charismatic man who held a swagger stick at his side and a sub-machine gun in his hand. He greeted me with a smile and, through an interpreter, apologized for not speaking English. I, in kind, apologized for not speaking French. Over the crackle of small-arms fire in the distance, I listened as the military leader painted a positive picture of his country's war effort. His goal at the moment, he told me, was to pacify the villagers and clear the road of the insurgents. The morale of his men, he said, was high, and their goal in sight.

I keenly felt my vulnerability as I sat in the back of an open truck with a dozen other reporters, driving across Highway 3 back to where our car and driver were waiting. He raced us back to Phnom Penh, where we had a scheduled meeting with members of our diplomatic corps at the U.S. Embassy. We were told that, under the Nixon doctrine, there were no American troops involved in the Cambodian conflict at that time. However, since the U.S. was supportive of the current government in Cambodia, we were still supplying military equipment and providing air support with bombing missions when needed. I left with the distinct impression that the Cambodians were hoping that America would fight their war for them.

* * *

At the time, Cambodia remained one of the few places in the world where people could still legally escape to opium dens. After one of the daily press briefings, I received a unique invitation from colleagues at the United Press International and Reuters bureaus in Phnom Penh to join them as their guests at the local opium emporium. Despite my trepidation about the side effects the opium might have on my body, I felt that this was something I had to experience.

My hosts assured me that I would be fine.

The next evening, we entered the establishment on the outskirts of Phnom Penh. The den itself was a bungalow with several rooms. Measuring eight feet by eight feet, our room was tight, with walls of bamboo and straw. An attractive hostess fitted me with a sarong and made me comfortable on a bamboo mat.

A fan swirled above me, but did little to relieve the oppressive heat. Pesky mosquitoes swarmed around me. For 50 riel (the equivalent of about 20 cents) I was offered a relaxing massage that helped to relieve some of my anxieties. As my hosts and I chatted and shared a few jokes, I heard familiar voices in the adjoining room. I was certain I recognized them as some of the diplomats I had met the previous day at the U.S. Embassy.

Our hostess brought in an oil lamp and a pipe about 20 inches long, with a bowl in the center. Over a flame, she boiled a black paste—pure opium—and placed a small amount of it into the bowl. The scent was sweet and mild, like perfume. The pipe was then presented to me, the drug already vaporized in the heat and ready to be inhaled. As my friends watched, I took one long drag on the pipe and instantly choked, the vapors burning my throat. My fellow reporters had a momentary laugh at my inexperience as they each took their turn at the pipe, drawing in the vapors with slow inhalations. If only I had known that was the way to do it!

Lying back on the mat, I took another shot at the pipe. I began to feel a little lightheaded—but nothing more. Night had begun to fall, and I thought I was hallucinating when I heard what sounded like explosions off in the distance. I wasn't—American B-52s, I was told, were staging a bombing raid on Khmer Rouge targets, about ten miles from where we were… A bit too close, I thought. With the tropical heat, the flies and the mosquitoes, my discomfort level soon rose to excruciating. I asked to return to my air-conditioned hotel room, but was informed that the curfew was now in effect, and the only way I could make the risky return was by riding in a taxi with the interior lights turned on. My hosts had fallen asleep, and stayed the night in the opium den, and I held my breath in the taxi I chose, its interior lights burning brightly, raced across the empty streets to my hotel.

* * *

The Communist Khmer Rouge eventually overpowered Cambodia's government-backed forces and achieved victory in 1975. This initiated a period of genocide, during which the victors forced people out of Phnom Penh into the rural countryside and carried out political executions, along with torture and forced labor. During their bloody four-year reign, the Khmer Rouge was responsible for the slaughter of approximately two million people, in what came to be known as the Killing Fields of Cambodia.

One man who lived through the horror and survived to tell the story of his unremitting nightmare was Dith Pran, whose struggle to outlast the brutality in his homeland inspired the 1984 Academy Award–winning film *The Killing Fields.* Pran, who had been an assistant to Pulitzer Prize–winning journalist Sidney Shanberg, played a key role in bringing the war crimes of Pol Pot and his regime to the world's attention.

Pran became an American citizen in 1986, and brought his family to New Jersey. He was working at *The New York Times* as a photographer when we met and became friends. In 1996 I was proud to nominate him for an Ellis Island Medal of Honor—and pleased to be there to celebrate with him and his family when he received it.

21

CHILDREN OF TERROR

Midnight meeting with Palestinian leader Yasser Arafat in Beirut.

*W*ith a huge Ferris wheel dominating the pristine white beach stretching along the blue Mediterranean shoreline, and gleaming white hotels casting shadows across the sand, the setting looked more like Miami Beach than Beirut. The view from the air, as we made our final approach into Lebanon's battle-scarred airport, belied the realty below. A once-beautiful city, formerly considered the Paris of the Middle East, now lay in ruins, racked by an ongoing civil war. Many of the luxury hotels were vacant, reduced in places to rubble and pockmarked facades from the relentless shelling.

Armed soldiers glanced at me suspiciously as I made my way out of the airport, passing a gaggle of hustlers outside who offered me everything from cheap currency to sex with their "sisters." I was there to do a story about the "children of terror"—the offspring of the Palestinian refugees living under the banner of the Palestine Liberation Organization, or PLO, who called themselves "freedom fighters" but who, elsewhere in the world, were considered terrorists committed to the elimination of Israel. The PLO and its leader, Yasser Arafat, had gained global recognition through deadly acts of terrorism, including the hijacking of airliners to the Middle Eastern desert.

The heat was oppressive and the anxiety high as we drove into the cauldron of conflict in Beirut. Along the way we observed an incongruous cast of images. On one side of the road there were encampments of Syrian soldiers, armed with Russian-made AK-47 rifles, manning checkpoints, while on the other there were happy children on the beach, building sand castles and dashing in and out of the surf. Sandbags and fortifications lined the landscape, sandwiched between souvenir shops selling seashells and brightly painted spent bomb casings.

The intensity of years of fighting was clearly etched in the rubble of buildings in downtown Beirut. Armored tanks were positioned in front of the year-old Holiday Inn that was already in shambles, its walls riddled with bullet holes and concrete balconies in a state of near-collapse. The building stood at the epicenter of the so-called "Battle of Hotels," during which opposing factions had staged violent firefights from neighboring hotels. Christian militia fighters had occupied the abandoned Holiday Inn, while their Muslim counterparts had taken up positions in another hotel across the way.

The psychological scars of war were felt deeper in the generations of children who had grown up with conflict as a way of life. In 1981, during a weeklong visit to refugee camps, schools and orphanages in half a dozen towns and villages throughout Lebanon, I observed them playing with dolls, skateboards, bicycles—and guns. They laughed at popular American television shows. They cried in the middle of the night. They were children who appeared to be like children anywhere, except they were different. Theirs was a generation of hatred, born and nurtured in the hardships of the refugee camps. From the start, I was told, they were taught to fight for a land they had never seen. Before they reached adolescence, many of them were willing and able to kill for it. What they didn't learn from their instructors, they learned from their parents and grandparents, who subscribed to the doctrine of Syria's Minister of Education, written in 1968: "The hatred which we indoctrinate into the minds of our children from their birth is sacred."

In one camp, I watched a three-year-old on a tricycle pointing a toy rifle into the air and crying out, "Bing, bing, bing." Nearby, a nine-year-old carried a real one.

The younger boy's mother, watching over her son, told me, "He's been born in the worst of times. All he sees are the weapons. He has nothing else to play with. He *wants* to play with guns." Bursting with pride, she declared, "When he's nine, he'll have a real one." The battle against Israel was justified, she claimed, because "there is no meaning to life without your homeland."

A 22-year-old neighbor echoed her sentiment, saying, "I have my homeland in my heart. Death is no problem for me, if I die fighting for it." The deep crevices in her face and circles under her eyes bore witness to her years of struggle and hardship.

Tensions rose during a visit to the PLO offices, located on the ninth floor of a building in the Hamra section of Beirut. Below, there was a tractor-trailer loaded with crates blocking the street, the driver nowhere to be found. We heard a cacophony of blaring horns. I was unnerved and fearful that this might have been an abandoned truck heavily laden with explosives. An anxious 15 minutes passed before the driver finally showed up and moved his truck. I had just about calmed down when I got word of a massive anti-American protest that had erupted nearby, after two U.S. fighter jets shot down two Libyan warplanes. As many as a thousand angry demonstrators had congregated, and were burning the American flag and an effigy of President Reagan.

I kept my head down as my driver hustled me back to the Commodore Hotel, a heavily guarded sanctuary for journalists in the war-torn area. Around the hotel bar, reporters shared stories and talked about close encounters. We acknowledged that we were all fatalists, fully aware of the hazards we faced while in pursuit of our stories, but the things we saw and heard here, on a daily basis, were truly surreal. We saw a Syrian soldier kicking a mule with the heel of his boot, in an effort to move it along the street. We saw a well-dressed man getting a shoeshine in the midst of a cloud of dirt and dust whipping across the street, standing beneath a poster of a Palestinian martyr. Dozens of these posters hung throughout the city. We regularly heard the crack of gunfire from inside the hotel; once, hearing it very close to the back of the building, some of us went to investigate. We found an eight-year-old boy firing an AK-47 at a fence.

* * *

It was 8 o'clock on a Saturday night when the hotel concierge summoned me to the phone. My PLO contact was calling to inform me that tonight was the night. Yasser Arafat had agreed to meet with me at 11:30, for a half-hour exclusive interview. The other reporters at the hotel were surprised and envious that I had scored this hard-to-get interview with Arafat so quickly. Apparently, the PLO saw it as an opportunity to reach a vast American audience through the article I was writing for a national publication.

A couple of hours later, I was picked up and driven to a residential section of Beirut. After a cursory security check—very surprising, given the many attempts that had already been made on Arafat's life—I was led into the finished basement of what appeared to be a private home. The room was thick with smoke. Nearly 20 men were smoking Marlboro cigarettes and fondling their worry beads. Several Kalashnikov assault rifles lay on top of the large brown and beige squares that made up the carpet. I sat nervously, wondering whether or not the controversial leader would be responsive to my questions. Soon, the doors to an inner chamber opened, and everyone stood up. I hesitated for a moment, but was the last to rise as a man walked out of the room, much of his body wrapped in bandages. I would later learn that he was an anti-Zionist Jew, who had recently performed a covert mission for the PLO.

I was ushered into the inner chamber and introduced to Arafat, and we exchanged pleasantries in English and Arabic. For a man of such stature among the Palestinians, I was surprised to see how short he was, at 5 feet 2 inches. He was dressed in military fatigues, and wore his customary black-and-white keffiyeh headdress. He seemed more personable than I had expected, and spoke with me mostly in English, though he had an interpreter at his side. Before we began, his Harvard-educated communications director, Mahmoud Labadi, offered to take my picture with the chairman. As we posed, he snapped four frames with my camera. Curiously, I would later find that three of the photos had Arafat and me perfectly framed, while the second shot had me dead center of the frame. It was theorized that if the camera had been rigged as a weapon—a known assassination tactic—it could have fired its projectile with the second snap of the shutter.

Recognizing that my article for *Parade* magazine would have a potential readership of 70 million Americans, Arafat reiterated his message that it was the Israelis who were the aggressors in their conflict. He emphatically denied that Palestinian children were being conditioned to hate.

Asked if the children were serving as pawns in the conflict, he asserted, "We are obliged to push our small children to defend themselves against Israeli aggression," but insisted at the same time, "We are teaching them love of the motherland, not hatred of the enemy." Not entirely satisfied with his response to my question, I waited a few minutes to ask again.

Labadi leaned over to me, cupping his hand over my ear. "Don't ask the same question again," he said, "or the interview is terminated." In the final moments of the interview, I dared to ask it again. "The interview is terminated," Labadi shot at me.

"No, let him continue," asserted Arafat, who handed me a photograph to take back to what sounded like "Jew York." It was of an infant, Fahtmi Palestine, taken from the womb of her mother, who was killed in an Israeli bombing raid. As I looked at the photo, Arafat took exception with my use of the word "conflict" during the interview, telling me, "It is not fair to say conflict. It is aggression against our children. They are the victims." When I asked if the Palestinian children could coexist with Jewish children in a place called Israel, Arafat was quick to respond.

"Yes," he declared, "in the future, when they grow up—when they have their state and are living in a secure land." Drawing our interview to its close, he invited me to ask the children myself whether they were ready to live in peace with Israelis.

* * *

I visited an orphanage at Souk El-Gharb known as the School of Happiness of Children, built exclusively for the orphans of martyrs. I put that question to 13-year-old Tarek. But the school's headmaster translated the English into Arabic differently. I was suspicious, but didn't learn until afterwards that the question wasn't quite what I had asked.

My driver-interpreter informed me that the headmaster had actually queried, "Can you live in peace under a Zionist government that wants to destroy the Palestinian people?" It was no wonder the boy shook his head wildly with the predictable answer.

Out of the presence of their elders, the children of the PLO spoke much more openly and candidly. 14-year-old Khalel said he would have no difficulty living with Israelis as friends. He told me he was optimistic that through prayer and compromise, peace could be achieved. 13-year-old Hassan said he would like for there to be peace, so he could visit Disneyworld.

12-year-old Abdul wished for peace so he could have a bicycle—but then hesitated and said, "If I had to choose between a bicycle and peace, I would rather have peace."

Still, it was true that for many other children in Beirut, hatred of Israel had been passed down to them over generations.

"We teach our children that our country is Palestine," one mother told me, "and our enemy is Israel." Some children expressed this antipathy through their art. A drawing by an eight-year old Palestinian boy, for example, showed people on a rooftop shooting down a plane.

The caption read, "Don't worry, Jerusalem, tomorrow we will return back." A grotesque painting by an eight-year-old girl showed several people hanging from gallows, accompanied by the words, "Jerusalem, fight and struggle until you are liberated from the enemies. We will fight and struggle until we liberate you."

We drove south to the Palestinian camp at Rachidye, just four miles north of the Israeli border. Israeli planes had destroyed six important bridges in southern Lebanon, thereby shutting down the main roads south from Beirut and sending us on a seemingly endless meander along a single-lane highway, through monumental detours and traffic jams. Our guide angrily shouted expletives in Arabic against Israel. When our pace along the road slowed to an unbearable one mile per hour, our driver took a detour into a banana field to move us along. The heat was oppressive; our car's air conditioner wasn't working, and temperatures inside soared to 100 degrees as we swept past wide-leafed banana trees, kicking up clouds of dirt and dust that blanketed our clothing and left a dryness in our throats. My heart skipped a beat at one checkpoint, when the barrel of a rifle was suddenly thrust through the rear window and pointed directly at me. At the other end of the gun was a boy not more than 12 or 13 years old, his finger tight on the trigger, demanding to see my travel documents. Fortunately, shouts in Arabic by my escorts quickly defused the tense situation.

The sprawling Rachidye camp was a sandswept, squalid oasis of cinderblock-and-concrete houses, with television antennas sprouting from rooftops of tin and tile. Each family complex was 20 by 30 feet and encompassed two or three living areas, plus a kitchen and outdoor toilet. At a designated time each day, as the sun streaked lines of shadow across a large table in a meeting room, the children of the camp were gathered together to be shown anti-Israeli propaganda and old Nazi indoctrination films. In an open field in a remote corner of the camp, a group of boys in military fatigues practiced loading and unloading firearms; elsewhere, young boys were seen shouldering AK-47s and other weapons as comfortably as an American kid might carry a baseball bat. Some as young as seven or eight were heard boasting about how well they could fire them. Nine-year-old Mesa claimed she was not afraid of all the shelling, but her eyes told a different story.

"It's daily music we hear," she said. "We don't think about it anymore."

In the village of Damour, 15 miles south of Beirut, the children had learned to cope after the many bombing and shelling attacks they'd endured. When the planes came, they ran to shelters, and when the planes were gone, they headed out to play again. It was good to see these children laugh—though ultimately, the joke was on me. At one point I jumped when I was startled by the sound of an explosion, but it turned out to be the sound of an Israeli jet breaking the sound barrier, causing all the kids around me to laugh uproariously. Unlike me, these kids were well able to distinguish the sound of a sonic boom from an Israeli fighter jet overhead from a bomb or mortar shell.

Behind the laughter of these children lay deep scars. The frequency of the attacks on their villages had impacted them psychologically: many had developed a fear of the dark, suffered regular nightmares and experienced frequent episodes of bedwetting. Some children were noticeably withdrawn, and had difficulty communicating with others or showing emotion. In various ways, these children of war were urged to live, fight and, if necessary, die for the cause. Like children of war everywhere, they were taught at an early age that their lives had no meaning without sacrifice. Because of the pervasive terror and constant threat of death, these children grew up very fast. They had been robbed of their childhood.

* * *

When I returned to New York, I learned that my life had been threatened in connection my visit to Beirut. Callers, identifying themselves as members of the extremist Jewish Defense League, reached out to my editor to suggest that if I went to Beirut to write a positive story about the PLO, it would be a "one-way trip." My editor reassured the callers that I was an objective reporter, and would do a fair story; but this didn't satisfy them.

"We don't want anyone doing stories about the PLO," they insisted. "He'll fall for their propaganda. Let him go to Israel." I later found out that the JDL had learned of my trip by intercepting a telex from New York to the PLO headquarters in Beirut, advising the organization to cooperate with me for my story. Mysteriously, at around the same time my wife found a screwdriver embedded in the driver's seat of her car—an ominous message, we assumed. Fortunately, nothing ever came of the threats.

After my article in *Parade* was published, I was sought after to speak to a number of Jewish organizations, and met with universal disfavor when I suggested that Yasser Arafat was the best hope for peace in the Middle East. Of all the factions of the Palestinian movement, I explained, Arafat's was the most moderate. No one seemed to care; in the eyes of so many, he was still considered a terrorist. It was 12 years later, in 1993, that my view was confirmed when Arafat joined Israeli Prime Minister Yitzhak Rabin in a handshake at the White House, ratifying the Oslo Accord and marking what then appeared to be the beginnings of the peace process in the Middle East.

In 1995, I met Prime Minister Rabin in New York, and shared with him the negative response I had gotten to my suggestion that Arafat was the best hope for peace. I thanked him for giving credibility to that controversial statement, adding that "it took a Yitzhak Rabin to make it happen." He was appreciative, but told me there still was much more to be done for a lasting peace. He was never to see the realization of his dream. Two weeks later he was murdered by an assassin's bullet, and I was sent to Jerusalem to cover his funeral.

22

BRINGING CHRISTMAS TO OUR TROOPS

Dave Kimmel and I bring Christmas cheer to troops at Bagram Air Base, Afghanistan 2013.

*i*t began with the delivery of a father's hug to a son at war, and evolved into the massive embrace of hundreds of homesick soldiers far from home at Christmastime. And it was the proudest achievement of my entire career.

At the height of the war in Iraq and Afghanistan, I proposed to my editors at WPIX TV that we spend the Christmas holiday with servicemen and -women from New York, to let them know they hadn't been forgotten back home. Since 2004, we have made four holiday visits to Iraq and one to Afghanistan. Each time my colleagues, cameraman Dave Kimmel and reporter Jill Nicolini, and I have brought the soldiers taped greetings from local elected officials and celebrities, along with some of New York's world-famous local delicacies—bagels, hotdogs and cheesecake—which we were able to get DHL Express to fly directly into the base. Best of all, we arranged for a number of emotional reunions, which enabled the soldiers to talk directly with their families live via satellite during WPIX's morning and evening newscasts.

The experience began with the startled-to-joy expression on the face of Private First Class James Adelis Jr. when I located him at a base 40 miles north of Baghdad and delivered a hug from his father, who was instrumental in handling the logistics for our visit.

"This is from your dad," I said, embracing him. "I promised to bring it all the way to Iraq."

The location of Camp Anaconda in Balad, just north of Baghdad, was geographically Iraq; but the surroundings were more like those of a small city in the heartland of America, with a first-run movie theater, a Pizza Hut and a Burger King. With a population of 22,000 servicemen and -women, Camp Anaconda was the largest logistical support base in the country. The troops lived in so-called hooches, improvised housing units consisting of pre-fab trailers, some of which had satellite TV dishes and running water. The sound of hairdryers, competing with the rattle of armored vehicles, lured me into a small building, where I was surprised to discover a beauty salon on the lonely desert outpost. It was a bit incongruous to see M-16s and pieces of body armor resting alongside the manicure tables. Yet for the 4,000 women at this base, a little pampering was the best way to combat battle fatigue.

Still, daily life on the military outpost could be very challenging. Discomfort was the norm. The fine, oil-tainted sand blowing around consistently coated our throats and clothing, and left layers of grit on the vehicles. Any rainfall would turn the ground into thick mounds of clay that caked in the soles of our boots. The brilliance of the morning sun rising over the Tigris River seemed to contrast with the ominous clouds of violence that lurked just outside the razor wire of the compound.

My nerves were rattled the first time the sirens wailed. It was a "red alert," warning us of an incoming mortar attack. Our military escort rushed us into our flak jackets and helmets, and we took cover. Off in the distance, there was a loud crack of thunder that sounded like an explosion, and everyone flinched. In a matter of minutes the all-clear was sounded, and we learned that the "incoming" had been destroyed. But that wasn't always the case. The base had been hit so many times, it earned the nickname *Mortaritaville*. Shortly before our visit, a shell hit near our broadcast position, wounding ten people.

The spirit of Christmas was in the air. Santa made his ceremonial rounds with an M-16 rather than a sack of toys slung over his shoulder. Soldiers sang Christmas carols as lights flickered on a robust tree. Peace on earth and good will toward men was the prayer for the season—and sadly, not much more than a stated goal in a country deep in the throes of war. Still, the spirit of the soldiers remained high. As we arrived bearing our holiday gifts, some of them were delighted to see a familiar face from home.

"Hiya, man—so good to see ya," burst Sergeant First Class Antonio Baird, of Brooklyn. "I've been watching you on TV for years." As glad as he was to see me, though, he was more excited to hear about the bagels and hotdogs we brought along.

Not that they were in any shortage of food. The question I was asked most frequently back home was, *How do the soldiers eat there?*

"Quite well," I would reply. The tens of thousands of meals served daily at Camp Anaconda were surprisingly lavish. At breakfast there was a full omelette station; after dinner there was a Ben and Jerry's ice-cream counter for dessert. The menus there were quite diversified, and more than substantial. For Christmas dinner, they served turkey, Cornish game hen and—would you believe?—lobster tails. The spiked eggnog, however, was nowhere to be found. Unlike in previous American wars, when soldiers were permitted to drink alcohol, it was utterly forbidden in Iraq. Getting caught with booze at Camp Anaconda could quickly get you arrested and thrown into the brig. With the intense 20-hour days we had been working, Dave Kimmel and I figured we would need a few moments to relax. Before we left New York, we spirited vodka in a large empty mouthwash bottle, and added vegetable coloring. We took a shot or two before our naps in Iraq. But having failed to thoroughly clean the bottles, I have to tell you that Listerine Vodka was difficult to swallow.

* * *

The inbound Medevac helicopters brought us constant reminders of the realities of war, as they delivered the most recent casualties to the Air Force Hospital on the base. This was a 62,000-square-foot facility under canvas that would rival any major trauma center in the U.S. On staff was a medical team of 380 doctors and nurses I described in my reports as the "Healing Hands for Heroes." Dave Kimmel and I were on the pad as a Black Hawk helicopter landed and a medical team raced out to lift a wounded Marine onto a gurney and rush him into the emergency medical facility in a desperate attempt to save his life. The Marine had a serious head wound, and was not responsive. I watched with a heavy heart as doctors worked feverishly against the clock to stabilize and revive the wounded marine. Within hours, he was on a plane to another medical facility in Germany. His chances of survival, we were told, were very good. Unlike in Vietnam, where it had sometimes taken days to get the wounded to a field hospital, we were told that in Iraq, the wounded were transported from the battlefield within 30 minutes, contributing to the base hospital's 98% survival rate.

I had a chance to see the doctors at work when an orthopedic surgeon invited us to get into scrubs and join him in Operating Room 3. He was removing a bullet from the left arm of a 50-year-old Iraqi civilian, who got caught in the middle of a firefight. It was difficult to watch as he delicately removed the bullet from the bloody arm, then sewed up the wound. The operation finished, the doctor had barely taken off his facemask before he asked when we were going to serve those bagels we had brought.

"I haven't had a good bagel since I left New York," he said wistfully.

There was no discrimination to be found at this field hospital. Even enemy combatants were treated here, under the watchful eyes of armed soldiers. Civilians were regularly treated here too—including children. It was a chilling moment when I heard the cries of a three-year-old Iraqi girl, who was being treated for shrapnel wounds.

In a most unusual encounter, I sat with an enemy combatant in a gazebo outside the hospital. An armed soldier stood over him, keeping guard. The man looked deeply troubled. He didn't speak any English, but somehow we managed to communicate. He offered me an Iraqi cigarette, and showed me a photo of a little girl.

"Your daughter?" I asked. He nodded his head and held up four fingers, indicating her age. Through his gestures, and the fact that he was waiting outside the hospital, I surmised that his daughter was one of the wounded, and was in surgery. Tears suddenly filled his eyes, and he held his hands together in prayer. I placed my hands in the same position, and expressed in English my hopes that his daughter would come through all right. Sadness consumed him, but he seemed to understand. He held my hand for a moment, and spoke briefly in his language, saying what I believed to be words of heartfelt thanks. For those few moments, we weren't adversaries from different worlds, but simply two fathers, connecting over the common concern of the well-being of a little girl.

* * *

One night, we flew under the cover of darkness to a military base in northern Iraq. Boarding a Black Hawk helicopter just as a 9 p.m. curfew went into effect, we lifted quickly above the rooftops of

Baghdad. Lights flooded the deserted streets below us, the silence of the night punctured by the deafening roar of the chopper's rotors. The tranquility of the city belied the fact that we were smack in the middle of a war zone. Off in the distance we could see the flickering flames of an oil refinery, stark against the darkness.

Previous wars were fought in jungles and trenches, not along roadsides like these; and as dangerous as those environments were, there was something newly menacing about these seemingly innocuous highways, where faceless enemy insurgents could hide the improvised explosives responsible for at least 44% of American combat deaths in Iraq. During one of our visits, we learned how dangerous it was to drive along any highway in Baghdad. After being told that a helicopter flight to the Green Zone was not available, Dave Kimmel and I were placed inside a 15-ton vehicle known as a Rhino—essentially an oversized RV encased in armor—destined down Route Irish, the codename for one of Baghdad's most notoriously dangerous highways. Even in such a heavy transport, I had some trepidation about the 12-mile ground trip, and offered to abort if Kimmel didn't want to chance it.

"No way," he insisted—and we were off, under orders to wear our flak jackets and helmets.

As we exited Camp Victory, we heard a loud thud, and off the left side of the vehicle we saw a plume of smoke.

My heart began to race as the driver, Staff Sergeant Hector Morales, made the sign of the cross, exclaiming, "Did you hear that?" Tersely, he told us that we had just narrowly avoided a small explosive device, apparently spirited away inside a plastic bag in the middle of the roadway. Morales gunned the accelerator and we raced off under the escort of a Humvee just ahead of us, its gunner standing alert at the trigger of his 50-caliber machine gun. Kimmel, his camera already rolling, turned it on me, as I breathlessly described what was happening, a chill running down my spine.

As we raced along the stretch of highway, the streets whizzed by in a blur. Once we were safe in the Green Zone, the Staff Sergeant got out to inspect his vehicle, and found no damage.

"We got lucky," he said with a sigh, his voice remarkably steady. We were reminded that what had been a nail-biting experience for us had been just another day in Staff Sergeant Morales's job. Still, he was not unappreciative of our narrow escape. "The man upstairs, he carries you around," he said, looking skyward. "We pray before we go to mission every morning—and he did his job today."

We were relieved to get through a most harrowing experience. But we were later told that it never happened. Three days after the incident, I received a call from a public-affairs officer in Baghdad who attempted to dissuade me from running the story in my broadcast, claiming that we hadn't had an IED encounter at all. The officer, a Marine colonel, told us she had never received a report of the incident. I suggested that perhaps there had been no report because it caused no damage or casualties. She insisted that there was no story here, claiming that maybe the driver was exaggerating.

She finally declared, "So you were hit by a firecracker." Fearful that the colonel might block the transmission of our story via military satellite, I remained respectful and held back what I really wanted to tell her. Fortunately, our account aired as scheduled.

* * *

Flying along over Baghdad at just under 1,000 feet, our helicopter cast a racing shadow across the sun-drenched landscape. We watched farmlands morph into rural and urban neighborhoods. Once a beautiful biblical city, Baghdad now bore the unmistakable scars of war, with many of its buildings in ruins.

These included Saddam Hussein's 12 opulent former palaces—marble-and-granite edifices the infamous tyrant had built as monuments to himself—along with the shacks and shanties they dwarfed: the homes of most Iraqis. Off in the distance, we could see the palace that Hussein had planned to name *Victory Over America*.

His defeat had reduced the unfinished palace to rubble. Another, named *Prosperity,* was leveled to an impoverished hovel, its floors collapsed. The palaces were a part of the Camp Victory compound in Baghdad, as was Al Faw Palace, which U.S. forces had turned into a military command headquarters. We landed to visit the building, marveling at the flashy remnants of the former tyrant's reign. A three-story chandelier reflected light off the towering marble columns; the bathrooms retained their gold plumbing fixtures. A Christmas tree with colorful lights incongruously adorned the rotunda. I couldn't resist sitting on a throne given to the former Iraqi leader by Palestinian president Yasser Arafat. Like the palace itself, this too was glitzy but beginning to show the wear of time, the fabric fraying and discolored from the multitude of visitors who parked themselves there long enough to take a picture. Similarly, as we hovered over other palaces—including one in Saddam's hometown of Tikrit—we were told that one had been fitted with a gold toilet for the despot's mother, while another was provided with a "torture playroom" for his sons.

The surroundings outside of Al Faw Palace were as pristine as those of the Taj Mahal. This, too, was a magnificent structure surrounded by a moat; Hussein, we learned, had closed down farmers' irrigation canals in order to redirect the water to encircle his palaces. The pool around this one was murky, with terrible secrets rumored to lie beneath its depths—the remains of scores of dissidents executed during Saddam's reign of terror.

As we prepared to leave the Green Zone, we stopped at a command center where soldiers were hosting a Christmas party for Iraqi children, many of them orphaned by the war. There was a jolly and rotund Santa—with a real white beard—and many happy, smiling children being weighed down by presents. It was a rare bright moment out of so many dark ones for them. As for me, my heart began to pulse as I watched one child, all of 11, being led up to Santa in a wheelchair. The boy's face lit up with delight as he spoke to the man in the red suit. Both of his legs were gone. It was sobering to see yet another innocent casualty of this awful war.

* * *

I was often inspired and emboldened by the courage and perseverance of the young men and women engaged in this far-off war, a war that met with so much opposition and created so much controversy back home. Many of these were citizen soldiers, members of the National Guard or Army Reserves. All of them showed exceptional dedication. In on-camera interviews, they expressed their support of the war, the feeling that they were accomplishing something. Off-camera, some of them expressed disdain and opposition to the war. But that sentiment was not reflected in the base hospital, where I spoke with an injured Marine sergeant, who cried because he was being sent home.

"I'd rather stay with my men," he said, teary-eyed. "I should go home when they go home." Nearby, a wounded 22-year-old Marine was equally eager to get out of bed and rejoin his men in Fallujah, where several were wounded and one killed in a battle with insurgents.

For a reporter, it was exhilarating to be able to boost the morale of our men and women who stand in harm's way, to bring them the spirit of Christmas and let them know they hadn't been forgotten back home. The high point of our visits with the soldiers was always the live hookups with their families. These were always uplifting, and very emotional.

"Hello, Amy, it's your old grandma," bellowed one woman to her granddaughter in Iraq, Lieutenant Amy Updike. "I'm so proud of you!" Sergeant First Class Alarik Talbert's wife and five children gathered around a Christmas tree as they spoke with him via satellinte.

"I have your butter cookies—I'll send them to you," his wife said, adding, "you look healthy." Master Sergeant Paul Raimondi, a retired telephone worker, got choked up as he spoke to his wife, four children and seven grandchildren on Long Island.

You could feel the emotion as his tearful daughter burst out, "I miss you, Daddy—I love you so much. I'm so proud of you!" Raimondi could barely express his thanks.

His voice faltered as he said, "This means so much to me."

Senior Airman Olamady Quinone's two-year-old daughter, sitting on her grandmother's lap in New York, interrupted the conversation to ask, "Why are you crying, Grandma?" Private First Class Tai Barbee was so moved by the outpouring of love from his large family in the Bronx, he couldn't hold back his tears.

"I want to apologize to New York City for a grown man crying," he said. I quickly reassured him that it was quite all right to shed tears of happiness.

The base commanders always gave us a place to host our holiday parties. It would be decorated with a beautiful tree and colorful trimmings. Fellow reporter Jill Nicolini—who joined us on two of our trips—and I would don our Santa hats and serve the bagels and cheesecake, while Dave Kimmel would put his camera down long enough to grill some hotdogs. It was always a joy to hand out gifts from home, including plush teddy bears outfitted in military fatigues that, with a press of a button would sing, "Proud to Be an American." For many of the homesick soldiers, Jill was the star attraction. A former Playboy model, she had no difficulty captivating and charming them.

During one of our visits to Iraq, she put on a Santa suit, entered the crowded room and asked, "Does anybody wanna to sit on Santa's lap?" To this day I can still hear the hoots, stomping and laughter that filled that room.

For me, their expressions of gratitude were the greatest gift I could receive.

I'll never forget the moment when a soldier thrust his hand into mine and said, "Thank you. You made a difference for my Christmas."

Another female sergeant embraced me with a bear hug and expressed her gratitude, telling me, "You don't know how much this means to us." And we touched the lives of many family members back home, who flooded our inboxes with emails of thanks.

One parent presented me with a bronze plaque that read, "Not only did you bring Christmas to Iraq, but your daily reports brought joy, calm and peace to the families of troops shown on your daily broadcasts. You are a true humanitarian and an American treasure." It was signed, "Proud Parents of an American soldier." Along with a commander's coin given to me by General David Petraeus, it remains one of my proudest possessions.

For the soldiers, marines and airmen we visited, our holiday celebration was a momentary respite. But there were always vivid reminders of the ongoing conflict that swirled around them. The most sobering moment for me came when I first arrived in Kuwait for a transfer to Iraq. I had just gotten off a plane with 200 soldiers beginning their deployment. My cameraman was collecting his equipment as I waited on the tarmac. My eyes drifted in the darkness toward a cargo plane nearby. I noticed what I thought to be hands raised in salute. As my eyes focused more clearly, I observed an American flag moving up a conveyor. It was a casket, bringing another soldier home. Tears began to stream down my cheeks. I stood silent for several minutes, and raised my hand in salute. The reality of war struck me hard.

on reporting

23

EXCLUSIVES: THE AGONY
AND THE ECSTASY

Remains of TWA Flight 800 recovered from the depths of the Atlantic and assembled at a nearby hangar.

*e*very reporter strives to get that exclusive story—to be the first to break the news of something important. Over the years I've had my share of exclusives, but I've also been scooped by competitors on stories I was still working on that were not quite ready to broadcast.

With all of the on-air and Internet news outlets today, the rush to be first to break the story has increased, and often compromises the accuracy of news. The basic industry rule is that no exclusive report should be released unless the information comes from at least two reliable sources. Generally, this serves as a good safeguard against inaccurate reporting. Believing in that tenet, I have always relied on two or more sources for any story I have uncovered—except on the night of May 1, 2011, when Navy SEAL Team Six took down Osama bin Laden.

It was early in the evening that Sunday when the White House announced that President Obama would be speaking to the nation on a matter of national security. Almost immediately, speculation and rumors surfaced that the most wanted man in the world, Al-Qaeda leader Osama bin Laden, had been captured. The longer the President's announcement was delayed, the more intense the speculation became. I reached out to several sources in Congress and at national security agencies, with the hope of nailing down the story. While most said they had no direct knowledge of what the president would be announcing, one trusted source—someone I had relied on in the past, who held a position that would have him in direct contact with President Obama—told me he could not discuss anything at that moment, but that he was about to get a call from the White House.

"Call me later," he advised.

As the hours passed and we still had no definitive word about what the president was going to say, speculation continued to mount that the mastermind behind the September 11th attacks had been captured and was dead. Still, no news entity was prepared to state it as fact. I joined anchor Jim Watkins during our live broadcast, to fill the void while waiting for the president to speak. At around 10:30 p.m. I placed another call to my source. He confirmed that he had just gotten off the phone with the president, and was sworn to secrecy. Though I told him I respected that, the tenacious reporter in me continued to press him. He said he had to go, but before he did, I tried one more time.

"Is it true?" I asked. There was a momentary pause, then the words that sent a rush through my body.

"Yes, but you didn't hear it from me," he said—and hung up.

"I got it! Bin Laden's dead!" I immediately told my producer.

It was now 10:39, and I was eager to break the story that PIX11 News had learned definitively that bin Laden was dead. But…not so fast. As I continued working the phones, my producer said that she first had to get the okay from News Director Bill Carey. He had concerns about breaking the story, she said, and didn't want me making that declaration without a second source. I pleaded with my producer, insisting that my source was unimpeachable—someone who had just been briefed by the president himself. But it was not enough; they needed a second source. Frantically I reached out to other sources I trusted for corroboration, but none of them had as much knowledge as my first source. I hedged around it as I spoke with Watkins on the air, coming awfully close to stating what I knew as fact—but as tantalizing as it was, I couldn't break the story.

At 11 p.m. it became a moot point. If memory serves me correctly, it was John King on CNN who first stated that bin Laden was dead and that this was what the president was going to announce. *Damn,* I thought. *I could have reported that 20 minutes earlier and scooped everyone!* What a coup that would have been for a local news station.

In Bill Carey's office the following morning, I told him I respectfully disagreed with his decision. He explained his concerns, among which was the matter of national security. He had feared that some lone wolf, an Al-Qaeda sympathizer, would hear the news on Channel 11 and immediately decide to retaliate by strapping on a bomb vest and going into a public place, and expressed the belief that news of that magnitude should come from the president. But Carey admitted that these examples were only used to foster his argument, but were not the determining factors for his decision.

"It wasn't the public safety issue that caused my decision… though I did offer that as an argument," he explained. "Rather, my decision was based on the fact that it was not ready to air. It needed a second source." It was simply a question of professionalism—and though it wasn't what I wanted to hear, I did understand his position. "I am confident you did your job well that evening," Carey told me, adding, "But so did I."

Ultimately, my only regret was that I didn't call the news director at home myself that night. I was so busy working the phones that I allowed my producer to do my pitching to him—and Carey would later concede that, had we spoken directly to one another that night, and had I revealed my source to him, I probably could have persuaded him to let me break one of the biggest stories of the decade before anyone else.

* * *

Because I've gained the trust and respect of so many newsmakers over the years, they know that I can be trusted to never reveal any of them as a source, or anything told to me off the record. I've often stated that I would be willing to face jail time rather than reveal a confidential source; fortunately, it has never come to that. And aside from the bin Laden episode, I've always had multiple sources for every exclusive story I have ever broken.

There were two-and-a-half sources back in 2009, when I reported that New York Governor David Paterson had selected Congresswoman Kirsten Gillibrand to fill Hillary Clinton's seat in the U.S. Senate when Clinton was named Secretary of State. It was the source of much speculation at the time; Caroline Kennedy, daughter of the late president, had been mentioned as another likely successor. I received my initial tip from a reliable source, who told me it was "a done deal." Then I spoke with a congressional source, who said he was told the Gillibrand announcement was imminent. The half-source was another member of Congress, who was given the information secondhand. That much was considered hearsay— but the two other sources were solid enough to enable me to break the story before the competition did.

Immediately after the story aired, I received a call from the governor's office, denying the accuracy of my report, and claiming that the governor had not told anyone in Congress of his choice. Perhaps not—but someone had leaked the news to a few people in Washington, and one of them had helped me chalk up a good exclusive. It wasn't long afterward that Governor Paterson made the formal announcement, with Gillibrand at his side.

* * *

Back in the seventies, I was credentialed to cover the United Nations. I would spend time in the delegates' lounge, often sharing coffee with foreign diplomats. Nurturing those sources paid off on a few occasions.

It was a foreign diplomat, for instance, who tipped me off that Saudi Arabian interests had offered to help bail out New York during one of its worst financial crises in 1975. I then received confirmation from a source in city government that a foreign money broker had a lender who wanted to offer New York a $250-million loan. The terms, my diplomatic source revealed, were for a 20-year loan with 7.7% interest, compounded annually and payable in one lump sum at maturity. I reached the money broker in Germany— my third source—who confirmed the terms and identified the would-be lenders as Saudi Arabian.

This was big news. My report was quickly picked up by national news outlets. The then–City Comptroller, Harrison J. Goldin, told me the city hadn't sought the loan, but said that the offer had been made by a foreign entity. Goldin said the offer was rejected because the terms "were out of line and not competitive"—in the end, he said, it would have involved too high a cost to the city.

* * *

I had confirmation from four sources before I revealed that New York Yankee legend Joe DiMaggio was hospitalized with terminal lung cancer. It began with a tip from a New York attorney who knew DiMaggio's close friend and attorney Morris Engelberg. Privacy rules made it difficult to get any information from the hospital where the iconic slugger spent 99 days. I reached another source who had once been a nurse at the hospital. She was reluctant to share any information with me, but when I told her what I knew and asked if it was true that DiMaggio was being treated for lung cancer, she confirmed it. In the course of that conversation she also revealed that he'd had several setbacks from lung infections, and even fell briefly into a coma. Subsequently I was steered toward another hospital worker, who not only corroborated the former nurse's story, but also told me that at one point a priest had been summoned to administer last rites to the ballplayer. Finally, before running my exclusive report, I reached out to the man closest to DiMaggio—Morris Engelberg himself. For his part, Engelberg didn't add anything to the information I had, but he didn't refute it either. Once I told my producers I had four sources who had confirmed my information, we all felt comfortable enough for me to report it; and again, the story was immediately picked up by national media.

The next morning, I almost cut my face shaving as I listened to a local radio newscast. The reader was well into his story when I tuned in, and I was startled when the first words I heard were, "The family is denying…" It was the millisecond from hell. Had I screwed up, I wondered? The rest of the sentence dealt with the administering of last rites, which the family said had never occurred. But there was no denial of the rest of what I had revealed. On March 8, 1999, Joe Di Maggio succumbed to his illness. He was 84 years old.

* * *

The trust I gained among my sources by withholding information that I was told to "sit on" often paid off in positive ways. But there were other times when a story was ready to break and I had the details, but was unable to get the news on the air.

Such was the case in 2003, when Libya finally struck a deal to offer $10 million to each of the families of the 270 victims of the Pan Am 103 bombing. My source for that story was James Kreindler, the lead attorney representing the families, who had told me ten weeks earlier that negotiations for a settlement were underway.

"We're very close," he said, and explained that the talks, in which he and a partner were directly involved, were at such a sensitive stage that any premature reporting could be detrimental to the negotiations. I agreed to hold off on the story, and Kreindler promised to give me the first shot at it when the agreement was reached.

He kept his word. Immediately after adding his signature to the agreement, Jim called me from London to give me the heads-up. His associate added some details. It was around 2 p.m., and we were between our morning and evening newscasts. Now I had a scoop, and I had to get it out there. But while it was a big story, it didn't warrant breaking into regular programming with a bulletin—so I had to do the next best thing and turn to social media. I wrote and posted the exclusive news on the PIX11 website. Within minutes CNN picked up the story, but failed to give us credit and attributed the report only to "a local New York City television website." It was not long after that that other media outlets began running the story. But it was my exclusive.

* * *

There have been times when other reporters have scooped me on stories because I would not betray sources who had given me information off the record and with my assurances of confidentiality. Win some, lose some, I say—it's always better to retain the trust of my important contacts.

James Kallstrom was one of them. The Assistant Director of the FBI's New York office, Kallstrom was given the daunting challenge of leading the criminal investigation into the crash of TWA 800 in the summer of 1996. He pledged to "leave no stone unturned," and assigned hundreds of agents to the investigation to determine whether the crash of the jumbo jet over the Atlantic—which had killed all 230 people aboard—had been an accident or an act of terror.

Kallstrom and his wife Susan had become friends of my wife and mine, with whom we occasionally socialized. I knew that Kallstrom had a personal interest in the TWA probe; the wife of a fellow FBI agent was a flight attendant on the doomed plane. So quite naturally, the investigation usually made the leading topic of conversation when Kallstrom and I would meet for lunch at the Friars Club. He felt comfortable talking to me about it, knowing that if he said anything I found to be newsworthy, I would ask his permission before using the information on the air. When I did, the answer was usually no—or a slightly more drawn-out form of refusal.

"Give me a couple of days and I'll let you know when you can go with it," he would sometimes say. I would follow up with calls to his office and he would tell me to continue to hold onto the story each time.

On a few occasions, while I was sitting on Kallstrom's stories, NBC's Robert Hager and others were breaking them. One exclusive I was eager to report was that investigators had fired missiles through the fuselages of abandoned aircraft at the China Lakes test range in California, attempting to determine if the missiles left any traceable forensic evidence as they passed through the skin of the plane. I had been holding the story for a couple of weeks when Hager broke it, and I immediately let Kallstrom know that I was pissed off. He apologized and assured me that Hager's information had not come from him or his office.

A similar situation occurred about 16 months after the crash, while the FBI investigation was winding down. It was a Tuesday evening when I learned from another source within the FBI that the federal investigation was over, and that no evidence of criminality had been found. I was told that letters were going out to families of the crash's victims, informing them that the FBI had determined that an accident—an explosion in the fuel tank—had brought the plane down. I immediately reached out to Kallstrom, and got him on his cell phone in his car. He neither confirmed nor denied the story, but told me to come to his office on Thursday and he would give me the whole story. He assured me that no other news-media outlet had advance knowledge that the FBI had reached a conclusion about the cause of the disaster. I took him at his word. A couple of hours later, my executive producer interrupted me during an editing session to show me some copy that had just come across as a bulletin from the Associated Press. Under a Paris dateline, the story revealed that families had received letters informing them that the FBI had determined that TWA 800 was brought down by an accident, not a missile, and that no criminal act was involved.

"Damn it, I *had* that story!" I shouted angrily as I raced to the phone to call Kallstrom. When I reached his public-affairs officer, I told him to inform Kallstrom that he had just lost a friend in the media.

Two days later, when I showed up for the news conference, I snubbed Kallstrom, who knew I was angry with him. After presenting the findings of the FBI's lengthy investigation, he opened up the news conference for questions. Without mentioning their names, he called on reporters raising their hands. Mine was up when Fox News's Eric Shawn got called. Shawn asked the same question I was hoping to ask. Moments later, I heard Kallstrom's voice calling out the only name he had mentioned during the entire news conference.

"Mr. Scott...the *distinguished* Mr. Scott," he said—his subtle way of apologizing for costing me an important scoop.

Kallstrom would later explain that special delivery letters had been sent to families in Paris, with instructions for them not to be delivered before the news conference. Someone had failed to get the message, he explained, and one of the letters' recipients called the Associated Press's Paris office to give them the story. I had missed out on a big one, but not by any intention of Kallstrom's—and I won his praise for being so trustworthy.

24

THERE'S GOLD IN THOSE ROTTING FERRYBOATS: A CLASSIC INVESTIGATION

The dilapidated ferry boat, Binghamton, resting half sunk in the Hudson River.

*t*here is no greater achievement for a reporter than to bring about public awareness of wrongdoing, flaws or abuses in our system, and to uncover the evidence that results in corrective measures. Investigative reporting is the hallmark of journalism, and where it leads us can be quite unpredictable.

It was a dilapidated, age-old ferryboat sitting in the murky waters of the Hudson River that led me on such a mission in

1975—a journey that would take me all the way to the White House and through the halls of Congress. The ferryboat, originally christened the Binghamton and pulled from the graveyard of vessels on Staten Island, was destined at that time to be converted into a restaurant on the shores of New Jersey. Though the boat was not proven to be part of any illegal transaction itself, it played a pivotal role in leading me to a pattern of extremely dubious practices by individuals at the highest levels of government, who were acting in collusion with the maritime industry.

During our three-month investigation, researcher Stanley Pinsley and I studied hundreds of documents and met with government officials, shipping-company executives and more than 30 maritime industry sources, on occasion wearing concealed recording devices. We found that shipping companies were the beneficiaries of certain loopholes in maritime law that enabled them to secure obsolete but still-viable ships for private conversion into cargo vessels. Of particular interest was the Vessel Exchange Act, a provision under the Maritime Act of 1960 and 1965, which was designed to help non-subsidized shipping companies improve the quality of their fleets.

The law provided that shipping companies could trade in old vessels that weighed more than 1,500 tons for newer and more efficient ones left over from World War II and still sitting in mothballs. Along with the trade-in, these private companies would pay a nominal sum of money for the government vessels, which had each been built at a cost of $2.5 million. For the shipping companies, this was a great deal—critics of the program in Congress likened it to trading in a secondhand Ford for a Cadillac.

The intent of the law was that oceangoing and Great Lakes vessels be used for the trade-ins. But our investigation found that shipping companies were not playing by these rules, and were dredging up rotting old ferryboats to turn in for the trade. Some of these, we found, even failed to measure up to the required 1,500 tons—in which case the shipping companies resorted to a process called "box-topping." A company we located at the World Trade Center provided this service, whereby they would build a phony plywood superstructure atop an existing boat, giving the impression that the boat conformed to the weight requirements for the trade-in. Our source likened it to a child sending in a cereal box top for a prize: after a transaction was completed, the "box-top" was removed and used on another underweight boat.

Our investigation determined that at least 30 decommissioned ferryboats had been traded in, some using this box-topping practice, by at least ten corporations including SeaLand Services and Alcoa Steamship. We also found that on August 10, 1961, Malcolm McLean, then-president of Waterman Steamship Corporation, told a congressional hearing that the Vessel Exchange Act was "a give-away not in the public interest"—then, five years later as President of SeaLand Shipping, dipped into the pot himself, and became involved in at least three of the transactions we uncovered.

* * *

The scandal went further. One of the primary beneficiaries of the trade-in, we found, was the Waterman Steamship Corporation itself—which, curiously, was one of the heavier contributors to Richard Nixon's reelection campaign. The company succeeded in exchanging at least half a dozen rotting ferryboats for valuable government vessels, one of which was the Binghamton. According to Coast Guard records, three days after Waterman purchased the boat from Ruscon Industries, it turned it over for the government trade. The government never picked it up, and for $50,000 turned it back over to the company from which Waterman had originally bought it—though documents showed that Waterman actually wrote the check. The Binghamton was subsequently acquired by the New Jersey restaurant consortium, and we never got an explanation for this transaction, which was certainly questionable at the very least. But we did learn that just seven days after taking office as part of Nixon's new administration, Commerce Secretary Maurice Stans—who had been Nixon's chief fundraiser—had approved the ferryboat swap for Waterman, whose CEO's name was prominent on a list of contributors to the Nixon campaign.

We brought this information to the attention of Connecticut Senator Lowell Weicker, a member of the Senate Commerce Committee, who called on the Justice Department to investigate. Concerned by what we had uncovered, he sent a letter to Attorney General Edward Levi, requesting that Levi look into allegations of "highly questionable, if not fraudulent transactions between the government and the shipping industry." Senator Weicker said that other elements of our reports deserved scrutiny as well, particularly "subsidies, both direct and indirect, which the industry has been receiving over the years, and certain relationships between the industry and members of the Senate and House of Representatives."

In the course of our investigation, we found that while the U.S. demonstrated its loyalty to American shipping interests, the maritime industry didn't always show its loyalty in return. Over a period of several years, $6 billion in taxpayer money was shelled out in building and operating subsidies to shipping companies—some of which, data showed, then abandoned the U.S. flag and registered their vessels in foreign countries like Liberia to avoid U.S. taxes and exploit cheap labor.

As we dug deeper into our investigation, sources told us they had knowledge of politicians being in the pocket of shipping companies that were reaping huge benefits, including government subsidies and favorable-treatment status. As I unveiled these findings on the air, I suddenly became rather popular with a few shipping magnates. One of them was Spyros Skouras, then-CEO of Prudential-Grace Lines, who invited me to a meeting, sending a station wagon to bring me to his office in lower Manhattan. Sitting behind a desk in his opulent office, he was charismatic but business-like, and we chatted amicably for a while. While I was hoping he was going to offer me some usable information, it turned out he was fishing for what I might have had on *him*. A high-level contributor to the campaign of then–Vice President Spiro Agnew, and closely tied to Nixon himself—who had once served as his attorney—Skouras was in tight with the Nixon administration, and reportedly pledged to give $5 million to the Nixon campaign if he named Agnew his vice president and made other Skouras-friendly appointments to the Maritime Commission.

As we probed deeper into the inner workings of Washington, sources pointed us to information showing how other officials in high places "extracted" political contributions from the shipping industry. We reported that Helen Bentley, Nixon's hand-picked chair of the Maritime Commission, was on record admitting that she had solicited at least $20,000 from shipping companies for Nixon's 1972 campaign. One of her predecessors told us, "She turned the commission from a monitoring agency into a lobbying agency that benefited the private companies." Former Congressman and Commerce Secretary Rogers Morton had questionable transactions with the maritime industry, too. Mike Trupp, who had served as director of international affairs for the Maritime Commission, said he had seen firsthand what he called "a shakedown" by Morton, in the form of high-priced ticket sales to congressional fundraising events.

The scope of our probe broadened rapidly as we began hearing stories about irregularities along the waterfront, including the mandating of no-show jobs by the unions. My reports, which were broadcast in both New York and Washington, were noticeably beginning to touch some nerves. Law firms and communications directors of companies and individuals we had named began to reach out to us, seeking transcripts of our reports and denying that their clients had done anything illegal. Stanley Pinsley and I knew the stakes here were high, and worked hard to remain responsible with what we were reporting—for each bit of information, we had at least two and sometimes as many as five sources.

Still, at times I found myself looking over my shoulder. One afternoon, I received a call from a man who claimed to have information I would find valuable. He wanted me to meet him aboard a freighter that was loading cargo on the Brooklyn docks. With some trepidation I headed for the rendezvous, alerting my news desk to look for me if they didn't hear from me by 6 p.m. It felt like a scene out of a movie as I walked across the dock and into the bowels of a freighter preparing to leave for Hong Kong. Once aboard, I met with the disgruntled ship worker—who, it turned out, was simply looking to vent about poor working conditions.

* * *

We were beginning to wind down our investigation when it took another dramatic turn. Trupp, the former Maritime Commission executive, suggested we take a look at President Ford's past dealings with maritime interests, asserting that when Ford was the House Minority leader, he received payoffs in the form of fees for speaking engagements before the Maritime Trades Department of the AFL-CIO. According to Trupp and other sources, Ford and other congressmen were invited to weekly cocktail luncheons where they would deliver speeches, frequently written by the labor group, and receive honorariums in return. Ford was said to be among the highest-paid of these beneficiaries. Justice Department records confirmed that Ford's name was on a list of favored congressmen who received contributions through secret bank accounts; but while several industry and union leaders were found guilty of illegal activity, Ford and other elected officials were never charged—because, as it was explained, there was no proof that they knowingly accepted illegal contributions. Nevertheless, our last report rattled the inner sanctum of the White House, and prompted a call to me from the office of the President's Press Secretary. While it was acknowledged that President Ford, as a member of Congress, accepted fees for speaking engagements, it was again emphasized that he had done nothing illegal.

In the weeks and months following our reports, federal authorities clamped down on maritime unions and made a number of arrests on racketeering charges. The Justice Department informed Senator Weicker that it was dropping its criminal investigation into the seemingly fraudulent ferryboat exchanges we had brought to light, because the statute of limitations would prevent potential prosecution. The special Watergate prosecutor who closely studied our investigative reports informed us that his office had no jurisdiction to probe allegations of political corruption prior to 1972. As for the Vessel Exchange Act, it expired in 1972 as well, because the U.S. reserve fleet had by that time been depleted of ships available for commercial trade.

It was an exciting journey for a local reporter. Beginning with a tip about a dilapidated ferryboat and developing into a trail of information that led us through the highest levels of government, our probe allowed us to uncover facts, seek the truth and create a new public awareness of political greed that led to subsequent reforms. And it garnered professional recognition, too: seven months after our exclusive exposé, *The Washington Post* "broke" a similar story that gained national attention. The following spring I was proud to receive my first Emmy Award, for Outstanding Investigative Reporting.

25

THE READING TEST SCANDAL

AN ACT

to amend the education law, in relation to unlawful acts in examinations

The People of the State of New York, represented in Senate and Assembly, do enact as follows:

1   Section 1. Subdivisions seven, eight and nine of section two
2   hundred twenty-five of the education law are hereby renumbered to
3   be subdivisions eight, nine and ten, respectively, and two new
4   subdivisions, to be subdivisions seven and eleven are hereby added
5   thereto, to read, respectively, as follows:
6   *7. Willfully and wrongfully disclose or transmit to any person the*

EXPLANATION — Matter in *italics* is new; matter in brackets [ ] is old law to be omitted.

Portion of the legislation enacted as a result of my investigation.

*i*n 1974, I found that tens of thousands of New York City schoolchildren were being cheated out of a proper education by being provided answers in advance to a standardized reading test. My reporting resulted in several reforms, including legislation that made it a criminal act for anyone to provide advance knowledge of test answers.

It began with an anonymous call from a teacher at a school in a minority neighborhood in Brooklyn. He told me that the school's 1400 students had gained advance knowledge of the Metropolitan Achievement Test through extensive coaching by teachers. He told me he could document his charge, and agreed to meet with me outside a motel on Long Island and conduct an interview with me, provided I shielded his face. When I arrived at the motel, he wasn't there—but he had left an envelope with the desk clerk. On mimeographed sheets were "Word Knowledge" and "Practice Reading" questions, identical to those on the actual published test.

The next day, I visited what was then Junior High School 263, which two years earlier had shown the lowest reading scores in the city. Teachers spoke to me off-camera, many expressing pleasure that I was exposing what they called "these dishonest practices." They showed me a memo that they claimed was written by the acting principal, directing them to give students practice tests on four separate occasions—and to burn the practice tests afterwards. They were shocked the day they administered the actual test and discovered that its questions were identical to those on the test they'd been using in the practice sessions. The advance knowledge produced extraordinary results: an 800% improvement in reading scores. Only five percent of the students had been reading at the proper grade level two years before; now almost 25% of the students who were coached in advance were reading well, according to the test results. Two classes had perfect scores. Many students had supposedly advanced two, three and four years in their reading ability; some scores jumped so high, teachers told me, they had to be doctored downward. All of this was in sharp contrast to the overall findings of the citywide test, which found reading deficiencies in 66 percent of the city's half-million elementary and middle-schoolers.

The principal at JHS 263 denied having directed teachers to coach students with actual test questions. He said that he had instructed them to compile old test questions for practice, and insisted he had no knowledge that current test questions were being used. Others asserted that the finger-pointing at the principal, who was black, was racially motivated by white teachers, who were "out to get him."

My initial report on WNEW-TV's *Ten O'Clock News* opened a Pandora's box. The following morning I was flooded with dozens of calls, most of them anonymous, from teachers at other schools throughout the city, reporting similar practices at their schools and noting that helping students cheat on standardized tests was quite common. As I probed deeper, I learned that coaching was only one facet of the cheating scheme; another widespread practice involved re-testing students until they got a good grade. One teacher revealed to me that she was instructed by her school supervisor to discard her students' lowest scores, and to withhold not more than five students in each class. Another told me that, rather than turn in a poor test paper, she was told to mark the student absent. Some students were re-tested as many as four times in pursuit of acceptable scores.

One tip led me to the tests' publisher, where I learned that identical tests were administered every four-year period, making it possible for teachers to get their hands on old tests with which to coach their students. Poor security made these tests easily accessible. One old test had the name of the student who had taken it four years earlier, still written on it. The Schools Chancellor, Irving Anker, had told me that no one was supposed to hold on to standardized tests.

I continued to receive mail and calls from teachers and parents as my exposé gained traction. Other media began picking up on the story. Dr. Edith Gaines, Executive Director of Education Planning and Support for the Board of Education, who was responsible for developing new teaching methods, called the allegations "horrendous and insulting" to the children, and called for an immediate investigation. After determining the validity of my reports, education officials invalidated 5,000 previously administered tests, and ordered the re-testing of 55,000 students.

As I continued my investigative series, I received additional information about testing irregularities and some of the reasoning behind such actions. The most frequent rationale was accountability. Principals and teachers expressed the belief that their value as educators was being measured by how well their students performed, and said there was competition between school districts to achieve higher levels of student performance. Some principals acknowledged that students had often been helped to pass exams in part because of pressure by both parents and education officials to get higher scores for New York students, in order to make them competitive with the national averages. One principal said that many students in his minority neighborhood school were poor readers who felt inferior and defeated, and that the reading tests, which didn't truly reflect students' learning ability anyway, were a good chance to boost their confidence. "They must be encouraged and get a sense of achievement," he said, rationalizing that by having them pass tests by whatever means, they might learn better in the future. Another principal, at a Manhattan school, said that students were often pushed along despite poor test scores, in order to prevent leaving overcrowded schools with holdovers.

In response to these reports, angry parents and educators began to pressure city and state officials. Soon the New York City Council called for an investigation, as did the state legislature. Assemblyman Leonard Stavisky, who chaired the Committee on Education, held a public hearing and asked me to be the lead witness. Lawmakers were shocked to hear what I had learned. My exposé prompted investigators to focus on 150 classes in 31 schools, where they found many abuses involving the reading tests. One principal, saddened by the fraudulent practices, said the real victims were the students.

"They are being cheated out of a proper education," he said, and contributing to the alarming statistic of one million American kids between 12 and 17 who at the time were listed by the National Center for Health Statistics as "illiterate"—unable to read as well as the average fourth-grader.

Two months after my initial report, new tests were given to 55,000 students. The public was assured the tests were secure. A day in advance I sat down for a television interview with Anthony J. Polemeni, an acting director of the Board of Education, who informed me that reform measures were already being implemented and that future tests would be secure.

"What about this re-test—how secure is it?" I asked.

"Quite secure," he declared, claiming that exhaustive measures had been taken in advance to make certain it would not be compromised. Reaching into my back pocket, I pulled out a copy of the actual test to be given the next day and asked, "Then how is it I have received a copy of it?" Recognizing that he was on-camera, Polemeni kept his cool, but voiced his dismay and questioned whether the copy I had was actually identical to the real test. When I said it was, he promised to look into the matter. Once off-camera, he castigated me for embarrassing him—he had been cooperative with me during the extent of my investigation, he said, and thought I should have given him the courtesy of letting him know what I had before the on-camera interview. I apologized for the embarrassment, but respectfully defended my action as journalistically legitimate.

The new test was administered in a number of schools selected at random, as well as in the schools where cheating had been suspected. It provided a powerful comparison between the two tests: 51% of students received lower grades in the second test, 37% higher grades and 12% showed no change. At JHS 263, students who had done well on the rehearsed test two months earlier dropped two or more years below level on the re-test.

In addition to the re-testing of students, disciplinary action was taken against several educators. An assistant principal was demoted, several teachers were transferred to other schools and formal reprimands were issued to a few non-tenured teachers. The Board of Education initiated reforms for future testing, and found a new supplier for its tests who guaranteed security safeguards, including the assurance that tests would not be delivered to schools until 24 hours prior to testing.

27 months after I had been tipped off to what became known as the Reading Test Scandal, I was honored to receive the pen with which Governor Hugh Carey signed into law Assembly Bill 5886-A,

an amendment to the state education law. The bill, introduced by Assemblyman Stavisky and 37 co-sponsors and approved by both chambers of the legislature, made it "unlawful for any person to willfully and wrongfully disclose or transmit the questions and or answers to an examination prior to the test." The legislation defined the violation as a misdemeanor, with a provision for punitive measures established for violators.

The copy of that bill, now beginning to yellow from age where it hangs on my wall, is among my proudest possessions. Next to it hangs the letter from Assemblyman Stavisky, acknowledging my pursuit of a story that would guarantee a better education for millions of New York schoolchildren.

"It is not often that a newsman becomes a newsmaker," he wrote, "but you have earned both designations as a result of your superb investigative reporting."

* * *

The new law was put to its first real test 23 years later in 1999, when 52 principals and teachers at 32 schools were accused of giving students answers to citywide reading and math tests. It happened at a time when educators nationwide were under intense pressure to improve student test scores, and at the time it was considered the biggest cheating scandal in the American public-school system's history. All of those suspected of involvement were suspended, pending the outcome of the investigation. Five of the implicated educators immediately resigned or were dismissed, escaping further charges. Several others were reassigned elsewhere in their school districts. After a year-long investigation under the never-before-used state law, punitive action was taken against half the group. Charges against others were dropped for lack of evidence of wrongdoing.

Outraged that educators would engage in such activity, one legislator decided at the height of the scandal that it was time to take action and get some media attention. Assemblyman John Ravitz called a news conference to announce he was introducing a bill "that would make it a crime for teachers or school administrators to help students cheat on standardized exams." His press release said that there were no laws in New York for these actions, concluding, "We must have a law on the books to help make sure that never happens again." After reading the release in advance of the assemblyman's press conference, I called his office to inform them that Assembly Bill 5886-A was already part of the state law, and did exactly what Ravitz was proposing to do. They were totally oblivious, and went ahead with their news conference anyway. Ravitz succeeded in getting his face on the evening newscasts, but his bill never made it out of committee to become law. The original 1976 bill, inspired by my investigation, remains in effect to this day.

26

BECOMING MY OWN STORY

Filing a report from the Channel 5 newsroom.

a story I was investigating never made it on the air, because I got scooped by the very people I was investigating—and I became a focal point of the story.

It all began when the New Jersey State Commission of Investigation attempted to get an ex-convict with mob connections to speak to me for a television report, as part of a purported plot to embarrass the New Jersey State Police. SCI attorney Alfred Genton first reached out to me in 1977 to offer me the incredible story. Over drinks at a motel, Genton told me that the state police had hired the ex-con, James Jelicks, as an undercover agent, and ordered him to break into the home of a local horse breeder to get evidence that he was drugging race horses in order to "juice them up" before races. Genton said that Jelicks was essentially paid by the department to commit burglary, and that on their behalf he had stolen drug records and set up electronic eavesdropping devices to record Sunday-morning meetings between horseracing ticket agents, drivers and trainers.

Genton was now encouraging Jelicks to tell me the full story, and offered to put us in touch. This was ostensibly to embarrass the New Jersey State Police, who were in the midst of a power struggle with the SCI. Yet Genton didn't put it to me this way. According to Genton, Jelicks himself wanted to go public with the story, and "was ready to blow up and blast the story all over the place."

"He was like a time bomb, ready to go off, and I gave him a reasonable out," Genton would later explain. "I felt, if he was going to blow up, he should have the name of a responsible reporter."

After several cancellations, I finally met with Jelicks. He told me he had been involved in so many unsavory acts, that the mob had placed a price on his head; and that he was betrayed after his break-in on behalf of the State Police. Despite assurances that "the state would take care of everything," he claimed he was arrested and beaten after his dirty work was done, and was sentenced to six months in jail. When he got out of jail, he went straight to the SCI, and agreed to cooperate with the Commission. Genton, he informed me, told him he wanted the story out "so the SCI could step in and investigate."

Furthermore, Jelicks claimed that SCI chairman Joseph Rodriguez had told him, "It's about time the State Police's little white castle crumbled."

Though the story Jelicks told me during our meeting and several telephone conversations was intriguing, he was never able to provide me with any documentation to back it up, aside from false identification cards and three social security cards he claimed he used in his undercover work. He did pass a lie detector test—administered by the SCI—but he was disavowed altogether by the State Police.

The State Police Superintendent at the time, Clinton Pagano, was reportedly incensed when he learned that Genton had reached out to me to get Jelicks's story on the air. Pagano strongly denied Jelicks's allegations, denouncing Jelicks as "a pathological liar" and claiming that the whole incident gave weight to his claim that the SCI didn't cooperate properly with the State Police, and was attempting to undermine his operation with the investigation. Genton denied that his motivation was to embarrass the law enforcement agency, and said he never told Chairman Rodriguez about his efforts to get Jelicks to tell his story on television.

* * *

I was almost two months into my investigation and getting ready to break the story, when the New Jersey State Senate Judiciary Committee let it out by announcing that it was planning a hearing into the assertions of police wrongdoing and the information leaked to me to embarrass the State Police. At that point, nobody knew that Genton had been my source in SCI, so I called him to assure him that I would never reveal his name. He informed me, however, that he intended to come forward and confess that he was my source.

I received some interesting looks when I showed up for the hearing at the statehouse in Trenton. When I introduced myself to State Police Superintendent Pagano and asked him about the veracity of Jelicks's claims, I received a dagger-like look in response. During the hearing, I heard my name echo repeatedly through the chamber as I sat in the gallery taking notes. Under questioning, Alfred Genton was asked repeatedly about his contacts with me, why he had called me, when we had met and what we had talked about.

Superintendent Pagano was visibly angry as he testified about the dangers involved in the leaks of information about his agency.

When the Committee Chairman asked him, "What is the hazard of Marvin Scott broadcasting the allegations?"

Pagano adjusted his glasses and responded, "The greatest hazard is that law enforcement must have the confidence of the people," adding, "To have those kinds of allegations brought out publicly, and to have the organization's members unjustifiably impugned, would diminish the public's confidence in that organization." Shortly after testifying, Genton resigned from the SCI, admitting that his referral of Jelicks to me had been an "indiscretion."

As I listened from the gallery, filming the proceedings and taking notes, a reporter from the *Newark Star-Ledger* realized that I was the guy the senators were talking about, and approached me.

"How could you, personally, be covering this?" he asked, noting how prominently I was being mentioned in the hearing that I was reporting on.

My response was quick and simple: "Just the way I cover any other story—objectively."

27

THE KID REPORTER WHO
BECAME A CHIEF

Television whiz kid, John Miller, reporting at the age of 15 with me in 1978, and again at the age of 37 2015.

Some reporters are made; others seem to have been born for the business. John Miller was both. At 12, Miller was a news prodigy who chased stories on a bicycle equipped with a police radio on the handlebars. On the way up in his career, he had an exclusive interview with Osama bin Laden in Afghanistan, co-anchored with Barbara Walters on ABC's *20/20* program and was a senior correspondent at CBS News. He currently has access to national-security secrets as the New York Police Department's Deputy Commissioner for Intelligence and Counterterrorism. But the whiz kid of news got his start as the youngest assignment editor and reporter at a New York television station, where I got him his first job.

The tenacious blue-eyed kid from Montclair, New Jersey, wanted to be a cop until he was 12, when he decided he wanted to be a reporter like his father—because, he said, "I couldn't wait to be a cop." He would chase police and fire department calls in his hometown, often racing on his bicycle to accidents, fires and crime scenes where he took pictures and sold them to local newspapers for $5. Seeing his name in the credit line printed below the picture was the fuel that kept him going. Figuring he would have a better opportunity to shoot salable pictures when staff photographers were not on the job, at night Miller kept a police radio by his pillow and if something happened, he would have his father drive him to the scene in the middle of the night. He hit it big with a picture he took of a spectacular accident, for which he received $25 from the *Newark Star-Ledger*. Over a period of two years, he sold about 50 photos to newspapers. While Miller had a reporter's perseverance, he lacked the working press card required to pass police and fire lines.

"So I borrowed my father's press card and made a pencil tracing of it," he confessed. "I took the forgery to a printer, who charged me $15 for 100 copies. It worked. From three feet away, you couldn't tell the difference between the real press card and the counterfeit."

Montclair police became concerned about Miller's safety, because he would show up at crime scenes on his bike before police got there. A police captain visited his parents, and expressed fear that their son could get killed if he continued to do that.

"Leave my kid alone," bellowed Miller's father, suggesting that instead of worrying about his son, the captain should get his officers to move faster.

Being a kid had its drawbacks for Miller, because many people wouldn't take him seriously. In effect, they'd tell him to get lost. On the other hand, he said, it was beneficial, "because those who did talk to me candidly figured that because I was a kid, the information they gave me wouldn't go anywhere." An affable young man, Miller was well liked by the cops, firefighters and politicians he met. Even early on, he knew how to make friends and develop sources in important places.

It was because of one of those sources that Miller and I encountered one another, and developed a relationship that would ultimately change the course of the young man's life. Miller received a tip that a suspect had been arrested in the biggest murder case at the time—the 1972 New Year's Eve stabbing death of 28-year-old teacher Roseanne Quinn. It was a grisly murder that horrified New Yorkers and later became the basis for the book and movie *Looking for Mr. Goodbar.*

The now-14-year-old kid, who was doing some work for a biweekly publication in New Jersey, couldn't do anything with his information, so he decided to call me as a return favor for providing him with information on a story I had done a month earlier. He informed me that police had arrested a 23-year-old fugitive, John Wayne Wilson, in Indianapolis, and said his source told him that detectives had evidence that Wilson had stabbed the woman 18 times after they had sex. I thanked Miller for the tip and tried to get confirmation from my own police sources, who were tight-lipped because, as I later learned, police had hoped to keep news of the arrest quiet until they had Wilson back in the city to charge him with Quinn's murder. I finally reached one high-level police source, who would not provide details but, after being aggressively pushed for answers, acknowledged, "I don't know where you got the information, you son of a bitch, but yes, we do have a suspect."

I broke the exclusive story on our 10 o'clock newscast, and immediately received calls from friends at other news outlets seeking the information they were unable to get from police. My story was headline news in the morning newspapers, and was such a great scoop that it got me a congratulatory note with a gold star from the news director.

I had not yet met Miller personally. All of our conversations were over the telephone. He had a deep, mature voice, and I had no idea he was just a teenager. He would call me quite frequently, offering tips to stories that always seemed to pan out. He became an incredible, reliable source, who enabled me to break a number of exclusive stories.

As an incentive and a way to say thanks for all those valuable tips, I had the station cut a check for $50, which I hadn't sent yet when I finally came face to face with him at the scene of a hostage standoff in Brooklyn. The tall, lanky kid with acne all over his face and three cameras slung over his shoulder bowled me over when he approached and introduced himself as John Miller. "

You're John Miller?" I exclaimed in disbelief. I couldn't believe he was only 14.

His passion for news was evident, and despite his young age, he seemed to have a better sense of how to get a story than many veteran reporters. Shortly after we met, I got Miller a part-time job working on the assignment desk at Channel 5. The teenager would take a bus into the city after school, and his mother would pick him up afterwards.

He failed gym twice because he often didn't show up—which he justified by saying, "I couldn't jeopardize my television job."

The after-school job led to a summer assignment in the newsroom. As good as he was in generating stories, Miller was an arrogant kid and alienated many of the reporters, who got angry with me for bringing him to the station. One day he had the tenacity to dress down a lead anchorman for coming in late.

"My greatest asset," Miller would say, "is that I know how to listen to the police radio and recognize what's important." He did indeed. He was so adept at it, he knew how to change chips in the radio to communicate directly with officers in the field. At times he even feigned being a member of law enforcement himself, in order to get firsthand information.

Miller's news intuition produced many stories, and on occasion, when a staff reporter wasn't available, Miller would be sent out with a camera crew to hold the microphone and ask some questions. The questions were good enough to make his editors take notice.

"But the reporters resented me," he said. "And the anchormen did everything they could not to use my name on the air."

Still, Miller earned his stripes. After the night assignment editor quit, Miller—then a news assistant—was awarded the title. At the age of 15, he became the youngest night assignment editor ever appointed at a television station. Slowly, the other reporters' resentment turned to respect.

As Miller remembers it, "It was sort of mind-boggling, telling these veteran reporters—who had been in the business longer than I've been around—how I thought they should handle a particular story."

It was only a matter of time before Miller began reporting stories on-camera. Sure, he was young—but he was a damn good reporter who produced remarkable stories. His boyish charm and piercing blue eyes were assets in his pursuit of news. When he was 16, Miller did a series of reports on the problem of prostitution of young boys in New York City.

"I stood on Manhattan street corners for two nights and got a good number of solicitations. One guy offered me 50 bucks to go to a hotel with him." But Miller never left the street. Everything was recorded through a wireless microphone he was wearing, and by a camera concealed in a nearby van.

A year later, Miller exposed one of the nation's largest banks as the landlord of a townhouse that housed a swank brothel.

"The only way to know for sure was to go in and find out," Miller recalled. It was a club that accepted credit cards, so while his crew waited outside, Miller went inside with an American Express card. He returned half an hour later with his proof—a receipt for $70. Moments later, he went back into the club with his camera crew, and was promptly thrown out. Police raided the place, and Miller's revelations made for a sensational television report. The story created a stir when it got on the air—and not just among its viewers.

"My mother wasn't thrilled with it," Miller recalled. Nor was the cameraman whose credit card he had borrowed.

* * *

Miller knew how to play the role of super reporter. He would show up at crime scenes wearing a long trench coat, with a hat pulled over his right eye and a big cigar in his mouth. When he was old enough to drive, he bought a used police car—a blue Plymouth with four antennas—for $1,000. Miller was so convincing when he pretended to be part of law enforcement that in 1977, when President Jimmy Carter made a surprise visit to the South Bronx, Miller placed a dome light on top of his car and managed to enter the presidential motorcade.

He certainly knew how to ferret out a story, and the images to go with it. In 1978 he wanted a shot of fashion designer Calvin Klein and his daughter after she was safely released from a kidnapping. While other cameramen staked out at several locations on the street, hoping to catch a shot of them, Miller had a better idea. He chartered a helicopter and had it hover over Klein's Manhattan high-rise. Klein and his daughter came to the window to check out the noise, not knowing they had just been caught on-camera.

When Miller turned 18, he was given a party in the newsroom, and was presented with his own legitimate press card. By then, he had earned the respect of the entire staff. News Director Mark Monskey felt Miller was such an asset to the news operation, and had such a bright future ahead of him, that he encouraged the kid—who'd flunked out of high school—to get a college education at the company's expense. Miller enrolled at Emerson College in Boston. His assignment was simple: attend school four days a week, and work as a weekend reporter for the other three.

Miller was somewhat of an enigma at Emerson. Not even his roommate knew that he was a reporter back in New York. He set up a police radio in his dorm room, programmed to Boston police frequencies, and would receive phone calls in the middle of the night from police and other officials. His beeper would go off in classrooms, and police in marked and unmarked cars would pick him up and drop him off in front of his dormitory. After a while, Miller's fellow students had him pegged as an undercover narcotics cop.

Although he had already made it to the big time in New York and received several awards, Miller apparently wasn't ready to make it on undergraduate radio and television stations at Emerson College.

"At the radio station, I was told that I needed experience and a few journalism courses," he recalled. "I was told to work on my delivery." Same thing at the school's television station, where he was told after an audition that he needed some more work. Although he had already worked for six successful years as a professional journalist, Miller only managed to get a B in Mass Communications from his unsuspecting professors. He never let on that he knew better.

"Better they shouldn't know what I was doing," he reasoned. "If I told them I was doing what they were teaching, they might have gotten intimidated and thought I was trying to tell them something they didn't know."

After college, Miller went on to have a distinguished career as a journalist. He continued to work at Channel 5 for a while, then joined the local NBC television news team in New York as its investigative reporter, and gained attention as the only reporter Mafia boss John Gotti ever spoke to. He later joined ABC News, where he managed to get that exclusive interview with Osama bin Laden three years before bin Laden orchestrated the terror attacks on September 11th. And he won the coveted role of co-anchor of the network's *20/20* broadcast, sitting next to Barbara Walters.

In 1994, at the age of 36, Miller finally realized his childhood dream of being a cop when Police Commissioner William Bratton tapped him as his Deputy Commissioner for Public Information in the New York Police Department. This time around, he was the source being quoted by others. When Bratton took over as Chief of the Los Angeles Police Department, he appointed Miller Chief of the LAPD's Counterterrorism and Criminal Intelligence Bureau. In 2005, he became Assistant Director for Public Affairs at the FBI, then a Deputy Director of National Intelligence for Analytic Transformation and Technology. He had a brief return to television as a senior correspondent for CBS News, appearing on the morning news and occasionally on *60 Minutes.*

When Bill Bratton came calling again to serve as New York's police commissioner, he wanted Miller at his side, and appointed him New York City's Deputy Commissioner of Intelligence and Counterterrorism. Now Miller has come full-cycle—from getting his information from a police radio hooked to his bicycle, to tapping into satellites in the ongoing fight to keep America and New York safe. The kid from New Jersey was truly a natural, and I feel proud to have had a hand in helping him launch his incredible career.

28

WORKING THE STREET

You never know who is going to show up behind you during a live shot.

erhaps the most challenging part of the job for a television reporter is dealing with people during assignments on the street. While most are respectful and understanding of the fact that we're working, others seem to have a burning desire to harass us, or feel that the presence of a live TV camera is their ticket to their five seconds of fame. Consequently, when we're on live television, we never know what to expect.

During the 2016 presidential campaign, for instance, I was in the final seconds of signing off from a live location when two malcontents appeared from out of nowhere: a woman with rings through her nose and her male companion. The two jumped into the shot, middle fingers pointing eastward, and shouted, *"Fuck you, Donald Trump!"*—the woman adding a few words about the candidate's eating a certain part of her anatomy. It went out live, and there was nothing we could do to stop it.

* * *

Another day I was taping a report on a crime in New York's Jewelry District. It is not uncommon for curious bystanders to eavesdrop on what I'm reporting; but on this particular day, a group of Hasidic Jews gathered around us in such large numbers, they totally blocked the camera. First there were only a few, who stayed out of camera range as they came in close to check out what I was saying. But then, slowly, the crowd of men in black coats and hats grew, and pressed so close my cameraman had to call "Cut"—and we had to find a different location to complete the report.

* * *

During the Christmas blizzard of 2010, I was doing a series of live reports from Times Square. While most New Yorkers heeded the warnings to stay inside, many tourists remained outside in a festive mood, frolicking in the snow along the Great White Way. I included many of these folks in my live shots.

A couple of minutes before one of our broadcasts, a couple of girls approached me, one of them holding a snowball.

She held up the icy glob and, in a heavy Swedish accent, asked, "What do you call this?" Not thinking anything of it, I innocently responded, "Snowball."

POW! Before I could react, the girl smashed the snowball into my left eye and the two ran off. I delayed my live hit as I removed the snow from my eye and stopped it from tearing, having been served another reminder of just how vulnerable we reporters are when working the street.

* * *

On another occasion I was preparing to go live from in front of Madison Square Garden when I started to get hassled by a couple of guys who had just come from a Rangers hockey game. After a few minutes, the group disbanded except for one young man, who stayed behind to tell me how much he wanted to be on television. I humored him by saying there wasn't room for the two of us to do the report—"So you do it," I jokingly suggested, thrusting the microphone into his hand. Surprisingly, he grabbed the microphone and immediately began to walk away with it, making me chase after him to retrieve it. I never expected him to actually walk away with it.

* * *

The photobomb gestures people make in the background of live broadcasts are outlandish and sometimes quite humorous. If only these people could see what they look like! One of my favorites was the woman who walked into camera range while I was doing a live report from the city's Department of Education. With her tongue hanging out in a grotesque twist, she placed her hands under her breasts and raised them for all to see. I had no idea she was behind me until my cameraman told me about it afterwards. We had a good laugh over that one. That's live television—and all in a day's work!

interviews

I have interviewed more than 30,000 people in my career. I met most of them while covering stories on the street, but a good number of these interviews have been conducted in studios or during my travels as a contributing editor for *Parade* magazine. On the nationally syndicated Independent Network News program *Midday Edition,* and on the *INN Magazine* program, I held one-on-one interviews with various politicians and foreign leaders, including Presidents Jimmy Carter, Gerald Ford and George H.W. Bush, Secretary of State Henry Kissinger, and Israeli Prime Minister Shimon Peres. Evangelist Billy Graham and I stared one another down during an intense interview following his return from a visit to the then–Soviet Union. Watergate burglar G. Gordon Liddy insisted that President Nixon had no advance knowledge of the infamous break-in that led to his resignation. I played straight man to King of Comedy Jerry Lewis during an interview that garnered an Emmy Award. I was mesmerized by the beauty of Sophia Loren and enchanted by the charismatic Liberace, who played the piano for me. There have been so many wonderful interviews over the years, it's difficult now to single out my favorites.

I can certainly tell you my least favorite. That was a sit-down interview with impressionist Frank Gorshin, most famous for his portrayal of the Riddler on the television series *Batman,* who was my guest on a live segment. During the interview I gave him ample opportunity to promote the Broadway show he was currently appearing in, then I asked about the origin of his uncanny impressions of notable people. I knew that as a young man, he would go to movies starring James Cagney and study his voice and every movement, at times even mouthing the words Cagney was saying on the screen, right along with him. In particular, I wanted Gorshin to tell me about that. But he was resistant. All he wanted to talk about was the show in which he was performing—and when he seemed to be done promoting that, he started talking up the show his publicist was representing across the street from his theatre! I finally got him to tell the Cagney story, but only by prompting him directly during our live broadcast. Gorshin was an utter bore, and if the interview had been pre-recorded, I would never have allowed it to be aired. Another forgettable interview was with the actor Mickey Rooney, who turned every question about his legendary career into a promotion about his new life as a born-again Christian. I tried again and again to bring him around to the more publicly interesting side of his life, but he remained resistant—and at the end of the nationally broadcast interview, ungraciously declared, "Nice trying to talk to you."

Fortunately, interviews like that have been the exception rather than the rule. The bulk of my interviews, with celebrities and everyday people, have been enlightening and informative. On occasion, I've been asked if I have any particular technique for conducting these interviews. I do, and in describing it I use the acronym CLASP. The acronym breaks down like this:

C is for *caring*—first and foremost demonstrate, through your knowledge of the guest, that you care enough about them to have studied up on who they are.

L is for *listening*, something interviewers often fail to do in their rush to ask the next question. Listening to the interviewee's response to the previous question is critical in determining whether that question requires a follow-up before moving on.

A is for *anticipating*. Consider ahead of time the potential unexpected curveball responses your guest will provide, and be prepared to deal with them.

S is for *staring*—maintaining eye contact. The eyes are very telling, and can sometimes reflect whether the interviewee is being forthright. I've also found that if I stare a guest in the eye after they have responded to a question, they will invariably continue talking. This particular technique has resulted in some of my best sound bites, and for some guests, in their saying some things they wish they hadn't.

Finally, the P is for *preparing*. This one's a no-brainer. Simply do your homework, and know as much about your guest as possible and what he or she is currently doing in order to formulate intelligent questions.

I have successfully utilized this technique in thousands of interviews. The following is a microcosm of the more memorable interviews I've conducted over the past half-century.

29

JERRY LEWIS:
KING OF COMEDY

Jerry Lewis joking with me on Ellis Island where he was honored with the Ellis Island Medal of Honor, 2011.

Jerry Lewis has long been acclaimed one of the greatest comedians of the 20th century, and has truly earned his title as the King of Comedy. His comedic elixir has intoxicated millions of people the world over, and his films have grossed almost a billion dollars. Conducting an interview with him can be a raucous experience, with the interviewer soon finding himself playing straight man to the comedic genius. I've done four interviews with Lewis, one of which won an Emmy Award for Outstanding Entertainment Programming. In those interviews, I delved behind the mask of the clown to find a man of brilliance and philanthropy. But this was also a man who endured so much pain in his life that he was once on the verge of committing suicide.

At the very core of Jerry Lewis's humor is the child in all of us—the sense he retains of himself as a child.

"I think what made it work for me is that I never allowed myself to get any further than nine," he said. "I've been nine since 1933, and I've been nine all of my life." It is what has sustained him through many generations. Approaching 90 at the time of our interview, Lewis dismissed that number as his chronological age, saying, "In my head and my heart, I'm nine. It's too much fun to allow yourself to get beyond 10 or 11, and then to adulthood," he mused. "Nine is innocent, sympathetic, compassionate, forgiving. All of those elements that were nine, I took and placed in the body that I pictured would make people laugh." The comedian said he doubted he would have been as successful, had he not continued to consider himself a child. "I've kept the nine-year-old in the forefront of everything I've ever done as an adult, and I think that is the secret to my success. I get paid for doing what most children get punished for," he added with a raucous laugh. "It's a miracle." Turning a bit philosophical, Lewis counseled, "The world would be a better place if people recognized we all have a child within us, and had fun with it. That child never leaves."

There was an effervescence about this funny man when he talked about his ten-year partnership with crooner Dean Martin back in the 50s and 60s. "He was my big brother, my father figure, my everything," Lewis proclaimed. "And when *he* smiled at something I did—you couldn't give me an Oscar in place of that." He expressed guilt that critics often gave him the credit for their acts' success. "Dean was a brilliant performer," he said. "He was not given critical acclaim because he was the straight man. He was underrated for ten years." He credited Martin with the success of their act—which earned the pair $250 million over a ten-year period—and expressed the sadness he felt when they broke up their act. The two performers went their separate ways then, creating a schism that lasted 20 years before Frank Sinatra reunited them on Lewis's Labor Day telethon for the Muscular Dystrophy Association in 1976. With a lump in his throat, Lewis told me, "That was an incredible moment for both of us."

Lewis hosted the annual telethon for 60 years, raising more than two and a half billion dollars. Though he's been asked repeatedly over the years, he has never disclosed why he dedicated himself to that particular cause. When I asked, he told me, "There is no why. From day one, I said it is not *why* I do what I do—it's just vital that I do it."

All the time Lewis was making audiences laugh, he was living a life of excruciating pain. His estimated 1,900 comedic pratfalls came at a price. During one performance, he took a fall and landed on his spine. He had to cancel the rest of the performance and was rushed to the hospital, where he remained paralyzed overnight and doctors informed him that he had come within millimeters of severing his spine. It was the beginning of a painful existence that lasted for the next 35 years. Four failed surgeries, steroids, painkillers—nothing relieved the pain.

It got to be so bad, Lewis contemplated suicide. "I was going blind, losing focus, the pain was so severe," he recalled. One day, he decided to do it, reached for a Beretta nine-millimeter and started to load the clip. As he placed the fourth bullet in the clip, Lewis said, he burst out laughing.

"Even in devastating moments like that, there can be humor," he reflected. *"Why do I need four bullets in there?* I asked myself. *I'm going to shoot myself four times?* I got hysterical—it was so funny, at that moment." As he was giggling to himself, his 12-year-old daughter Danielle walked into the bathroom and saw the gun. "My heart dropped," he said. But he thought fast, telling her that he used a gun in his act and was practicing a routine. She bought it and left him alone—but his daughter's unexpected presence was sobering. It gave Lewis reason to reconsider his action. "I thought about never seeing Dani and my wife anymore," he said, and changed his mind.

At that point Lewis called his dear friend, heart surgeon Dr. Michael DeBakey, and shared with him what he was thinking of doing. "He said that if I could put my suicide on hold for about an hour, he would have the top pain specialist in Las Vegas come to my home," Lewis recalled. When the doctor arrived, he gave Jerry treatment and a device to help relieve the pain. To this day, Lewis still uses a "pain pacemaker," an implanted device called a spinal-cord stimulator, that sends electrical impulses to the spine and blocks the pain.

During our most recent interview, Lewis shared two of his proudest moments with me: one in 1977, when he was nominated for a Nobel Peace Prize, and another in 1995, when he had his debut on Broadway in the musical *Damn Yankees.*

Throughout his life, despite all his successes, Lewis's late father would tell him, "Ya ain't done nothing till you've done Broadway." Jerry beamed. "I finally did…I looked up and said, 'Look Dad, I made it!' I felt his presence that night. It was simply incredible."

Lewis also revealed something that was not commonly known at the time—his friendship with President Kennedy and his 19 secretive visits to the White House.

"He flew me in on Air Force One, and he never allowed me to come in the front way," he explained. The press corps, too, had been kept in the dark about his presence there. Kennedy was concerned that if his critics knew of his friendship with Lewis, they might take it out on him by not contributing to Lewis's telethon.

Lewis got a bit reflective when I asked if there was anything he hadn't done and still wished to do. "Hate to say it," he shot back, "but I've done it all. I haven't done it all perfectly, so I'd like to continue to redefine my life—go back a couple years and fix that element, and do a better job." When future generations look back on him and his comedic era, he said, "I just hope that they'll know that all I had done was done with a lot of love in my heart." As we brought the interview to a close, he shared with me a copy of his credo, which reads, "I shall pass through this world but once. Any good, therefore, that I can do, or any kindness that I can show to any human being, let me do it now. Let me not defer nor neglect it, for I shall not pass this way again."

30

CHUCK YEAGER: AVIATION PIONEER

Chuck Yeager was a test pilot who flew to the edge of space. Photo Courtesy: NASA Archival Photo.

*g*eneral Chuck Yeager was an aviation pioneer who flew to the edge of space before the first spacecraft ever left the launch pad at Cape Canaveral. By flying experimental planes faster than the speed of sound, Yeager pushed the boundaries of modern aviation, and showed courage that paved the way for the earliest American astronauts. He has since been acclaimed as America's greatest test pilot.

During a 1985 interview with me to promote his newly released autobiography, Yeager was quite blunt when I asked him to what he attributed his historic success as a test pilot.

"The secret to my success," he said, "is that I always managed to live to fly another day." He sure had his share of close calls—particularly the one in 1947, when his super-secret Bell X-1 test plane was dropped from the belly of a B-29 and he discovered that his batteries had failed, leaving him with no power to operate any of the key systems onboard, even the instrument panel.

"We had no way of talking to anybody, and no way of knowing how much fuel I had aboard," Yeager remembered. The young pilot, however, kept his cool. Using the craft's manual-jettison system, Yeager was able to dump enough liquid oxygen and alcohol to enable him to pull off an emergency landing on a dry lakebed in the Mojave desert. Gesturing with his hands, Yeager related the hair-raising danger of the situation, and the concentration it took him to come through it.

"You sit and sweat it out—you sweat it out. Fortunately everything worked out, but it was very close," he sighed. "When you can walk away from a flight like that, that's all that counts."

Despite his legendary skill, the great test pilot said he was never comfortable being referred to as a guy with "the right stuff," as author Thomas Wolfe characterized the initial group of trailblazing astronauts.

"It doesn't mean that much to a pilot," he said. "It's like saying, just because you have the right stuff, you're an outstanding pilot. That's not true—you need a lot of other things to help you, like experience and being at the right place at the right time." He was delighted, for instance, to have been born in 1923 rather than 1963. "It made me the right age to serve in World War II," he said, where he was able to fly escort missions for bombers "and, as a test pilot, to make the transition from prop airplanes to jets, to rockets, and right on into the space program."

I asked Yeager to describe the feeling of breaking the sound barrier by traveling at Mach 1—faster than 760 miles per hour. He had difficulty doing so. "Sitting up there at 45,000 feet, strapped in the X-1, monitoring systems, you're working hard: controlling pressure, keeping the airplane heading where you want it to go and running into buffeting. Not knowing the outcome of the test flight, you have no time to think about feelings," he confessed. "The day we broke Mach 1, we didn't know we were going to. I remember watching the Mach meter and getting into heavy buffeting, then suddenly it stopped, and we began a smooth flight as the Mach meter jumped off the scale. We had gone beyond the 1.0 on the dial. They didn't have a lot of confidence that the X-1 would go beyond Mach 1." With all the calm of someone describing a less stressful job, Yeager said he couldn't believe it when he became the first human being to break the sound barrier. "I was expecting the airplane to do a lot more—like trying to disintegrate—and I'm happy it didn't."

Yeager said he was not disappointed that he wasn't asked to join the first team of astronauts. "They required a degree, and I only had a high-school education. I was having my fun flying research airplanes, and they were riding in capsules." He laughed. "I had a lot more fun than they did anyway." Even so, when I asked him if there was anything left that he would like to do, he shot back, "I'd like to get a ride in the space shuttle. I would enjoy something like that." Sadly, the space shuttle program came and went without an invite to the intrepid test pilot.

Chuck Yeager went on to a happy retirement, holding onto—as of this writing—93 years of memories. His tremendous courage is matched only by his humility. When I asked how he would like to be remembered by aviation historians, Yeager paused, smiled and replied simply, "As a military pilot who did his job."

31

ED KOCH:
NEW YORK'S TENACIOUS
CHEERLEADER

Mayor Bloomberg pushed me into the middle for this photo, during an 80th birthday celebration for Mayor Koch.

*i*t's a journalist's job to ferret out the news, ask the hard questions and remain objective. But oftentimes, there is a bonus that comes from the job: the friendships that evolve from our professional relationships with newsmakers. New York mayor Ed Koch is one of those people who I'm proud to say became a friend over the years, particularly after he left City Hall. Professionally, he always took my calls and responded personally to my emails, and rarely—if ever—turned me down for an interview. As a matter of fact, Koch was probably the most frequent guest on my weekly PIX11 *News Closeup* program, ever since it went on the air in 1992.

Koch often gave me credit for his initial media training back in 1969, when the then-congressman from New York's Silk Stocking District would appear with me on a monthly interview program on Manhattan Cable Television, broadcast in black-and-white from a moving storage building across from Lincoln Center. From the outset, I found him to be on the quiet side and a bit introverted, but always outspoken on the issues. He became more confident with each broadcast, and the shoot-from-the-hip liberal soon began to loosen up and inject some levity into our chats. It was an early evolution of the famous Ed Koch charisma.

"Ask me whatever you want," he would exclaim in his high-pitched voice—and I would. He would be electrified with animation, his eyes popping wide open. He had a knack for coming up with a zinger that would elicit a laugh from the studio crew.

Covering Ed Koch during his years as mayor was such an enjoyable experience. He loved dealing with reporters, often holding court in the lobby of City Hall. He deftly fielded questions, and answered them scrupulously—except when someone asked something he thought was stupid, at which point he would simply shout, "That's ridiculous."

Of his years as mayor, Koch told me, "I like my job. It's challenging. There are so many pleasurable moments, painful ones as well—but I've never had a boring day." He was a passionate mayor, with an unyielding love for New York and a common-sense way of speaking; his trademark question, "How'm I Doing?" received a positive response from voters, who elected him for an historic three terms. Koch felt that one of his finest hours came in 1980, during a transit strike that crippled the city. He stood firm with the transit union.

"I said, 'We're not going to let these bastards bring us to our knees'—and we didn't," he said. After 11 days, Koch beamed, "They surrendered. We crushed it."

Koch had a zest for life that showed in just about everything he ever did. During one interview he told me, "If something is worth doing, it's worth putting your heart into it." He relished practically everything he did. I'll never forget the Christmas broadcast he did with me, in which I had him read *The Night Before Christmas*. It was a moment as classic as Mayor LaGuardia reading the comics to kids back in the thirties. Another of my favorite Koch moments came in 1981, after a massive power outage in lower Manhattan. The outage happened just before the homeward rush, and all subway service was knocked out. Thousands of people descended on the Brooklyn Bridge to walk home. I was following them with my camera crew when I heard a familiar voice closing in. It was Mayor Koch in shirtsleeves, apologizing to the people for the outage and pledging, "We'll overcome this." Approaching one woman, who appeared to be having trouble walking, he told her he would get her a ride home, then darted into the roadway, flagged down a car and instructed the driver to take the woman home. He gingerly helped the woman into the car before returning to the cheering crowd on the bridge.

"You're the hero of the hour," I shouted, to which he retorted, "No, I'm just doing my job."

It was moments like that that endeared Ed Koch to so many New Yorkers. He had an uncanny way of connecting with them, of making them feel that he really cared about them. (Years after the incident on the bridge, Koch revealed to me what he had told the driver of the car in which he had placed the woman: "I told him to take her straight home, and no funny business—or else.") Koch also wrote many books, including his best-selling *Mayor,* in which he was not particularly kind to many of the people he had worked with. He offered no apologies, telling me, "Historians are not supposed to be kind, they're supposed to be accurate."

On Koch's 80th birthday, I covered a party Mayor Michael Bloomberg hosted for him at Gracie Mansion. At one point, I asked to be allowed into the reception not as a reporter, but as a friend, hoping to wish the former mayor a happy birthday. Koch and Bloomberg were taking pictures with guests, and as soon as my head popped into the room, Koch—in that high-pitched voice—shouted to me to get in the picture. Mayor Bloomberg shuffled me into the center as I tried to argue that Koch should be there.

"Look into the camera and smile," I was instructed. A month later, I received a copy of the picture from City Hall. It was a great photo of the two mayors and me, and Koch had signed it, "To Marvin, my friend." Bloomberg had added his signature too, along with the inscription, "Marvin, you and I should look this good at 80."

In his last interview with me before his death in 2013, Koch seemed almost resigned to his fate, telling me prophetically, "I've had a wonderful life. I don't know if I'll live another 24 hours or another ten years. Whatever God gives me—and he's given me a wonderful life—I'm happy. I'm satisfied." When I asked how he would like to be remembered, the indomitable former mayor replied, "I hope they will remember me as someone who loved the city of New York and its people, and did whatever was in my power to make their lives better." Above all, he added, he wanted to be remembered for "giving a spirit back to New York." It is his spirit—the unique spirit of my friend Edward Irving Koch, and all that he accomplished as the city's 105th mayor—that remains his legacy.

32

WALTER CRONKITE: THE MOST TRUSTED MAN'S HERO

Introducing Walter Cronkite the Phil Simms during a taping of the television pilot *First Meeting* in 1994.

*W*alter Cronkite was long revered as "the most trusted man in America." As the anchorman of *The CBS Evening News* for almost 20 years, he was the personification of television journalism, and set the standard by which all others who followed have been judged. With his calming and reassuring baritone voice, Cronkite guided the nation through moments of tragedy, like the assassination of President Kennedy, and uplifted our spirits in times of triumph, like when Neil Armstrong landed on the moon.

Having always admired Cronkite as a personal role model, I felt privileged to spend a day working with him on a television pilot in 1994. He was the celebrity guest on the new program, entitled *First Meeting*. The idea behind the program was to introduce each episode's guest to the person he or she most wanted to meet. Cronkite, surprisingly, selected New York Giants quarterback Phil Simms.

As host of the program, I got to spend the first few minutes interviewing Cronkite before we made the introduction. In keeping with the show's theme, I asked Cronkite who, among all the people he had met in his world travels, left the best impression on him during their first meeting. Cronkite hesitated for a moment, then—to my surprise—he identified the late Yugoslavian dictator, Josip Tito.

"He came on much friendlier, more human-style than I would have expected from the dictator of Yugoslavia," he explained. And, he said, he was taken by Tito's sense of humor and his interests in the social welfare of his own people. Despite this initial reaction, Cronkite did admit, however, that "first impressions are not necessarily sustained." I then asked the iconic newsman, if he could go back in time and interview any historical figure, who would that be? "Other than Cleopatra?" he mused. With a bit of a pensive look, he said, "Columbus, Magellan—they would have been fascinating interviews."

The moment came for me to introduce the legendary newsman to Simms. As the towering quarterback entered the room, Cronkite— who had met presidents and kings with cool-headedness—rose from his chair, an adolescent smile crossing his face and his eyes widening in a gee-whiz moment. The giant of news excitedly shook hands with the giant of the gridiron. "Never thought I'd get to see you this close," gushed Cronkite, and added, "I hope I can call you Phil."

Why, I asked quizzically, of all the people in the world, had Walter Cronkite selected Phil Simms as the person he most wanted to meet?

"C'mon, I'm an average American," he beamed. "I sit there

every Sunday afternoon, either in the stadium or at home, watching Simms at work. For heaven's sake, I've admired his work for so long. Who else would you want to meet?"

I sat back for a few minutes as the two chatted about football and Cronkite, the spirited fan, asked one question after another of his sports hero. At one point, he wanted to know if Simms ever got nervous on the field. Simms said he was too engrossed in the game to think about it. The question prompted me to ask Cronkite the same thing.

A smile crossed his face as he replied, "I get far more nervous addressing a group of 100 people than going on the air with 150 million people." Still, at a time when many television news personalities are well coiffed and seemingly perpetually focused on their appearance, Cronkite said he was never concerned about that.

"My desire always was to communicate the news," he said. "The news was the thing. How I looked and what the atmosphere around me was didn't matter."

During the interview, Cronkite and Simms continued to connect like two old buddies, and the revelations were surprising. "Where did that nickname 'Old Iron Pants' come from?" Simms inquired. Once I had reassured him that it was okay to fess up about this on television, Cronkite revealed, "It's because I didn't have to go to the bathroom as often as everybody else. I sat in the anchor chair for hours and hours." We had always known of Cronkite's love of sailing, but during our interview he also revealed a passion for racing cars. "The minute I got in that car and revved up the engine, it seemed to catch hold," he told us. "It was just cool driving." He said he didn't have to win a race to feel a high from it. "Just finishing a race, I had such an adrenaline explosion. I was just high as a kite," he bubbled.

And I learned something else about Cronkite during that interview: his professional fantasy. His eyes sparkled as he told us, "I've always wanted to be a sports hero, all my life. I dream of hitting that home run and winning the World Series, or doing what Phil did, making a 30-yard pass in the last 20 seconds to win the game." But, he said, he knew early on that he wasn't destined for a career in sports. "I tried it in high school and just wasn't good at it," he confessed.

Cronkite had his gee-whiz expression all over his face once again when Simms presented him with a signed football and a New York Giants jacket. For the man his fans called Uncle Walter, this was a special moment, seeing the news giant play the role of an everyday sports fan. And Simms's impression, after their first meeting, of America's most trusted man?

"He's just a real down-to-earth person," he said.

As the man himself would have said in his signature sign-off, that's the way it was—on the day I got to work with Walter Cronkite: March 24th, 1994.

33

SOPHIA LOREN:
JUST CALL HER MAMMA

I was mesmerized by Sophia Loren's beauty and charm during a 1983 interview.

i was tantalized as I stood face to face with Marilyn Monroe, hypnotized as I gazed into Elizabeth Taylor's violet eyes, and mesmerized by the beauty of Sophia Loren. As a reporter, I was fortunate to snag interviews with some of Hollywood's brightest stars and most beautiful actresses. Of them all, Sophia Loren stood out as a woman of timeless elegance and charm. She was my prized interview in 1983, when she came to New York to serve as Grand Marshal of the Columbus Day Parade. Her smile was electrifying and her femininity intoxicating as we greeted one another. As I began our interview by introducing her as one of the world's most glamorous women, her eyes dropped sheepishly and a bright smile exposed her pearl-white teeth.

"No, no," she demurred. "I don't like the image of me being glamorous and sophisticated at all." Her real ambitions, she told me, lay elsewhere. "I really fought all my life to get rid of the image of being a sex symbol and to become an actress," she said. "Since I started in this business, I wanted to be an actress with a capital A—that's what I was reaching for, and that's what I *think* I reached. But who knows?" she added with a laugh and a twist of her head.

I assured her that a legion of her fans would certainly agree that she had achieved that goal. Her 1962 Best Actress Oscar, for her portrayal of a mother protecting her daughter from the ravages of war in the film *Two Women,* was a testament to her skills. But her striking looks were not to be denied. She was 49 at the time of our interview, and she looked as elegant as ever in a red sequined dress and bolero jacket, with candelabra earrings dangling from her ears. As we talked about classic beauty, she told me that "beauty is how you feel inside, and it reflects in your eyes." Her own hazel eyes were shielded behind her signature tinted designer glasses.

It was difficult to believe that during her childhood, Loren had been considered an ugly duckling. Apparently she was so thin, she earned the moniker *stuzzi cadenti,* or "little toothpick!" "Look at me now," she said laughingly. The secret to her enduring looks, she told me, was simple. "I'm happy. I live a wonderful life. I live for my family," she added, referring to her Italian movie-producer husband, Carlo Ponti, and their two sons.

Surprisingly, despite her international acclaim as a movie star and her recognition as one of the world's most beautiful women, Loren said she didn't want to be known as an actress, but as a mother.

"For me, I am first—before anything else—a mother," she exclaimed. "I'm a mamma!" She said she loved her sons more than life itself. She told me she was very proud of them, and admitted that while she made every effort not to spoil them, she was known to have weak moments—with limitations.

"Often?" I asked her.

Waving her index finger back and forth, she retorted, "No, not at all."

It was impressive to see how relaxed and down-to-earth the megastar remained as she responded to my volley of questions. "I may look calm and collected, but I'm extremely emotional," she conceded. Still, her approach to life was refreshingly grounded. She noted, "I like to live life day by day. I'm somebody who doesn't take life in a crazy way. I always want to know where I am, what I'm doing and what I'm going to do."

When I asked my last question, "If you could live life all over again, is there anything you would do differently?" her eyes widened and her smile broadened. "Nothing, nothing," she declared, adding, "I'm quite content with what I have."

34

DOG DAY:
THE ROBBER WHO
WANTED A BANK JOB

John Wojtowicz told me he wanted to work as a bank guard after he was released from prison.

Some of the people I've met in my career have had such unusual names that it once prompted my wife to observe, "You have the strangest friends." These were my news contacts, I explained: guys with names like Bear, Hurricane, Meatballs and Dog Day, who sometimes would leave cryptic messages on my home phone.

John "Dog Day" Wojtowicz was quite a character. He got his moniker from the steamy "dog days" of August in 1972, when he decided to rob a bank to pay for his boyfriend's sex-change opera-tion. It was a crime that riveted the nation, bringing all eyes to the Chase Manhattan bank in Brooklyn where Wojtowicz and an accomplice held nine hostages and kept FBI agents and police at bay for 14 hours. Wojtowicz became something of a folk hero during the heist, positioning himself as the little guy against a financial giant and bringing many of the hostages and onlookers over to his side. A crowd of 2,000 gathered outside the bank and stood for hours in the tropical August heat, cheering and rooting for him; at one point the 27-year-old, openly gay, married father of two threw money out to the crowd.

Frightened but determined, Wojtowicz tried to cut a deal with hostage negotiators to let him get away with $29,000. It didn't work, and the day-long siege ended with the hostages being released unharmed, Wojtowicz's 18-year-old accomplice Sal Naturale being shot and killed by FBI agents, and a destitute Wojtowicz being convicted of bank robbery and sentenced to 20 years in prison.

Dog Day's escapade became the stuff of legend and inspired the film *Dog Day Afternoon,* starring Al Pacino. When he was paid for the movie rights to his story, Wojtowicz was finally able to pay for his lover's sex-change surgery. But a year later, Ernie Aron—now Liz Eden—ditched Wojtowicz, saying she never wanted to see him again. The bank thief, still imprisoned, made an unsuccessful attempt to kill himself; and in 1978, after serving more than six years of his sentence, Wojtowicz was released to a halfway house in Manhattan, with the parole proviso that he immediately find a bona fide job or return to prison to serve out the rest if his term.

That was when he reached out to me, hoping my broadcast would help him snag a job. Short and not particularly good-looking, Woj-towicz turned on the charm with me right away, speaking rapidly of his frustrations trying to find a job.

"They tell me they can't give me a job because I'm an ex-con," he whined. "But they can't use that excuse. They could say I'm not qualified, but how could they justify that I'm not qualified, for example, to be a ticket taker or a cashier?" Then he asserted, "I've been in banking for eight years, so no problem—I could be a bank teller, no problem. I know all that stuff."

As we walked and talked, the man everyone knew as Dog Day said he understood why people didn't want him handling money, given that he was a convicted bank robber. But he said he saw no reason why he couldn't get the job he *really* wanted—as a bank security guard!

"If I can hold off half the New York City Police Department and half the FBI for two days, I know I could guard a bank, or anything else," he said confidently. "If I'm guarding you, who's going to mess with you?"

Eventually, Dog Day Wojtowicz found a few odd jobs, including one cleaning toilets and providing other janitorial services on Park Avenue. Yet he never forgot what made him famous. Periodically, until his death in 2006, he would return to Brooklyn to stand in front of the Chase Manhattan bank, signing autographs and wearing a T-shirt proclaiming, "I robbed this bank."

35

CHRISTIE BRINKLEY: THE KNOCKOUT WHO FOCUSED ON KNOCKOUTS

Christie Brinkley and me. 1982.

*b*londe, blue-eyed cover-girl model Christie Brinkley is a daz-
zling beauty to this day, and has graced the covers of more
than 500 magazines in her career. *Playboy* readers voted her
one of the 100 sexiest women of the 20th century, and she has also
been labeled "one of the 100 hottest women of all time."

What few know about her is that this knockout in front of the
lens was also enchanted with knockouts in the boxing arena. Early

in her career, Brinkley had a passion for boxing, and spent a lot of time photographing fights. She was 27 when I wrote about her photographic interest for *Parade* magazine. Despite her success as a model, she said she got a greater thrill seeing one of her boxing pictures in print. Her first photo appeared in the boxing magazine *Ring*.

"It was an outstanding photograph of a fighter's face flying off the side of his opponent's glove," she told me excitedly. It was the first time the glamorous model had gained recognition for something other than her sensuous beauty, and the $50 fee and credit line it brought her seemed to buy her more pride than the thousands of dollars she received daily for modeling shoots.

"Modeling is fun," she told me at the time, "but photography is so much more challenging. I love to capture the action and to compose my pictures. It's so stimulating."

Brinkley said she knew absolutely nothing about boxing until friends invited her to join them in the third row at the heavyweight championship fight in October, 1980, between Muhammad Ali and Larry Holmes in Las Vegas.

"I both surprised and impressed my friends by learning as much as I could about the fight," she recalled.

She brought three cameras to the bout.

"There was such excitement—the whole audience was screaming," she said. "It was like a concert. I could hardly load my film." She remembered that her hands were trembling when, 30 seconds into the first round, Ali took a punch "that knocked the expression of confidence off his face." Brinkley's blue eyes radiated as she described the events of that night, admitting to being a bit squeamish when she first saw the blood and brutality of the sport.

"I was in tears behind the camera, but too caught up with what was happening to stop shooting," she said. By the time Ali's manager stopped the fight in the 10th round, Brinkley had shot 35 rolls of film. "Thank goodness I wasn't on assignment," she explained. "Most of my pictures were out of focus and poorly exposed. Also, because I didn't know how to anticipate a punch, I got lots of shots of outstretched arms and faces with blank looks."

Brinkley was clearly in focus herself at the post-fight party. There she met the editor of *Ring,* who had noticed her taking pictures during the fight. He offered to give her an assignment, which she assumed was simply a polite party gesture. A few weeks later, he actually offered her an assignment to shoot a fight at Madison Square Garden. Her greatest fear was that she would be resented by the cadre of male photographers there, who earned their living shooting the fights. She tried to hide her curvaceous body under a conservative tailored suit, and tucked her long blonde mane under a rimmed hat. However, despite her concerns, Brinkley was immediately accepted as one of the boys by the veteran ringside lensmen.

While most boxing photographers are out to catch the crucial punch, Brinkley said her interest was in looking beyond the brutality of boxing, and explained that she wanted to capture "the rich atmosphere in the arena and the human drama written on the faces of the people in and out of the ring." Explaining further, she said, "I look for the shot of the guy who won after he was sure he was going to lose, or the wives of the fighters on the sidelines."

Her efforts to capture the complete boxing experience in her pictures paid off at the November 1980 Roberto Duran–Sugar Ray Leonard fight in New Orleans, where Duran stunned the boxing world by quitting in the middle of the match. Afterward, the boxer maintained that he had a terrible stomachache. Yet no one recalled seeing any sign of illness during the fight—except Brinkley, who thought it was so unusual to see an icepack on Duran's stomach that she took a picture. Her photo provided irrefutable evidence that Duran had indeed been ill before he threw in the towel.

Brinkley won other praise for her photographs. "Her work stands up to her looks," one photographer said. "It's of the highest professional caliber," said another. The then-editor of *Ring,* Randy Gordon, was impressed by the sensitivity of her pictures, noting her "marvelous sense of timing. She could almost feel when the guy is about to let the punch go, and get a picture of one fighter's fist on the other guy's chin, with the face all distorted."

While she said that she never wanted special treatment, Brinkley admitted she was always grateful for those rare moments when her good looks gave her the edge over other photographers—like the time she watched a young fighter take such a terrible beating that the referee had to stop the fight. As the defeated boxer slumped in the corner, Brinkley jumped into the ring to get some close-ups. "His face was badly mauled," she recalled. "He looked as if he had been in an auto accident. Suddenly there was movement in one of his closed, puffy eyes. It opened and shut in a wink as he looked up at me and pursed his swollen lips. How many photographers can say they have a picture of a defeated boxer throwing them a kiss?"

Brinkley also told me she believed her photography helped her become a better model. For one thing, she said, it helped her to be more patient, and enabled her to develop a better understanding of just what a photographer looks for. It has certainly paid off for her. These days, Brinkley continues to model and act in film and television, owns exclusive lines of jewelry and skincare products, and is successfully involved in real estate—leaving her with a reported knockout worth of $80 million.

36

EDDIE FISHER:
THE KISS I NEVER
SAW COMING

I had to coach Eddie Fisher before a live broadcast of *Midday Edition* in 1982.

*d*escribed by some as "the Frank Sinatra of our time," Eddie Fisher was one of the most popular singers of the early 1950s. From the beginning, his life seemed to contain all the elements of the Horatio Alger rags-to-riches story, a fairy tale about a poor Jewish boy from Philadelphia who grew up to sing for princesses, dine with presidents and marry not one, but three of Hollywood's most glamorous stars. He had talent, popularity and money—until he made the journey from star to has-been, from millionaire to bankrupt, from heaven to hell.

In November of 1981, Fisher came to the studio to tell his story and promote his memoir, *Eddie: My Life, My Loves*. It proved to be one of the most challenging interviews I ever did. And for the first time in my career—and quite uncharacteristic for me—I had to admonish and lecture my guest.

Fisher appeared sleepy when he showed up with two publicists for a morning taping of the interview, to be used on a future broadcast of the syndicated show *Midday Edition*. Still boyish-looking at 53, thanks in part to a facelift, Fisher was very laidback as I told him about the format of the interview and what I hoped to cover in the four minutes allotted for the segment.

We began the interview. "In a brutally revealing autobiography, Eddie Fisher talks candidly about his life," I said as part of my introduction, then welcomed Fisher and led into my first question by noting that he was the guy who had it all, and blew it. "What happened?" I asked. Fisher twisted uncomfortably in his chair. A nervous smile pierced his lips and, after a slight pause, I got a "Well, umm," then another pause.

"I took a fork in the road," he said finally, then followed it with another strained laugh, adding, "I don't know, I think I got married." He seemed to be rambling already.

"Were your marriages the problem?" I asked.

There was another pause, then, "I…umm…ahh, I got away from music," he said. "I got interested in other things…that we really don't want to talk about." He dropped further back into his chair. "We want to talk about music."

"Okay," I said, "let's talk about music. What happened to the man and his music?" Again rambling, Fisher repeated what I had just said, then retorted, "I just told you, I—umm"—another long pause—"some other things took priority, which was a mistake." Trying to hold the interview together, I asked Fisher to elaborate about some of those priorities, but still he had no answer for me. "I've talked about it so much, and—ahh—umm..."

At this point I had already realized that the interview was terrible, and would have loved to start over. But we had to prepare the studio for our live broadcast. We had two minutes left for the interview, and I still hadn't learned anything about Fisher's scandalous divorce from Debbie Reynolds, or his volatile marriage to Elizabeth Taylor, who had humiliated him when she ditched him for Richard Burton. I was hoping he would tell me, as he had written in the book, that living with Elizabeth Taylor "was like living in the eye of a hurricane," or that he would repeat any of the other dirt he had dished in his memoir, like the story he told of confronting Burton after learning that he and Taylor were having an affair during the filming of *Cleopatra*.

"Richard, leave my wife alone," he told the actor—to which, according to Fisher, Burton replied, "You don't need her. You're a star already. I'm not. She's going to make me a star. I'm going to use her, that no-talent Hollywood nothing."

I also knew that Fisher's career began to tumble after his divorce from Taylor, after which he got hooked on methamphetamines in so-called "vitamin cocktails" supplied by "Dr. Feelgood," Max Jacobson, the man who shot up the stars. He blew money carelessly, living so high on the $20 million he earned in his career that he finally hit bottom and filed for bankruptcy. All of this was fascinating stuff, and would have been very compelling for our viewers to hear—but he told me none of it during our interview. The only decent quote that came out of it was when Fisher acknowledged that he was his own victim.

"I thought I could do anything," he confessed. "I was very young, and I thought I knew everything. I thought I had everything. But I didn't know everything." He said he should have focused on his singing and "not let my head get turned away in another direction—but we all make mistakes." On the verge of making another comeback, Fisher declared, "I consider myself one of the luckiest people on the face of the earth."

The taping session ended. I thanked Fisher for coming in, and said goodbye to him and his publicists, who didn't look too happy. I dashed back to the newsroom to check my script for the upcoming live newscast. A few minutes later, an embarrassed Fisher showed up and asked if there was any chance we could tape the interview again. He was apologetic for not being very responsive the first go-around. My producer told me another taping was okay if Fisher was willing to wait until after our live broadcast. Fisher and his publicists were thrilled, and agreed to wait. About 20 minutes before our broadcast, however, my producer informed me that our scheduled live guest for that day had failed to show up. "Do you think Eddie can go live?" she asked. I hesitated, then said that it was worth a shot—but I wanted to talk to him first.

Pulling Fisher aside from his publicists, I picked up on what he had told me during the interview, that he considered himself lucky.

"Well, today is your lucky day, Eddie," I said, "because you're going to get a second chance to do that interview. Are you up to doing it live?" Fisher's face lit up and his eyes widened.

"Live? Oh, yes, I'm ready. I love you, Marv," he declared. But we weren't done. I told him how disappointed I was that he hadn't been responsive to my questions in the first interview.

"You're promoting a book, and it should be expected that you are willing to talk about what you have written," I counseled. In no uncertain terms, I added, "If you want to embarrass yourself, do it somewhere else—not on this network, on my program or to my viewers." Fisher was most apologetic, and assured me he would handle the live interview better.

Seconds before the segment went live, I again encouraged him to be upbeat and responsive. He smiled affirmatively. I began by showing a photo I had taken with him 25 years earlier, when he had just gotten out of the Army. "Look how adorable I was," he laughed.

Holding his head up and no longer slumped in the chair, Fisher said he felt great, declaring, "I gotta sing, I gotta sing!" Raising his arms, the iconic tenor took me by surprise as he burst out with lyrics from the hit Broadway musical *Cats*, bellowing, "Midnight—not a sound from the pavement." Seizing a moment when I wasn't on-camera, I blinked my eyes, nodded my head approvingly and gave him a thumbs-up. This was a different Eddie Fisher, a different interview. "Wait a minute," he beamed with a smile. "Did I just do that? I'm crazy—I feel wonderful."

Though he never did get into his relationships with Debbie Reynolds, Elizabeth Taylor or Connie Stevens, he was much more forthright than before about his failures.

"I got lost," he confessed. "I got involved with women, with gambling, and I loved buying women jewelry—rubies, diamonds and emeralds—and I loved to give it all away. I was a victim of Eddie Fisher, whatever that means." He exuded energy and there was a sparkle in his eye as he went on. "Singing is my true love," he said. "I feel like I'm sitting on top of the world right now, because I've been given a second chance." I wrapped up the interview with a quote from Fisher's memoir: *A future of promise is possible only when you have made peace with the past.* Eddie Fisher has made that journey, and we wish him well."

The broadcast was over and the lights came down. Fisher's publicists couldn't have been happier. Fisher himself was thrilled with the interview—just how thrilled, I was about to find out. "I love you, Marv," he declared again, embracing me. Abruptly, he gave me a kiss like I'd never had before: a soul kiss, in which he placed his tongue in my mouth. I immediately recoiled in surprise as Fisher laughingly told me, "The only one I ever did that to before was Dean Martin."

Well, at least I was in good company!

37

THE HOLOCAUST DENIER:
A DIFFICULT INTERVIEW

Dr. Robert Countess.

*i*n commemoration of the opening of the Holocaust Memorial Museum in Washington in the spring of 1993, I invited a Holocaust survivor and a historian to join me on my weekly newsmaker program, PIX11 *News Closeup.* It was a time when anti-Semitism and neo-Nazism were on the rise, and one in five Americans did not believe that the Holocaust had ever occurred. In light of the graphic images from the concentration camps, the tales of Holocaust survivors and the bodies of six million Jews, I found this incomprehensible; yet in the interest of fair journalism, I decided to invite a Holocaust denier on the program as well. Jewish groups were not pleased, claiming that "to engage them in debate would give them the undeserved legitimacy they crave," but I felt it my responsibility to cover both sides.

My guest was Dr. Robert Countess, a revisionist historian. Countess was active with the Institute for Historical Review, an organization at the center of the international Holocaust-denial movement. I began my interview by noting that in journalism school they taught us that there are two sides to every story—but as the legendary broadcaster Edward R. Murrow once observed, some stories just don't have another side.

"The Holocaust," I said, "is one story that doesn't appear to have another side."

Almost before my sentence was finished, Countess shot back, "I would say that every story has three or four sides." I insisted that I was simply interested in hearing *his* side, to which Countess responded by flat-out denying that there had ever been a systematic policy to exterminate the Jews during World War II.

"There was a Nazi effort to relocate Jews out of Germany control," he asserted, "but never any talk of extermination." He went on, explaining that the Jews had simply been sent to internment camps until they could be settled elsewhere.

"Was Auschwitz a death camp?" I asked.

He quickly answered, "No," then modified his answer. "Yes, in the sense that people died there—mostly from typhus," he said.

"Why were crematoriums built there in the first place?" I pressed him.

"Because they anticipated, as well as experienced, a great outbreak of the disease," Countess retorted. Bodies were burned and thrown into large open pits, he said, because it was the best way to deal with the epidemic of typhus deaths. I reminded Countess that even the camp's longtime commandant, Rudolf Höss, had confessed that Auschwitz was a death camp, before being found guilty of war crimes and hanged—but Countess had an answer to that too.

"He was tortured," he said, adding that Höss "was kept up 48, 72 hours, was beaten, and didn't know what he was saying or doing when he signed the confession."

Countess then tried to suggest that so many people had died in the camps because the camps had fallen into chaos due to allied bombing. "People were dying left and right," he declared. He also insisted that the figure of six million Jews killed during the war was "highly exaggerated," and claimed the figure was closer to 300,000—"possibly."

I was getting increasingly agitated as I listened to this diatribe, but maintained my objective demeanor as we continued. During our seven-minute interview, Dr. Countess failed to offer any substantive argument to support his claims, and those of his fellow Holocaust deniers. Before we ended, I asked for his reaction to a statement by an anti-Jewish group, which read, "In our view it is nothing more than an international racket by Jews to bleed, blackmail and ter-rorize their many enemies around the world into silence about the crime of subservients to their aggressive designs."

Countess concurred with the statement, noting, "There are a number of American Jews who would say that it is a racket." He added that Holocaust survivor and Nobel laureate Elie Wiesel "would be the high priest of this racket."

At that point I thanked my guest, and announced that the pro-gram would continue after the commercial break. Right or wrong, it was my desire not to shake this man's hand—but the camera was late in getting out of the shot, and caught Countess thrusting his hand into mine. Before the taped program aired, I had the hand-shake edited out.

My following guest, Holocaust survivor Valerie Jakober Furth, could not believe what she had heard.

"This man has the gall to come here and tell me that it didn't happen," she said emotionally, telling me how painful it had been to listen to Countess's denial. "His lies were so outrageous, I got upset," she said. "How does he have the nerve to say that in face of all the evidence?" She feared that by permitting such deniers to continue spreading lies, the Holocaust could happen again. The best way to combat such ignorance, she said, was through education, by continuing to tell the truth and bear witness to what had occurred.

With tears in her eyes, Mrs. Furth powerfully did just that. "I know this man is a liar, because I know the truth," she said. "I'm a witness. I smelled the smoke, the burning flesh. I was almost gassed. My family was gassed. I saw the lake where they threw the ashes. These were my people, soaked with our blood."

38

ELIE WIESEL:
BEARING WITNESS

Elie Wiesel interview on PIX11.

"I have tried to fight those who would forget. Because if we forget, we are guilty, we are accomplices."— Elie Wiesel

*e*lie Wiesel's mission in life was to bear witness, and not allow the world to forget the inhumanity of the Holocaust with its annihilation of six million Jews. A survivor of the Nazi concentration camps who lost his mother, father and younger sister in the camps, Wiesel emerged as a voice for the voiceless—"a messenger to mankind," as the citation read on the Nobel Prize for Peace he received in 1986—whose strong message of tolerance lives on as his rich legacy. When Wiesel revisited Buchenwald with President Obama in 2009, the president called him a "living legend."

Wiesel was 82 in 2011, when I met him at a social event and encouraged him to join me for an in-studio interview. It turned out to be one of the most emotionally inspiring interviews I have ever done.

Having spoken extensively and eloquently about the haunting atrocity of what had happened and the lessons the Holocaust should have taught us, Wiesel told me he felt "close to despair" over public opinion polls that showed that 35 million Americans bore hatred for the Jewish people. "If Auschwitz didn't cure the world of anti-Semitism, what could and what would?" he asked. "It's stupid," he added. "The anti-Semites hated me before I was born. The anti-Semites who hate me have never seen me. Nevertheless there is hatred in them." He questioned where they learned this hatred, noting, "Somebody has to teach them anti-Semitism—you've got to be taught to hate." To counter that, he insisted that it is imperative to continue to speak out, not just against anti-Semitism, but against hatred, bigotry and intolerance in all its other forms as well. "To give up is not an option," he declared.

If he were a judge, Wiesel said, he would institute a new way to mete out justice for an anti-Semite who was charged with a hate crime. "I would put him in a cell for a whole week, and force him to read certain pages, certain messages and testimonials, and show him pictures, all relating to the Holocaust. That would force him to face the realities of those times."

As for those who deny that the Holocaust ever happened, the Nobel laureate asserted, "They exist to our embarrassment. Just as there are mentally ill people, there are some morally ill people. Why should I waste my time and energy to discuss anything with them? We don't live in the same world." Wiesel said he had encountered deniers himself who tried to provoke him; one even tried to kidnap him. "He said he would take me into custody and force me to admit that the Holocaust is a lie," he sadly related.

But the scholar who came to personify the Holocaust survivor knew all too well the realities of the horror. He expressed anger that the United States remained silent about the Holocaust while it was going on, and failed to intercede to try and stop it. "Why didn't the American Air Force bomb the rails leading to the camps?" he asked. "They could have at least delayed the process for days, weeks—perhaps saved some lives. Every day, from ten to 15,000 human beings—men, women, children—were being gassed and burned… every day, every night." The deep lines in his aging face tightened as Wiesel told me how disgusted he was that the superpowers were aware of the depravity that was going on at Auschwitz and Buchenwald, and did nothing to intervene. "To remain silent and indifferent is the greatest sin of all," he proclaimed, and expressed his belief that had there been social media back then, the Holocaust might never have happened, since there would have been no way to maintain its secrecy.

Wiesel wasn't sure what helped him to survive his own experience. "No one ever said I had to survive so I could tell the tale," he said. "As long as my father was alive, I wanted to live, because I knew, if I died, he would die immediately after me." Having lost his mother and sister at Auschwitz before being transferred to Buchenwald, he was forced to watch as his father was beaten with an iron bar, and later cared for him as he succumbed to dysentery and starvation. "I had no more tears," Wiesel recalled in his trailing voice. "After my father died, my life was not a real life. I let myself live. I didn't do anything to remain alive." A few months later, the war was over and the death camp was liberated.

When he was freed from Buchenwald in 1945, Wiesel was 16 and orphaned. He couldn't speak about his nightmarish experience, no less write about it, until more than a decade later. He told me he delayed discussing it because "I wanted to be sure that I had the proper words. I'm still not sure I found the right words. How do you explain something like that?" He said he rarely spoke about those events. "I go around it," he explained. He said only four or five of his 60 books relate to the Holocaust.

Wiesel's famous chronicle of his ordeal, *Night,* was written in Yiddish and originally entitled *And the World Was Silent,* a title later changed by his publisher. The book has since been critically acclaimed and translated into many languages, and has sold well over 10 million copies worldwide.

During our interview, and for the first time on television, Wiesel agreed to read the book's most renowned passage, about his imprisonment at Buchenwald. His eyes dropped and his speech slowed as he began: "Never shall I forget those flames which consumed my faith forever. Never shall I forget that nocturnal silence which deprived me, for all eternity, of the desire to live. Never shall I forget those moments which murdered my God and my soul and turned my dreams to dust. Never shall I forget those things, even if I am condemned to live as long as God Himself. Never!" Even 65 years later, I could sense the heavy emotion consuming his body as he read the passage. "It's painful," he conceded, "because it was a moment in my life that outweighed all others for me. Life is not made up of years, but of moments."

When I asked him, "All these years later, can you forgive?" his response was terse.

"I am not a judge, really," he said. "Only God can forgive, if He so chooses."

I asked the scholar of the Scriptures, as so many before me had asked, "Where was God when six million Jews were being slaughtered?"

Wiesel paused and took a deep breath before responding, "I have heard the question; I don't have the answer." Though Wiesel too had asked the question and voiced disbelief over the slaughter around him, he said he never stopped believing in God. "I cannot live without God," he said. "There is the greatness of my tradition. We may question God, even if he doesn't answer."

39

RUDY GIULIANI: SHEDDING A TEAR LIKE THE REST OF US

Mayor Giuliani at Ground Zero.

rudy Giuliani was nearing the end of his term as the 107th mayor of the city of New York when terrorists struck our country and forever changed our lives on September 11th, 2001. Almost caught in the destruction of the World Trade Center himself, Giuliani emerged as the unquestioned hero of the day, acting as the father figure who guided us through the dark cloud of terror that hung over our city and our nation.

My relationship with the mayor went back to 1983, when he was the United States Attorney for New York. His then-wife, Donna Hanover, co-anchored a midday broadcast with me on the Independent Network News. He became a friend during that time, and always made himself accessible to me for an interview.

We recorded many interviews, particularly during the annual observance of the 9/11 terrorist attacks. On the fifth anniversary, I found Giuliani more reflective and more candid than he had ever been before as he talked to me about that day, and shared with me the moment he cried. He started by telling me he had conflicting sentiments about 9/11.

"Sometimes I look back on that day with anger," he began. "I have tremendous feelings of sadness. It was the worst day in my life—the worst day in the life of my city, my country. But there were other aspects of that day that made it an uplifting day, because of the incredible acts of nobility and bravery people displayed. I witnessed so many people helping other people."

As President George W. Bush was being flown to a secure location, Giuliani became the comforting voice updating a stunned nation about what had happened. His most difficult announcement was in response to the question about how many casualties were anticipated from the collapse of the two towers.

"The number of casualties will be more than any of us can bear, ultimately," was his response, the grim reality written over his somber face. "I didn't want to give an actual number," he told me, "because we just weren't sure." Initially, he had been told to expect 12,000 casualties, then 6,000, then 8,000. "I didn't want to give them a number I wasn't sure of. I didn't know how many we would recover." Ultimately, the final figure was placed at just under 2,900 lives lost.

Giuliani was so stoic during those days—such a pillar of strength. We saw a different Rudy Giuliani that day.

"What changed you?" I asked.

"The event changes you," he replied. "All of us are different people under different circumstances. In a situation like that, you need unity of purpose—compassion that hopefully will bring out your very best instincts."

The way he handled himself on 9/11 earned Giuliani the admiration of the nation and the nickname "America's Mayor." He admitted to feeling the same anger, anxieties and sadness as everyone else in the country during that time, but said he refused to allow himself to succumb to those feelings.

"I just kept saying to myself, 'You can't give into this now, you can't break down.'" Giuliani said he resisted being overcome by emotion by telling himself, *I've got to save that for another time. I've just got to remain focused—got to remain alert—because I don't know what decision I have to make next.* He did admit that had he not been the mayor, with such daunting responsibilities that day, and been simply another bystander to that horror, he probably would have broken down and cried, particularly after viewing the unthinkable—people jumping from the flaming tower.

But Giuliani did concede that he couldn't hold back the tears in his office when he reached his longtime friend, U.S. Solicitor General Ted Olsen, on the phone. September 11th was Olsen's birthday, and his wife Barbara had delayed her trip to Los Angeles by one day so she could celebrate with him. Barbara was one of the passengers killed aboard American Airlines Flight 77 when it crashed into the Pentagon.

"Ted was one of my closest friends," Giuliani remembered. "I was at their wedding, and he and his wife had recently visited my office." He said he had heard that there was a tape of Barbara making a desperate call to her husband just before the crash. "It was overwhelming, talking to Ted that day. During the conversation, I cried," he recalled sadly.

The former mayor's head dropped and he fell silent for a moment as he remembered shedding tears again, when he learned that Fire Chaplain Mychal Judge had been killed. "I felt a tremendous sense of being alone when I lost Father Judge," he said. He had turned to Father Judge for guidance at moments like this, he told me. "He's the one who could help me explain this. He's the one I would sit down with in a private room and ask, 'Father, how do I explain this to all these people who lost loved ones?' and he would always find a better way to do it, to help me explain it." When he realized he had lost Father Judge, Giuliani said tears filled his eyes. "I felt so alone, and said to myself, 'You're going to have to do this one for yourself now.'"

Giuliani acknowledged that families would never get over the pain of a day the world should never be allowed to forget. But out of the ashes of that day, he said, America came together in a way we hadn't seen before. "We were united as a nation, and we were supportive of one another. Somehow, goodness trumped evil."

40

LIBERACE:
THE DAY HE PLAYED THE
PIANO FOR ME

Liberace captivated me when he played the contemporary Mack The Knife as if might have been interpreted by Mozart.

*i*t was a cloudy spring day in 1985 when sunshine suddenly brightened the studio with the arrival of the incomparable Liberace. His warm smile showcased teeth as white as the keys on the piano; and dressed in a cream-colored striped suit, pale-blue shirt with sky-blue tie, and jewel-encrusted rings on both hands, he charmed everyone in sight. He greeted me like we were old friends, and we discussed the interview we were going to do live for the

Independent Network News's *Midday Edition,* which I co-anchored at the time with the former First Lady of New York, Donna Hanover.

Though outwardly flamboyant, the megastar showed a more reserved, humble side as we spoke one-on-one prior to our interview. While I had many questions for him, he wanted to know about me, too: where I was from, and how long I had been in the news business. He seemed genuinely interested, and if I wasn't a Liberace fan before, I certainly was one now. I understood instantly why he was so popular around the world. When I left him in the green room to begin our broadcast, I told him I would rejoin him in the last segment. He placed his hand in mine, thanked me for inviting him and told me to feel comfortable calling him Lee.

I began the segment by introducing him with the words, "His costumes are his trademark, his talent his hallmark." As the camera came in for a tight close-up of him, I explained that he had returned to New York after 30 years away from its clubs, for 21 performances at Radio City Music Hall. He told me performing there was the fulfillment of a career-long dream.

"I have so much fallen in love with New York," he said. "This town has so much energy, it's given me a vital spurt."

I asked to what he attributed his enduring popularity. Without hesitation he replied, "I feel fortunate to appeal to a general type of audience, which includes people of all ages—kind of a family-type audience." He said he had never been a "cult-type performer like so many others," and cited dangers in dealing with cult audiences, explaining, "One day you're hot and the next day you're not. I've been fortunate to grow into new generations."

As for the inspiration behind the signature candelabra on the piano during each of his performances, he explained that he had been so impressed by the presence of the candelabra in the 1945 film *A Song to Remember* about the life of Chopin that he went out the next day, bought one and placed it on the piano for his opening night in the Persian Room of the Plaza Hotel. "It became an instant trademark," he said, beaming with that effervescent smile.

As we were conducting our interview over a piano, I couldn't resist making a request.

"Might your fingers be itching a bit?" I teased. He was graciously receptive.

"I don't think many people realize that Mozart was a very young and very popular composer," he noted, his eyes turning to the piano, and added, "I have often thought if he were alive here today he would probably enjoy our pop music very much. He would probably play, in his own inimitable Mozart style, *Mack The Knife.*" For the next mesmerizing minute or so I listened and watched as Liberace's fingers sailed ever so gently across the ivories, his jewel-encrusted rings glistening in the spotlight. It was such an unforgettable moment.

As we wrapped up the interview, he told me how pleased he was that *Amadeus* had just won the Oscar for Best Film. "It's wonderful to see a movie of such caliber get recognized like that," he said. He expressed the hope that he, too, could wind up on the silver screen as one of his musical heroes.

"Maybe there's another composer's life that someday I might be able to interpret on the screen," he smiled, with a sparkle in his eyes.

He never got to do that. Less than a month after our interview, Liberace was secretly diagnosed with HIV, and died of AIDS-related complications two years later at the age of 67. For me, I will never forget the day Liberace played the piano for me, and thanked me graciously for an "enjoyable" interview. I thanked him in turn for one of the most memorable interviews I had ever done—one that seems as fresh today as it did that sunny day in the studio in 1985.

short takes

At the heart of every story is a person. It is the people of all walks of life—the poverty-stricken and the rich and famous—of all faiths and religions, of all different shades of skin—who make the news; I'm simply the storyteller. And as a reporter, I've been fortunate not only to tell their stories, but to connect with many of them personally, including a couple of convicted murderers, a Mafia hitman, presidents and presidents-to-be. I've been to Hell and back, and was caught sitting in my car with a thousand-dollar-a-night prostitute; I've anchored the news in my skivvies and gotten the Concorde to land in the Hudson.

The best part of dealing with people directly is the gratitude they express when I meet them. Often I'll hear, "I've grown up watching you—thank you for your good reporting." I was most touched when an Italian immigrant, who had just become an American citizen, ran up to me to say thanks. "I have learned English by listening to you on television."

There are so many personal stories I could share from my long career as a journalist—some uplifting, some sad, some simply a look behind the scenes of a life in reporting. It would take volumes to tell them all. Here are a few of the shorter ones that have stuck with me the most.

41

THE ANGEL OF THE EVENING

*l*eaving the night shift one evening, I was approached by an attractive woman who asked if I would like to party. She was a working girl, attempting to proposition me for a sexual encounter. Being the reporter I am, I quickly turned the tables on her with a proposition of my own—an interview. It took a little sweet-talking on my end to get her to agree to such an unconventional request, but in the end she agreed to join me in my car, where I recorded a ten-minute interview.

She called herself the "Angel of the Evening." She explained that she was a housewife from Kentucky with two kids and an unemployed husband, who came to New York City a few times a year. She told me she made about $1,000 a night, and each time would return home with $15,000–$20,000 in cash.

The interview was terrific—but I had some explaining to do to a skeptical colleague, who spotted me sitting in my car with an attractive woman at 2 o'clock in the morning.

42

"MY HOSTAGE"

journalists can get very possessive when we feel we have something exclusive. Sometimes this can push us to ridiculous extremes.

In 1985, after Islamic extremists released 39 hostages from the recently hijacked TWA Flight 847, the hostages were flown from Beirut to Rhein-Main Air Base in Germany for medical check-ups. I was among a mob of reporters outside the hospital, clamoring for interviews. Observing one of the former captives out for a stroll, I attempted to flag him down for an interview. As I approached him, however, a producer from *The Today Show* appeared out of nowhere and grabbed his arm.

She turned to me, fire in her eyes. "You can't have him," she declared fiercely. "He's *my* hostage!"

43

THE NEWS IN BRIEFS

*i*t was a stifling July night when the police and fire radios bellowed an urgent call to the airport in Charleston, West Virginia. A commercial airliner had just overshot the runway and there were reports of injuries.

Alone in the two-man Capitol Bureau of WHTN-TV, I grabbed a camera and portable light and raced to the airport, where I discovered the light's battery was dead. I piggybacked off of competitors' lights, shooting while they were shooting to capture images of emergency operations, dazed passengers running to the terminal and a plane that had miraculously stopped short of running off the mountaintop runway. It was the big story of the night, and I had less than two hours to get it on the air.

By the time I returned to the studio, I was dripping with sweat, and my clothes felt like a wet towel. The studio was vacant but for myself and an engineer who came in to put my segment on the air, so I removed my jacket, shirt and pants and hung them up to dry, running barefoot and in my skivvies into the darkroom to hand-develop the film I had shot. Once the developing process was done, I wrapped the film around a drum made of dowel sticks, turned on a fan, and rotated the drum by hand to dry it. A rather primitive procedure, by today's standards!

Breathlessly, I dashed back and forth to the newsroom, calling police and hospitals and checking the teletypes for the latest information while attempting to write a script. The film wasn't quite dry when we went on the air at 11. The lead anchor in Huntington headlined the story at the top of the broadcast, telling viewers I had just returned from the scene and would be along shortly with film. (This was 1959, and there was no technology yet that would allow us to go live from the scene of breaking news.)

It was about five minutes after 11 when the film was finally dry. There was no time to edit it, or do anything else, for that matter—except get into the studio. I dashed into the newsroom and threw on my shirt, tie and jacket, not bothering with shoes or pants. Charging downstairs, I threw the film to the engineer while still buttoning my shirt, and was barely behind the desk when the anchor cut to me for the latest details. I was still perspiring heavily; sweat dripped visibly from my brow. A few seconds into the story, my horn-rimmed glasses fogged up, and anyone watching my eyes would have found themselves staring into two gray pits. The only thing that saved me was that we cut almost immediately to the film I had shot, giving me an opportunity to wipe my glasses.

It wasn't my best presentation, but I got the story on the air— and viewers never suspected that I was coming into their homes wearing my BVDs.

44

THE WITNESS

*i*t's amazing, people's weakness for their ten seconds of fame on-camera. While covering a story about a fire in a South Bronx apartment—which police later discovered to have been arson, intended to cover up the robbery and murder of an elderly woman—a young man approached me to tell me he had seen a man running from the apartment, carrying a television set. He said he gave chase, but failed to catch him. Naturally, I put him on-camera to describe exactly what he claimed to have seen.

It was a good sound bite—but as it turned out, he wasn't quite the neighbor he had claimed to be. The next day, detectives showed up at the studio, and asked to view the video. My eyewitness, they said, was the man they suspected of robbing and killing the elderly woman, and setting her apartment on fire.

45

BLAMING THE NEWS

*i*n the seventies, Peter Mocco, then-mayor of North Bergen, New Jersey, was indicted by a grand jury on corruption charges. Some of the evidence leading to the indictment was uncovered in a series of investigative reports I did for WNEW-TV, which the U.S. Attorney for New Jersey credited as relevant in the probe. The charges—of criminal conflict of interest and conspiracy—stemmed from Mocco's alleged involvement in arranging for the township to do business with a company in which he was accused of having a private interest.

From reliable sources, I had learned in advance that the grand jury was about to indict Mocco, and I broke the story exclusively on the air. Days later, after Mocco was arrested and formally charged, he claimed the indictment was the result of my report, and threatened to challenge WNEW-TV's FCC license. His argument—which ultimately failed—was that once the jurors heard the news on television, "they felt obligated to indict."

46

A BREAKING STORY
THAT HIT HOME

i was just finishing the weather report on my local noontime newscast when my producer burst into my earpiece to alert me to a breaking news story coming up. A writer slipped the copy into the teleprompter, which I began reading cold on the air, relating how firefighters were battling a stubborn blaze in a high-rise building in Fort Lee, New Jersey. The blaze had gone to several alarms and people were being evacuated from the building. Suddenly I found my delivery slowing and my pulse quickening as new information brought me to the realization that the fire was actually in the building where I lived! *Oh my God,* I thought, trying to keep my delivery calm. I couldn't get to a commercial break fast enough. At the break I called my son, who was living with his mother in an adjoining building. He said he had just heard my report on TV, but aside from hearing the fire engines, he knew less about the fire than I did.

After the break, I read an update on the fire, reporting that there had been no injuries and that the fire had been confined to the 21st floor. My apartment was on the eighth floor, and was undamaged. Still, it was one hell of a way for me to get the news that struck so awfully close to home.

47

HURRICANE CALLING

*i*t was a couple of weeks before Christmas in 1975. I had just completed an exclusive report stating that Rubin "Hurricane" Carter would soon be released from prison to await a second trial for murder. I had barely left the studio when a production assistant came running down the hall to inform me that I had a collect call in the newsroom from Trenton State Prison, from someone named Hurricane.

"Marv, is it true?" the excited voice asked when I picked up. My report was the first he had heard of Governor Brendan Byrne's intention of releasing him and his co-defendant, John Artis, under a form of executive clemency, pending the outcome of their upcoming appeal for a new trial.

I had met previously with the former middleweight boxer at New Jersey's maximum-security prison, where he had already served nine years of a life sentence for a crime he told me he didn't commit. Carter and Artis were found guilty of the murders of three white people in a Paterson, New Jersey bar in 1966; claiming they had been framed, they argued that their conviction was based on flawed and circumstantial evidence. Carter became an international symbol of racial injustice, inspiring Bob Dylan to write the song "Hurricane" and jumpstarting a movement, spearheaded by Muhammad

Ali and a legion of other celebrities, to get him and Artis freed.

Complicating the case were tales of Carter's fits of rage and violent nature, something that would continue to dog him long after the trial, and to which he would make reference in his autobiography, *The Sixteenth Round.* One major source of controversy was the circumstances surrounding the beating of Carolyn Kelley in 1976, while Carter was awaiting retrial. Kelley had been one of Carter's biggest supporters, and devoted more than a year of her life to raising funds for Carter's defense. During an argument in a Maryland hotel room, however, Carter punched Kelley, flooring her, then kicked her in the back.

Carter initially denied hitting her, and later offered different versions of what had happened that night—including one in an interview with me, conducted while Carter was out on bail, that would be brought up many times over the years. In his autobiography, he claimed that Kelley had faked the beating because they were having an affair, and she wanted to blackmail him out of $100,000. In my interview, however, he set the figure at a quarter of a million dollars, and told me Kelley had turned on him because he wouldn't give her the money.

"The Kelley matter affects me very horrendously," he told me, noting that because he was out on bail at the time, anything of a scandalous nature would get him back behind bars. Though Kelley never filed charges, Carter feared that her allegations would turn off the thousands of people who had come to help him. "But we're going to deal with it," he declared, looking straight into my camera. "We're going to keep on going…I'm going to win, 'cause I don't know how to quit."

During his six-week retrial, Carter kept up this cautious optimism, telling me that despite his wrongful conviction at his first trial, he still had faith in the criminal justice system. Those hopes were dashed when the jury of eight men and four women returned a verdict of guilty on all three counts of first-degree murder. It was a shocker—pain and anguish were clearly visible on the boxer's face. But in 1985, after Carter had spent a total of almost 20 years in prison, a federal judge overturned his and Artis's convictions, claiming the prosecutions had been "predicated upon an appeal of racism rather than reason, concealment rather than disclosure." Carter enjoyed 28 years of freedom before his death at the age of 79 in 2014.

48

WATCH WHO YOU'RE TURNING YOUR BACK ON

a cemetery seemed the perfect backdrop for the opening to a documentary I was filming, dealing with the high number of cancer deaths in New Jersey. The crew and I stopped in the cemetery office in Roseland, New Jersey, to ask permission to shoot on the premises. We waited for a while—and when no one showed up, we entered and began shooting discreetly, making certain we only had the backs of tombstones facing the camera, so as not to reveal any names.

After several minutes we were approached by a priest from the local archdiocese, who admonished us for filming there without permission and demanded that we leave immediately. I apologized for the intrusion and we began to pack up our equipment. Defusing his anger, he explained that he wasn't upset because we were trespassing, but was concerned because of where I had been standing. He explained that my back was to the tombstone of the son of a noted Mafia figure, who lived in a nearby gated estate that was rumored to have a gas chamber where he purportedly exterminated people who crossed him.

"He would be most displeased," the priest cautioned, "if he saw somebody's back to his son's grave."

49

JACKIE O'S ONE-WORD EXCLUSIVE

J acqueline Bouvier Kennedy, the woman we had come to know and love as Jackie, was a radiant First Lady. She was elegant and glamorous, a photographer's dream. Almost ten years after the assassination of President Kennedy, she was married to Greek shipping magnate Aristotle Onassis and living in New York with her children, John Jr. and Caroline, where they remained under the watchful eye of the Secret Service.

But there was another eye always on them, too—one pressed to the viewfinder of a camera. Notorious paparazzo Ron Galella became Jackie's nemesis as he stalked her and her children, earning a comfortable living off of the pictures he took of them. For years, Galella hid in bushes and behind coat racks in pursuit of candid Jackie shots. He would often say that his subjects were more like "targets," and Jackie was his favorite—"the perfect model of wife, mother, woman."

I had known Galella for years, and he would boast to me about how much he loved the chase and even claim that, despite her protests over his intrusiveness, Jackie actually loved his photographic stalking. Secret Service agents were concerned, however, that Galella was getting too close. He took pictures of John Jr. riding his bicycle in Central Park, and on one occasion jumped into his path to get a closer shot. Another time he interrupted Caroline during a tennis game. And he was accused of coming "uncomfortably close" to Jackie, pursuing her in a boat as she swam.

At one point Galella came so close, he was arrested by agents. That prompted him to file suit against them and Jackie, arguing that they'd violated his rights and his ability to earn a living. Jackie countersued, claiming invasion of privacy. That paved the way for a six-week trial in federal court that *The New York Times* called "the best off-Broadway show in town." It was certainly filled with drama as Jackie described in detail how Galella terrorized her and her children, relentlessly invading their privacy. In return, Galella complained that she was interfering with his livelihood and violating his First Amendment right to photograph any public figure. He even claimed Jackie had told her Secret Service detail to "smash his camera"—something she categorically denied.

"But," he noted, "she always kept a Galella smile on her face." The photographer left court each day with a bravado-filled swagger, always eager to talk to reporters about how he was the victim in the case.

Jackie, on the other hand, would invariably dodge the media, flanked by her legal team, and dash into a waiting car. I had become friendly with her lawyers, who were complimentary of my reporting of the trial, and I appealed to them to let me have a brief interview with their client. Several weeks into the trial, they agreed to give me an exclusive with Jackie if I asked her only one question. As she came down the courthouse steps, I eagerly approached her and asked, "Mrs. Onassis, are you pleased with the way the trial is going?"

With a faint smile, she responded with a simple "Yes."

That's it? I thought. If only I had phrased the question differently, perhaps I would have gotten a few more words out of her! I attempted another question, but her attorneys shut me out, reminding me that I had agreed to ask only one. *What the heck,* I thought—at least I got a yes out of her, and after all it was an *exclusive* yes!

The trial ended with the judge ordering Galella to stay 50 yards away from Jackie and 75 yards from her children. Galella appealed the decision, and a higher court modified the restriction to 25 yards. By his own admission, Galella subsequently violated that ruling "a hundred times"—but following several more years of wrangling and the threat of jail time and a $120,000 fine, he finally turned his lens away from Jackie. His dramatic courthouse encounter with the former First Lady was highlighted in the HBO documentary *Smash His Camera*—in which I play a cameo role, achieving my one-word exclusive with Jackie.

50

A HIT MAN'S SALUTATION

*f*rank "The Bear" Basto was a reputed member of the Gambino crime family, a man mobster Vincent Teresa identified as a professional assassin in his book *My Life in the Mafia*. Basto had a beef with federal law enforcement, and reached out to me to expose it. He claimed that prosecutors were securing convictions of mob figures by getting other mobsters to cooperate as witnesses against them. The feds would win over these truculent witnesses, Basto said, by "wining and dining them"—putting them up in good hotels and providing them with prostitutes.

During a late-night meeting with me, Basto insisted that he had no part in organized crime. "Hell no," he said with a laugh. "Organized? You ask my wife—she'll tell you I'm the most disorganized guy you ever met. I'm a thief, sure," he admitted, "but organized? Hell no." He and I corresponded after he was sent to prison on one of his convictions. The hit man was an interesting pen pal, with an unintentionally pointed way with words. In one letter, he congratulated me for winning an Emmy Award, signing it with the salutation, "Keep knockin' 'em dead."

51

THE FIRE THAT TAUGHT
ME A LESSON

*a*t times, reporters can get so caught up in the stories they're covering that they lose sight of their human sensitivities. I became one of those reporters—and learned a sad lesson—while covering the aftermath of a dancehall fire in Portchester, New York, in which 24 young people lost their lives.

It was just after midnight on June 30th, 1974, when wisps of smoke began to waft onto the dance floor of Gulliver's, a popular restaurant and discotheque on the New York–Connecticut border. There didn't seem to be any immediate need to panic, but when the bandleader announced that a small fire had broken out in an adjoining building, many of the 200 young people on the dance floor decided to play it safe by heading outside. Those who didn't soon found themselves trapped by acrid black smoke and flames that engulfed the room within minutes. All-out terror ensued, and many were trampled to death in the human stampede. Piles of discarded high-heel shoes near the exit served as mute testimony to the crowd's panicked escape.

When I arrived at the scene hours afterward, it was tragic to learn that the bodies of at least 24 young people who went out for a Saturday night of fun lay dead amid the fire-charred rubble. But I had a story to cover, and my camera crew and I immediately got to work looking for survivors to interview. I spotted a woman running frantically across the parking lot and gave chase, poking my microphone at her and inquiring why she was there. I should have guessed the answer and backed away—but instead I pursued the woman relentlessly, asking her over and over again, "Why are you here?" Suddenly, she let out a blood-curdling scream and collapsed to the ground. My camera and microphone captured every moment of it. *Great television,* I thought initially; but was disgusted with myself afterward when I understood why the woman was there.

She had just realized her worst nightmare: her little girl had failed to come home from her night out. Finding her daughter's car in the parking lot, the mother knew instantly that she had to be among the dead. As others came to her side, I tried to comfort the woman, who was now crying inconsolably. I directed my cameraman to stop shooting. I felt terribly guilty for pursuing her the way I did, shoving my microphone in her face. I realized I should have handled it very differently—common sense should have told me why she was searching the parking lot, and sensitivity should have kept me from getting so aggressively close. But in my quest for a good television report, I lost touch with the better part of my humanity.

Later, I stood over the editor as we cut the video for our evening newscast, and had him cut out my pursuit of the distraught mother, and discreetly limit the footage of her that we used in my report. But I never forgot what I learned from this experience. In the years ahead I covered many more tragedies, and I always dreaded approaching someone who had just lost a loved one. Sometimes they would welcome the media, finding it cathartic to speak out in their moment of grief. But remembering the lesson I learned at the Portchester fire, I'm more sensitive to the grieving people I approach, and I make it a point to begin by offering them my condolences and telling them that I wish, just as much as they do, that I wasn't there.

52

ONE HELL OF A STORY

i've traveled to the far corners of the world over the course of my career, but one of my most unique visits was to a place called Hell...Michigan. It's a small, picturesque hamlet 46 miles north of Detroit. I went there during the height of the Cuban Missile Crisis in 1962, after UN Ambassador Adlai Stevenson confronted Soviet Ambassador Valerian Zorin and, in a clear, lucid voice, told him he was willing "to wait until Hell freezes over" for an answer to his question of whether the Soviet Union had placed missiles in Cuba.

I stood by a dam and sat beside a waterfall in the little town, but it was only October, and Stevenson didn't have to wait for Hell to freeze over. After he presented irrefutable reconnaissance photos to the UN, the Soviets packed up their missiles and went home. As for me, I returned to Hell a few months later, to take pictures beside the town's snow-covered frozen waterfall.

53

CUFFED ON ASSIGNMENT

*i*t truly was an undercover assignment. I was conducting a radio news investigation to determine why so many so-called "massage parlors" were becoming a part of the landscape of our neighborhoods, and what was really going on beyond those obstructed storefront windows. Were these places simply a front for prostitution? There was only one way to find out: pose as a customer.

I checked out a place on Manhattan's West Side, looking to discover whether the women were in the country legally, and whether they really were licensed to provide massages. I never got the chance to find out. Within minutes of my arrival, the place was raided by police. Before I had a chance to identify myself as a reporter and produce my press card, I found myself being rounded up along with the other patrons and employees, and my hands being cuffed behind my back. Fortunately, the inspector in charge of the sting knew who I was, and promptly removed the cuffs. As it turned out, police had indeed determined that the establishment was providing prostitution services. Nothing like being on the spot for a breaking news story!

53

THE CONCORDE OVER LUNCH

*t*he Concorde Supersonic airliner was a triumph of modern technology and engineering. Perhaps it was ahead of its time—it flew at twice the speed of sound, and could cross the Atlantic in just over three hours while its passengers dined on champagne and caviar. There was something undeniably romantic about flying the Concorde at 60,000 feet. "When people talk about Concorde," wrote one columnist, "they describe it the way we might describe Marilyn Monroe: elegant, glamorous, classic, and peppered with oohs and ahhs."

In 2003, after 20 years of service, British Airways and Air France decided to retire their Concorde fleets, claiming they were no longer economically viable to operate. The airlines then each conducted a global search for permanent homes for its aircraft, at museums or similar institutions. Discussing this at lunch with my friend John Lampl, who was Vice President of Corporate Communications for British Airways in the United States, I suggested that he offer a Concorde to the Intrepid Sea, Air and Space Museum in New York Harbor. I noted that the museum was located at the same pier from which great luxury liners like the Queen Elizabeth and Queen Mary once sailed to Europe. He liked the idea, and once he was back at his office he ran it by airline executives in London. They too liked the idea, and asked if I could set up a meeting.

First I had to see if the Intrepid trustees were interested. Initially they were cool to the idea, concerned about the cost factor, so I arranged for a meeting between them and British Airways officials, who flew in from London. I was asked to sit in on the meeting, which concluded with a handshake and a deal for a Concorde to find a new home in New York. Six months later, Concorde Alpha Delta—the aircraft that set a world speed record of 2:52:59 for the transatlantic crossing—arrived at Kennedy International Airport on its final flight, and was transferred to a barge for its journey up the Hudson River to the Intrepid.

Credited with having initiated the deal, I was asked to speak at the dedication ceremony. Joined by representatives from the Intrepid and British Airways, I was also invited to ring the closing bell at the New York Stock Exchange. In reporting the arrival of the Concorde to New York on his evening newscast, my colleague Jim Watkins made note of my involvement, and quipped, "See, folks—have lunch with Marvin Scott, you never know what's going to happen."

54

MY MURDEROUS PEN PALS

*d*avid Berkowitz and Ronald DeFeo Jr. are among the most notorious murderers of our time. Berkowitz, better known as the Son of Sam, killed six young men and women during a shooting rampage in New York City during the summer of 1977; DeFeo—the scion of a family that occupied the infamous house in Amityville, Long Island, that was later claimed to be haunted by demonic forces—methodically murdered his mother and father and four siblings in 1974. Both men are currently serving lifelong prison sentences, their many appeals for early release having been rejected. Over the years, I've made many requests for one-on-one interviews with Berkowitz and DeFeo. In pursuing these personal meetings, I exchanged letters with the murderers, which are interesting for what they revealed about the character of the two infamous men.

David Berkowitz seemed enthusiastic about granting me an interview after I suggested bringing along Eddie Zigo, the New York detective who arrested him. Zigo, who became a friend after we met at a social event, initially agreed to join me on the prison visit for a special report I was preparing for the 20th anniversary of Berkowitz's arrest. Berkowitz, who hadn't seen the detective since the night Zigo put him in handcuffs, was so looking forward to seeing him two decades later that he made it a condition for the interview. Zigo, however, had reservations about the visit, and eventually decided not to go. In subsequently declining the interview, Berkowitz wrote me an apologetic typewritten letter.

"I would have felt more comfortable meeting him with my friends present," he wrote. "But he wasn't in agreement with it. I understand. No problem. In any event, please accept my apology."

This, it seemed, was a Berkowitz much mellowed by his decades in prison—very different from the 24-year-old murderous madman who terrorized an entire city for a year, killing six people and wounding seven. Known early on as the .44 Caliber Killer, Berkowitz claimed his murderous spree was inspired by the devil, who had transmitted his orders to Berkowitz through his neighbor Sam Carr's black Labrador retriever. In his bedroom, Berkowitz had scrawled the words, "Sam Carr—My Master," giving rise to his "Son of Sam" moniker.

Detective Zigo remembered the night he collared Berkowitz, and told me, "When I approached him, I said, 'Are you David Berkowitz?' He looked at me with that grin on his face, and said, 'No, I'm the Son of Sam.'" The detective shook his head, still in disbelief. "It just amazed me that he was so calm about everything, knowing what he did."

In his letter to me, Berkowitz said he remembered very little about the night he was arrested and his interaction with the man who had collared him, and would have liked to meet Zigo so many years after his egregious crimes. "I vaguely recall Detective Zigo because it was a long time ago," he wrote, "and the entire arrest incident was a traumatic ordeal for me. Nowadays I barely remember this period of my life. It's a blur. I don't even remember if I got to speak with Detective Zigo very much. Mostly I recall finding myself at the Kings County Hospital prison ward, and that's about it. Please wish Mr. Zigo well for me."

In the years since his crimes, Berkowitz has turned to born-again Christianity to help him cope with his actions and lifelong incarceration. In his letter, he expressed remorse for what he had done. "I am deeply sorry for the crimes I committed," he wrote. "I continually pray for those whom I injured as well as for the families of those who lost a loved one." In conclusion, he added, "I am thankful to have survived, and I wish to move on. God bless you."

* * *

In contrast to Berkowitz's apparent repentance for his crimes, Ronald DeFeo still vociferously denies that he committed his. Four decades after he was sentenced to six consecutive life terms for murdering his family, DeFeo continues to call for a new trial. His trial attorney initially attempted to plead an insanity defense after DeFeo claimed he had heard voices telling him to kill. In subsequent versions of his story, DeFeo accused the Mafia of committing the murders while he smoked marijuana in the basement.

In an exchange of letters with me in 1999, DeFeo suggested it was his sister Allison who killed everyone, and that he killed her in self-defense while wrestling for the gun. He claimed that prosecutors had used Allison's blood—obtained from a shell casing he had picked up and wiped on his pants—as evidence against him.

"Really, I need to find a real criminal lawyer, get the DNA testing done and I am out the door, because the truth speaks for itself," he declared in his handwritten scrawl. Angrily demanding a new trial, he went on: "The truth is in black and white. The problem is everyone is afraid of the truth… There was no insanity, only people talking about books, about movies, about me being possessed. All anyone wants to hear is possession stories."

The "Amityville Horror" phenomenon that developed in the aftermath of the murders was, in DeFeo's belief, a total hoax. "Amityville is about money, that's what it's all about, an industry," he wrote, accusing his attorney, William Weber, of having colluded with George and Kathy Lutz to create the whole occult story after they fled their home, claiming it was inhabited by demons.

Expressing the belief that he was being exploited, DeFeo first demanded that I pay him for an interview, and then denied my requests altogether.

"You get paid for what you do," he wrote, adding, "I am not doing nothing for free while you exploit me some more."

55

PRESIDENTS

*p*resident Harry Truman was just a couple of months out of office when he appeared on a television program with students on NBC. I was a high-school student back then, and as the media rep for the High School Press Association, I was invited to the studio to take pictures. When Truman arrived, he was very friendly as he greeted each of the students on the panel. As I was snapping photos, he approached me to say hello and ask how I was doing.

"Just fine, Mr. President—and you?" I responded nervously. What an exciting moment for a kid, to meet the man who had just been President of the United States! He was very engaging and seemed to be interested in photography, asking me about my camera and my hobby. While I took a couple of shots of him we continued to chat, and he surprised me by saying that he too enjoyed photography, but never took any pictures himself.

"Why not?" I asked.

"Because if *I* lifted up a camera," he smiled, "the only pictures I would likely get would be of press photographers taking pictures of *me!*"

* * *

Our first impressions of prominent people sometimes belie the image that is publicly projected of them. President Dwight David Eisenhower struck me as a man who was not comfortable in his role as military leader–turned-president. He had been out of the White House a few years when I met him at the U.S. Military Academy at West Point in 1965. He was certainly gracious when I approached him to ask about the history that was being made in space that day—his fellow West Pointer, astronaut Edward White, was staging the first-ever space walk.

"You must be proud, Mr. President," I prodded him—but he didn't seem to know who Ed White was, until an aide jumped in to fill him in. He stumbled over a few words, and finally provided me with what amounted to a 10-second sound bite. It's possible he was simply having a bad day.

* * *

Richard Nixon was always Richard Nixon—someone who struck me as a somewhat plastic, stereotypical political candidate. I traveled with him in 1968, covering his presidential campaign for the Mutual Broadcasting System. Though his minions were trying hard to project him as "The New Nixon" during that campaign, he came across to me as studied and ill at ease. He appeared to be facing an uphill battle against his expected Democratic challenger, Robert Kennedy—but that changed after Kennedy was assassinated, weeks before his party's nominating convention. Nixon, now running against Hubert Humphrey, was more dynamic, and knew how to excite the crowds of supporters who turned out for his rallies.

I got to see firsthand that the new Nixon wasn't much different from the old Nixon during a flight to Albany, New York, for a campaign stop. I was the pool reporter for radio that day, and got to fly on the candidate's plane, the *Julie,* named for his younger daughter. At one point Nixon, who was rarely seen in public without a jacket, came through the cabin in shirtsleeves with a cup of coffee in his hand. He chatted with the small group of pool reporters, talking about the campaign and the remarks he planned to make in Albany. There was a bit of mild turbulence during the 10 or 15 minutes we stood there, and throughout that entire time, I observed that Nixon tightly clutched the cup of coffee in front of him like a prop, with the cup never leaving the saucer. Right or wrong, I interpreted that as another sign of the rigid politician within—the same Richard Nixon we had known for years. Still, months later he went on to win the election.

* * *

I first met and had the opportunity to share a microphone with Gerald Ford when he was a congressman from Grand Rapids, Michigan, where I had moved for my second job. He was always approachable and friendly to the media, and was most accommodating the night I asked him to join me at radio station WOOD to provide analysis during our coverage of the gubernatorial election, in which George Romney won his first of three terms. Ford was an effective legislator, and was well liked by Democrats as well as Republicans. It was easy to understand how he comfortably transitioned into the Oval Office after President Nixon's resignation. Despite Ford's affability, though, his popularity dropped after he pardoned Nixon over the Watergate scandal, and voters replaced him with Jimmy Carter in 1976.

In subsequent years, Ford would grant me interviews whenever I saw him at political conventions. It was at a charity benefit, years later, when I greeted him on the dais where he was sitting next to iconic comedian Bob Hope. He was pleased to see me again, and to learn that I was now a television anchorman in New York. His eyes widened and a smile crossed his lips as he nudged Hope, boasting about how a kid who began his news career in Grand Rapids had made it to the big time. He seemed genuinely proud.

* * *

My impression of Jimmy Carter was that he was a sensitive, religious man who wanted to be liked. Ultimately, he failed to exert the leadership and support he needed to be an effective president; he didn't seem to have the stomach for politics, and by his own admission he wasn't enough of a horse-trader to succeed at the job. I covered the Carter White House in the summer of 1980, and my best memories of those years were the barbecue parties Carter held on the back lawn for staff and reporters. The big story in the final days of his presidency was the effort to gain the release of 52 American hostages being held by Iran, and I was also at the White House during those tense hours before a deal was finally struck and the hostages were freed—the day Ronald Reagan succeeded Carter.

I had the opportunity for three one-on-one interviews with Carter, two of them when he came to the studio to promote his books. They were good interviews, but contained nothing dramatically revealing. Carter was personally quite affable and easy to talk with; there didn't seem to be anything pretentious about him. And he graciously greeted my 10-year-old son Steven and 7-year-old daughter Jill, whom I allowed to play hooky from school one day to meet the former president and take a picture with him.

* * *

George H. W. Bush was President Reagan's vice president and was seeking reelection when I interviewed him at the Republican National Convention in Dallas in 1984. We talked about the upcoming race with Walter Mondale, and how he expected the nomination of Geraldine Ferraro as the nation's first female vice-presidential candidate would impact the race. It was quite evident that Bush had his own agenda with the message points he wanted to get across, regardless of what I asked him. But even with his prepared messages, I managed to get in some hard news questions.

He seemed very studied at times, and quite methodical—like

when he turned away from me to look directly into the camera while stressing a point. As someone who had taught media techniques to corporate executives, I immediately recognized what he was doing. After the interview, he thanked me for it, and as I complimented him on his handling of it, I couldn't help but ask if he had recently undergone media coaching.

"Yes," he responded with an uneasy laugh. "Was it that obvious?" I explained that I had done that sort of training myself, so to me it was obvious.

"Any suggestions?" he asked. I suggested that he try to sound less programmed, and make that turn to the camera less obvious. He expressed his gratitude for the guidance "from a pro," and as I left, he gave me a small penknife and a pen bearing the vice-presidential seal as a token of his appreciation.

* * *

President Bill Clinton had to have taken a page out of the JFK handbook. He is charisma personified: he has the uncanny ability to look you in the eye and make you feel that you are the only person in the room. I have watched him work crowds, and it's amazing the way he connects with each individual he meets. After the Monica Lewinsky episode, my wife thought Clinton was a scoundrel—until she met him and became silly putty. With hundreds of others in the room, Clinton held Lorri's hand for a moment, looked her in the eye, then looked over toward me and asked her, "Is he behaving himself?" Look who's asking!

56

THE PHOTO THAT BROUGHT A FAMILY TOGETHER

Photo I took as a teenager that inspired my career.

more than 50 years had passed since I had taken a photo of a raging fire in the Bronx when I received an email from a viewer requesting a copy of the picture. He saw it in a book in which I had written a chapter about the Bronx. Donald Mahoney said he was making the request because he recognized his late firefighter father in the photo, the only picture he had ever seen of him in his 37 years on the job.

With regret I responded that I had misplaced the negative, and did not have a print copy. However, I promised that I would save the email and reach out to Mahoney if I ever located the negative.

Five years later, in 2011, while combing through my old photo files, I finally located the negative. It brought back vivid memories of the night I took the picture. I was 15 years old and watching *The Steve Allen Show* at 11:30 p.m. when I heard fire engines whizzing by. I looked out the window; flames from a nearby catering hall had turned night into day. I grabbed my Rolleiflex, headed out and started shooting pictures before firefighters had even deployed their hoses. One of the pictures was a great shot of flames mushrooming from almost a dozen windows of the unoccupied catering hall.

It was that fire, and being first on the scene, that sparked my interest in a career in journalism. When I returned to my apartment building, my neighbors clustered around me to hear what I knew about the fire. You could say that was my first "newscast." Subsequently, I was thrilled when the *New York Daily News* bought my photograph, paid me $25 and gave me my first credit line under the photo. I was hooked! Coincidentally, it was 26 years later that I returned to the same building where I sold that photograph, to become an anchor and reporter at WPIX-TV.

With the newly found negative, I had an enlarged photo printed and framed, and alerted Don Mahoney that I had a surprise for him—the photo he thought he would never get. We arranged to meet at the Friars Club, where Don brought along his brothers, Michael and John. They marveled at the photo, and indeed recognized their father, James Mahoney, in the picture.

"It's his frame, the way he stood," John observed. "We couldn't see his face clearly," noted Don, "but we recognized that little white spot." He pointed to the ankles of the man in the photo. "He used to wear white socks, and you can see it in the picture." His brothers agreed that this was the confirmation they needed.

James Mahoney died 25 years earlier, and seeing his picture was an emotional experience for the brothers.

"He was a honey bear," Michael said. "He wasn't tall, but he was big."

"There was something about him," Donald added, remembering that his father had helped him to overcome a case of bulbar polio that afflicted his left shoulder. "Whenever you were with him, you felt very safe." John nodded in agreement. "You knew everything was going to be okay," he said. "The guys who worked with him said they would watch him to see what to do at a fire—they knew *he* knew what to do."

Bringing the brothers this experience, so many years later, was so gratifying for me. It was truly touching, watching them studying and reflecting on my photo of their father. It helped them to remember him, and share fond memories of their life together. "This means the world to us," Donald told me. "This is the only picture we have of our father fighting a fire, and you kept a promise you made to someone you didn't know, five years ago—that says something."

57

NICE TO MEET YOU

*a*s reporters appearing on daily news broadcasts, we become familiar faces in the city, and are often greeted by viewers who recognize us. Sometimes that recognition comes from unexpected places. Once, for instance, Stevie Wonder sat down with me for a brief interview after performing a concert in Central Park. We greeted one another, and I had barely spoken a sentence when the multiple Grammy Award–winning musical genius, who has been sightless since birth, paused for a moment and said, "I know that voice from television—nice to meet you." That was a kick, getting recognized by Stevie Wonder.

Equally surprising was the time I was approached by a homeless man on a cold February night. I thought he was looking for a handout as he stretched out his hand, but then he said he wanted to shake mine.

"I've been watching you every night on the news," he said excitedly. You really can't make assumptions about people, and I didn't want to be rude, but curiosity got the better of me as I looked at this man, standing beside the corrugated-cardboard box that was his home. I couldn't help but ask him how exactly he got to watch me out here in the cold street. He excused himself for a moment, reached into his cardboard house and pulled out a 10-inch black-and-white battery-operated television! Only in New York, my friends—only in New York.

INDEX